MANDATES, PARTIES,

AND VOTERS:

HOW ELECTIONS SHAPE

THE FUTURE

In the series *The Social Logic of Politics*,
Edited by Alan S. Zuckerman

MANDATES,
PARTIES,
and VOTERS

HOW ELECTIONS
SHAPE THE FUTURE

JAMES H. FOWLER

Department of Political Science, University of California, San Diego

OLEG SMIRNOV

Department of Political Science, University of Miami

TEMPLE UNIVERSITY PRESS
Philadelphia

TEMPLE UNIVERSITY PRESS
1601 North Broad Street
Philadelphia PA 19122
www.temple.edu/tempress

Copyright © 2007 by Temple University

Published 2007
Printed in the United States of America

∞

The paper used in this publication meets the requirements
of the American National Standard for Information Sciences—
Permanence of Paper for Printed Library Materials, ANSI Z39.48-1992

Library of Congress Cataloging-in-Publication Data

Fowler, James H., 1970-
Mandates, parties, and voters : how elections shape the future /
James H. Fowler, Oleg Smirnov.
p. cm. — (Social logic of politics)
Includes bibliographical references and index.

ISBN 13: 978-159213-594-3   ISBN 10: 1-59213-594-3 (cloth: alk. paper)
ISBN 13: 978-159213-595-0   ISBN 10: 1-59213-595-1 (pbk.: alk. paper)

1. Elections.   2. Political parties.   3. Voting.   4. Political planning.
5. Elections—United States.   I. Smirnov, Oleg, 1979-   II. Title.
JF1001.F68 2007
324.9—dc22   2006024645

2   4   6   8   9   7   5   3   1

CONTENTS

LIST OF FIGURES

LIST OF TABLES

ACKNOWLEDGMENTS

This project has spanned about five years, but the real spark started in the summer of 2001 in Santa Fe, New Mexico where we first met and began developing these ideas at the Santa Fe Institute's Complex Systems Summer School. We could not ask for a more energizing or creative environment, and we will heartily recommend the experience to our own students who seek to cross disciplinary boundaries in their work.

Since then, we have received a lot of valuable feedback from our colleagues on drafts of conference papers, journal articles, and chapters which eventually fused together to form this book. In particular, we would like to thank Jim Adams, John Aldrich, Jim Alt, Alison Alter, Stephen Ansolabehere, Robert Bates, Henry Brady, Ethan Bueno de Mesquita, Lars-Erik Cederman, Eric Dickson, Mark Franklin, Jeff Grynaviski, Laszlo Gulyas, Peter Hall, Daniel Ho, Robert Huckfeldt, Torben Iversen, Bob Jackman, Cindy Kam, Gary King, Ken Kollman, John Londregan, Lisa Martin, Ferran Martinez I Coma, Mikhail Myagkov, William C. Mitchell, John Orbell, Scott Page, Maggie Penn, Brian Sala, Ken Shepsle, Allison Stanger, Jim Stock, Walt Stone, Colin Teichholtz, and Liz Zechmeister. We also received helpful comments from several group discussions, including the Harvard Workshops on Positive Political Economy and Rational Choice, the Complex Systems Summer School at the Santa Fe Institute, the workshop on Empirical Implications of Theoretical Models at Harvard University, Summer 2002, and the Micro Politics Group seminar at U.C. Davis.

We would also like to thank the Institute of Governmental Affairs at U.C. Davis for research support and Skip Lupia, Diana Mutz, and the team at Time-Sharing Experiments in the Social Sciences for the opportunity to collect nationally-representative data.

We are grateful that the people acknowledged so far took time to read each of the papers and give thoughtful feedback. However, there are a number of other people to whom we owe a special debt of gratitude. We especially thank our dissertation committees, Robert Bates, Lars-Erik Cederman, Gary King, Ken Shepsle, John Orbell, Misha Myagkov, and William Mitchell. These advisors provided more than just feedback on papers—they guided us through the process of forming ideas, generating and designing models to test them, and then figuring out how to explain our findings. They were also extremely patient with us as we experimented with new methodologies and took circuitous routes through other disciplines on our way to saying something meaningful about political science.

Oleg thanks John Orbell for being an intellectual father and the biggest inspiration to conduct and enjoy research. Oleg also thanks James Fowler, his coauthor, for being a great mentor and, no less importantly, a wonderful friend.

James thanks Icarus, a small group dedicated to thinking about evolutionary game theory and interdisciplinary approaches to social science. Led by Eric Dickson, this group included Ethan Bueno de Mesquita, Noah Dauber, Amanda Friedenberg, and Matt Stephenson.

Finally, we must acknowledge the most important people in our lives— our families. In particular, James counts his lucky stars every day to have such a close relationship with his parents, Zora and Jim Fowler, his wife, Harla Yesner, and their two children Lucas and Jay. They provide inspiration and life satisfaction that make it easy to work long and hard. Without them, this book would not exist.

James H. Fowler
Oleg Smirnov

MANDATES, PARTIES,
AND VOTERS:
HOW ELECTIONS SHAPE
THE FUTURE

ONE

Introduction

Although George W. Bush won both the 2000 and 2004 presidential elections, the way his campaign organization characterized these two victories differed dramatically. After Bush won in 2004 by more than three million votes, his reelection team was quick to claim that the people had given him a *mandate* to govern. In contrast, there were no such claims in 2000 when Bush received half a million *fewer* votes than his opponent. Yet, according to the electoral rules of the United States, Bush won both contests. Why would the margin of victory affect the interpretation of an electoral response if the main purpose of elections is to determine who wins and gets into the office?

In this book, we highlight the importance of electoral margins in political competition. Our work primarily describes two-party elections like those held in the United States; however, some of our results will also have implications for multiparty systems (cf., Kedar 2005). The core of our argument is that electoral margins contain information about the preferences of an electorate whose preferences are not known with certainty. In other words, electoral *margins* help to determine whether or not a candidate has received an electoral *mandate,* or authority to act on behalf of the electorate. All things equal, larger margins of victory mean stronger mandates—more of the public is in support of policies favored by the winner. As a result, after an election is held, *both* the winning and losing party have an incentive to shift their policies toward the policy preferred by the winning party. The winner shifts in order to obtain more favorable policies and the loser shifts in order to remain competitive in the electoral system. Moreover, the size of the shift is increasing in the margin of victory, since larger mandates suggest larger shifts in public preferences. These dynamics have far-reaching implications for our understanding of democratic political processes. We study these processes by treating elections as a dynamic sequence, in which elections in the past affect policies in the present and elections in the future. As a result, both politicians and voters may see each election not as a stand-alone event but as a fragment of a larger picture, in which future policies and future electoral platforms are also important.

We emphasize that our main argument about mandates is a ceteris paribus argument. A landslide win by a party leads to a more extreme policy position by that party in the next election on the grounds that the median voter is much closer to that party. However, since this is not a unique and deterministic causal mechanism, the choice of a policy may be affected by a number of other factors like valence or partisan advantage of one of the parties, changes in the state of the economy, geopolitical factors, and even such variables as terrorist attacks and natural disasters.

We are not the first scholars to study electoral mandates. Several other authors (Stigler 1972; Kramer 1977; Stone 1980; Conley 2001) have suggested that politicians care about the margin of victory because it helps them implement their preferred policies should they win elections. Stigler (1972) and Kramer (1977) were among the first to suggest that the margin of victory in an election can be "valued in itself as a 'mandate' for the victor" (Kramer 1977: 317). In this case, larger margins of victory mean the party or candidate "can do considerably more" (Stigler 1972: 99). Examples of benefits from having a mandate include increased patronage, the election of legislators from marginal districts whose indebtedness to the party leadership ensures a more cooperative legislature (Kramer 1977: 317), and general political opportunity (Conley 2001). Similarly, voters care about mandates because they, too, have preferences over policies and they believe that politicians care about mandates as well.

Conley (2001) further argues that elections are uniquely important because they "convey information about public preferences to elected representatives so that these representatives know whether or not to adjust the policy agenda" (Conley 2001: 1). In particular, she argues that politicians have an incentive to react appropriately to the margin of victory in the previous election, or else "they will be punished at the polls in the future" (Conley 2001: 6). She also shows empirically that large margins of victory are more likely to yield large policy changes (see also Stone 1980).

The importance of mandates, however, has yet to be widely accepted by students of electoral politics. Perhaps this is just a historical consequence of the fact that early treatments of elections happened to be conducted through the prism of static elections, office-motivated politicians, and pivotal voter motivations.

MANDATES AND PARTY BEHAVIOR

The seminal spatial models of electoral competition assumed that parties are *office-motivated*. In other words, parties formulate policies in order to win elections (e.g., Hotelling 1929; Downs 1957; Davis et al. 1970). Similar to shopkeepers choosing where to locate their stores on a given street, political parties choose candidates and positions on an ideological issue space. Similar to consumers choosing the closest shop, voters choose a party or candidate with the policy position closest to their own preferred policy. The equilibrium analysis of different models of electoral competition with office-motivated parties provides us with two main types of results: political parties either (1) converge to the same position—the location of the median voter (Downs 1957), or (2) diverge chaotically, offering an infinite variety of policies across a multidimensional issue space (Plott 1967; McKelvey 1976). These predictions do not fit well with what we know about the actual behavior of political parties. For example, parties typically offer policies that diverge significantly from the median voter and remain relatively stable over time (e.g., Peltzman 1984; Poole and Rosenthal 1984; Grofman, Griffin, and Glazer 1990).

Observed party differences can be easily explained if we acknowledge the fact that politicians have policy preferences that differ from those of the median voter. In other words, we assume that parties are *policy-motivated*. The assumption of policy-motivated politicians is completely consistent with the spatial modeling framework. The main difference is substantive: politicians try to win in order to implement their preferred policies instead of offering policies in order to win. A seminal analysis of policy-motivated candidates was offered by Wittman (1973, 1977, 1983) who described an equilibrium concept that now bears his name.

According to Wittman, political parties have preferences over the issue space and choose policies in order to maximize expected utility. In equilibrium, this choice is governed by own-party policy preferences, the other party's policy preferences, and the probabilities of winning and losing the election. The probabilities of winning and losing are, in turn, a function of the offered policies and the distribution of voters. Each party simultaneously searches for an optimal trade-off—offering a policy closer to its most preferred policy increases a party's utility should it win the election, whereas offering a policy closer to the median voter's preferred policy increases a party's chances to win the election. Thus, politicians must balance their desire to implement favorable policies against their fear of losing the election and, therefore, not being able to implement *any* policies at all.

A critical component of Wittman equilibrium is uncertainty about the election outcome for a given set of offered policies. If political parties know the exact location of the median voter and voters know the exact location of offered policies, then the outcome of the electoral competition is certain. Under these conditions, if either party is even infinitesimally closer than the other to the center, then they will win the election. Since each party would prefer to win with a slightly less desirable policy, there is a race to the center. Thus, under certainty, the behavior of policy-motivated candidates is visibly the same as the behavior of office-motivated candidates in the traditional model.[1] However, when we introduce uncertainty about the election outcome, it creates a trade-off. Parties may be willing to give up a small increase in the probability they will win in order to have the opportunity to implement a more preferred policy (should they win). Under a wide range of conditions, uncertainty about the voter distribution causes parties to *diverge*, with both parties proposing policies away from those preferred by the median voter.

There are two main sources of election uncertainty. One possibility is that candidates know the exact location of the median voter but the voters do not know the exact location of the candidates' policy positions (e.g., Chappell and Keech 1986). In this case, policy-motivated candidates appear to be "fuzzy," which allows them to offer equilibrium policies that are different from the location of the median voter and still have a positive probability of winning the election. A more traditional way to represent uncertainty about the election outcome is through the parties' uncertainty about the location of the median voter (whereas voters have complete information about the candidates' locations). In this case, the location of the median voter is randomly distributed. The distribution reflects what parties believe about the preferences of the electorate. The mean of the distribution is the parties' best guess about the location of the median voter and the variance reflects how certain the parties are. By using polls, it is possible to substantially reduce the variance of this distribution. However, it is possible that fundamental changes in beliefs about locations of the median voter happen only after major elections. One need only consider the many election "surprises" that have occurred over the years to realize that substantial uncertainty about voter preferences can only be resolved at the ballot box.

Wittman equilibrium analysis has been utilized in a number of political science studies (an incomplete list includes Hansson and Stuart 1984; Calvert 1985; Chappell and Keech 1986; Kollman, Miller, and Page 1992; Groseclose 2001; Adams and Merrill 2003). It is possible to show under certain relatively strict conditions that, in equilibrium, candidates' strategies differ if politicians are policy-motivated and there is uncertainty about the election outcome. However, despite being intuitively simple, Wittman equilibrium is very difficult to solve analytically, especially once we begin relaxing some of the restrictions. As shown in Roemer (2001: 60–61), the model of Wittman equilibrium is "intrinsically badly behaved" because the underlying expected utility functions are not quasi-concave. As a result, relaxing some of the basic assumptions about the model can make the model analytically intractable. For example, models based on Wittman equilibrium typically assume that parties have identical beliefs about the probability distribution of electoral outcomes and preferences that are equidistant from the expected location of the median voter. Of course, the latter assumption is violated if the expected location of the median voter changes through time (except for a degenerate case when all elections end in a perfect tie). Thus, a dynamic model of policy-motivated parties poses serious challenges for an analytical treatment of the model.

The main model that we describe in this book is just that—a dynamic model of electoral competition based on the Wittman equilibrium concept under uncertainty. We assume that politicians are policy-motivated (or have mixed motivations, which lead to substantively similar results). We also initially assume that there is inherent uncertainty about the true location of the median voter, which is randomly distributed according to some probability (though this distribution is generated endogenously in Chapter 4). The nature of this distribution reflects parties' subjective beliefs about the electorate. Finally, we assume that political competition is a dynamic process with multiple elections sequentially taking place. Because of the dynamic nature of the process, we cannot restrict party preferences (and, consequently, equilibrium policies) to be symmetric around the perceived location of the median voter. As a result, our general models become analytically intractable.

However, we analyze them using alternative formal methods in Chapters 2 and 4 such as numerical equilibrium analysis and agent-based modeling. We then test the predictions of these models using empirical evidence in Chapters 3, 5–8.

MANDATES AND VOTER BEHAVIOR

There are two ways to interpret party behavior in our models. First, the electoral mandate may affect policies that the winner proposes *in the present*, either right after a poll (see Meirowitz 2004) or right after an election (see, e.g., Conley 2001; Razin 2003). Large leads in the polls or large margins of victory in an election mean that winners can shift the policies they offer toward their own preferred policies without substantially increasing the risk of electoral defeat or resistance from the opposition. Conversely, close polls and elections should make parties more cautious. Second, the electoral mandate may affect the platforms of competing parties *in future elections* (e.g., Shotts 2000). A significant margin of victory indicates that the location of the median voter is closer to one of the parties, the winner. Both parties use this information to update their beliefs about the voters' distribution. Consequently, changes in beliefs tend to affect the choice of policies that the parties will offer in the next election.

In both cases, the margin of victory serves as a *signal*, where and how far the voters want politicians to go along the issue space, either in the present or in the future (or both). The signal is important if two requirements hold simultaneously: (1) politicians respond to the signal, that is, move with the mandate, and (2) voters believe that politicians respond to the signal. In this book, we focus on both requirements by presenting a theoretical model and examining its empirical implications for both voters and politicians. We show that, indeed, politicians are responsive to the margin of victory: in our theoretical analyses both the winning and losing party shift their equilibrium policies toward the policy preferred by the winning party and the size of the shift is proportional to the magnitude of the margin of victory. We also show that voters understand and believe in such electoral dynamics.

A desire to affect the margin of victory and send a signal to politicians can be defined as a *signaling motivation*. The idea of signaling is not new in an electoral context. Lohmann (1993) examines signaling as a cornerstone of "informative and manipulative" political action. She argues that if politicians pay attention to the size of a protest movement, then an individual may have an incentive not to free ride and to contribute to the public good by joining the movement. The act of voting is subject to a similar collective action problem. However, if voters believe that parties are dynamic in the way we describe, then they may have an incentive to signal their preferences by voting in order to affect future policies offered by both parties. Thus, our model of electoral competition and empirical analysis is consistent with analysis presented by Lohmann. For example, extremists in either context— protest movements or elections—take political action in order to affect the behavior of politicians whereas less-concerned citizens (moderates) tend to free ride.

Other recent papers outlining the logic of signaling include Shotts (2000), Meirowitz and Tucker (2003), Razin (2003), and Meirowitz (2004). Shotts presents a two-period game theoretic model of elections in which candidates estimate voter preferences by using results from the first election. Thus, the first election affects candidates' behavior in the second election. As a result, voters have a longer time horizon and, therefore, make electoral decisions having *both* elections in mind. One of the implications of the model is that voters may have an incentive to signal their preferences for moderate candidates by abstaining in the first election (even when the cost of turnout is zero). Razin (2003) presents a somewhat different model in which election results affect post-electoral policies. He shows that voters may have a signaling motivation to vote if political parties are responsive. More-over, the signaling motivation is stronger than the motivation to be a piv-otal voter. We compare these two motivations using a decision-theoretic model and empirical analysis in Chapter 5. Meirowitz and Tucker (2003) suggest that the signaling motivation may be responsible for split-ticket voting in sequential elections (see also Alesina and Rosenthal 1995). Meirowitz (2004) extends these results from elections to polls, and shows that if voters believe parties respond to vote intention surveys by adjusting their policies, then polling results cannot be a reliable measure of public opinion.

A unified message from these papers is that voting determines not only *which* party wins an election but also *how* one wins. Whether the voters care about post-electoral policies or future electoral platforms, in either case they have an incentive to engage in signaling behavior as long as they believe that all votes count and that the political parties are responsive to the mar-gin of victory. Similarly, the signaling motivation lies at the heart of the the-ory of electoral mandates that we present here, since it makes the margin of victory the link between voter behavior and candidate strategies. Throughout this book, we consider theoretical evidence supporting the notion of a signaling motivation and test it empirically, providing support for the importance of electoral mandates in political competition.

Another message from these formal models of the signaling motivation is that a belief in responsive parties gives voters an incentive to behave strategically in contests between two alternatives. Specifically, we should expect different behavior from extremist and moderate voters. Both kinds of voters want their preferred candidate to win, and thus have an incentive to vote sincerely. However, they also have an incentive to move post-electoral policy as close to their own preferred outcome as possible. Extremists experience no conflict between these incentives. Each vote for the preferred party increases the probability of victory and moves post-electoral policy closer to their ideal point. Moderates, on the other hand, must consider a trade-off. If they believe that larger margins of victory cause the winning party to offer more extreme policies, then they may signal their preference for more centrist policies by voting for the expected loser—even if it means voting for their second choice. We call this type of strategic behavior *mandate balancing* (see Chapter 6).

PLAN OF THIS BOOK

In this chapter, we have introduced the reader to the two pillars of our theory of electoral mandates: (1) for politicians—a dynamic extension of Wittman equilibrium under uncertainty, and (2) for voters—a signaling motivation to vote. We will be returning to these themes throughout the book as we explore both theoretical and empirical evidence that supports our theory of mandates, and our main thesis that politicians behave according to the margin of victory and that voters know that. Here we outline the substance of each chapter of the book as well as some of the methodological contributions.

In Chapter 2, we begin with a game theoretic model of dynamic electoral competition under uncertainty. Building on the classical Wittman model, we study how policy-motivated parties behave when they use the previous election to update their beliefs about the electorate. For this model, we treat voter behavior as exogenous (although we will endogenize voter behavior in Chapter 4). Although the model is quite simple, it quickly becomes analytically intractable when we introduce repeated elections because candidates' preferences are no longer symmetric around the expected location of the median voter.

We examine the properties of our model through the use of computer simulation. We believe this is a methodological contribution to the spatial modeling of electoral competition. Very little work has been done to extend the Wittman model because of its analytical intractability. This is unfortunate because the model can be examined by means of numerical equilibrium analysis. In this chapter, we provide basic guidelines for how to derive numerical comparative statics, and hope that these guidelines will be used by other scholars when they face similar problems with models that cannot be solved in closed form.

Substantively, we show that *mandates matter*. An increase in the winning party's vote share in the previous election helps the winner and hurts the loser because it causes *both* parties to shift their platforms for the next election in the direction of the winner's ideal point. This result will be tested empirically in later chapters. The model also yields other novel results. In the context of more than one election, we have two different kinds of uncertainty—electoral volatility and confidence in prior beliefs. The impact of electoral volatility is well known (see, e.g., Roemer 2001 for a rigorous treatment). More volatile elections yield greater uncertainty about the location of the median voter causing both parties to offer more extreme platforms. Our model reproduces this result with one exception. A party that wins the previous election in a landslide will actually offer a more *moderate* platform as electoral volatility increases because the greater uncertainty decreases the credibility of claiming a mandate. The second kind of uncertainty, confidence in prior beliefs, has not been studied previously but we show it also has an important impact on equilibrium platforms. We also show that polarization in the electorate plays a critical role in the dynamic behavior of parties. A more polarized electorate allows the winning party to choose a platform closer to its ideal point, but it also makes the losing party choose a more moderate platform.

Chapter 3 is devoted to further development and empirical testing of a theory about the link between election results and candidate ideology. Parties use past election results to update their beliefs about the location of the median voter and then adjust the candidates they offer accordingly. If the median moves right (left), Republican vote share increases (decreases) and causes both parties to move proportionally to the right (left). Testing this theory, we find that past elections have a dynamic impact on the ideology of future political candidates in the U.S. Senate. Winning parties tend to offer candidates who are more extreme in the next election and losing parties tend to offer candidates who are more moderate. Moreover, the size of the victory matters. Close elections yield small changes in the ideology of future candidates, whereas landslides yield larger changes. An average increase in Republican vote share yields a shift to the right that is about one-quarter to one-half the size of the average shift in ideology. This suggests that parties and candidates pay attention to past election returns. One major implication is that parties may remain polarized in spite of their responsiveness to the median voter.

In Chapter 4, we endogenize voter behavior and explore the effect of local information and retrospection on voter behavior in the context of the Wittman model. Specifically, we model voters as boundedly rational agents who make turnout decisions on the basis of election results and simple learning mechanisms. Voters are situated in social networks and use "fast and frugal heuristics" to overcome cognitive limitations and informational complexities (Lupia and McCubbins 1998; Gigerenzer et al. 1999). Our goal in this chapter is to describe a model of repeated elections in which voters and parties act *simultaneously*. We place voters in a social context and let them interact with one another when choosing whether or not to vote. We also let parties choose platforms, and these choices may change from election to election depending on feedback from the electorate. This allows us to explore the endogenous interaction of dynamic platforms and costly turnout.

In Chapter 4, we also hope to make a methodological contribution to the study of electoral behavior. We believe that an interdisciplinary approach, based on contributions from several social science disciplines, will lead us to a better understanding of the subject. The agent-based model we propose in this chapter is built on a number of contributions by sociologists (social context of voters), psychologists (bounded rationality and use of heuristics), economists (platforms dynamics and turnout decision), anthropologists (cultural influence exemplified by imitation), and last, but not least, political scientists (interdependence of voters and candidates, dynamic nature of the electoral competition). Agent-based modeling makes it easy to add many variables to a model, but we believe that initial modeling efforts for problems like these should remain simple to provide a bridge to what may already be an extensive analytical effort. Such an approach will not only provide good predictive models of electoral politics—it will also generate hypotheses that inspire future analytical efforts to find related closed-form solutions and empirical efforts to test relationships suggested by the model.

Consistent with the previous chapters, our substantive results suggest that mandates play an important role in electoral competition and they also help to address some of the most serious challenges in the field of electoral politics. Our model yields significant turnout, divergent platforms, and new hypotheses about the importance of social networks and citizen–party interactions. Making citizens boundedly rational and placing them in a social context turns out to be important. A closer look at social neighborhoods in the model shows that local imitation inherently yields negative feedback dynamics that encourage turnout. The effect is further amplified by the natural limits on information-processing capacities of citizens such as the length of memory.

Our model also shows that political candidates in the model pay attention to electoral mandates as they try to estimate the location of the median voter to remain competitive. As a result, proposed policies correlate with changes in the positions of both the median *voter* and the median *citizen* (the set of all people who vote and who do not vote). Interestingly, the greatest polarization occurs when voters' preferences are highly correlated between neighbors—that is, when neighborhoods are *ideologically* segregated.

In Chapter 5, we proceed to a closer examination of voters on the individual level. In this chapter, we assume party behavior is exogenous, letting politicians behave as in the models presented in Chapters 2 and 4. For voters, we construct a decision-theoretic model of turnout, in which individuals maximize their subjective-expected utility in the context of repeated elections. The model focuses on a citizen's subjective but rational estimates of whether he or she is better off voting or abstaining. In the model, we examine the value of a vote as a signal of one's preferences. Three empirical implications of our theoretical model are that citizens with higher levels of *external efficacy*, *patience*, and *electoral pessimism* should be more likely to vote.

We find limited empirical support for all three implications using validated turnout from National Election Studies (NES) data (1976–1988). Turnout is higher among citizens with higher external efficacy, higher discount factors (note that higher discount *factors* correspond to lower discount *rates*, i.e., less discounting), and lower expectations about the proportion of votes their favorite candidate will receive. The decision-theoretic model and empirical analysis have important empirical implications. First, our analysis suggests why a citizen may vote when elections are *not* close and there is a clear favorite. Second, we find further evidence for the phenomenon of *mandate balancing*, which we outlined above and examine in detail in

Chapter 6. Mandate balancing may explain why a voter would rationally support a party that is farther from one's ideal point. This happens when moderates support a party that is more likely to lose future elections in order to keep future winners from becoming too extreme. We also suggest that the NES studies showing the importance of close elections for turnout may, in fact, be capturing the effect of the signaling motivation. When we include the expected proportion of votes for one's favorite candidate in the empirical model, closeness ceases to be significant.

Chapter 6 focuses on how voter beliefs about politics and electoral mandates affect their behavior. In Chapters 2 and 4, we show two formal models that suggest parties have an incentive to respond to electoral margins, and in Chapters 4 and 5, we show how party responsiveness might influence voter behavior. In this chapter, we provide evidence that voters do, in fact, believe that parties are responsive, and this influences how they vote.

Using experimental data from the Time-Sharing Experiments in the Social Sciences (TESS) internet instrument, we find that voters believe an increase in the electoral margin of victory causes (1) the winning party to support more extreme policies and candidates, and (2) the losing party to support more moderate policies and candidates. We also test an important empirical implication of these voter beliefs, which suggests that some voters may vote strategically. Voting for the winner causes the winning platform to be adjusted further away from the center. Thus, moderates may have a "signaling" incentive to choose the party that is more likely to lose in order to keep the winning party from straying too far away from the voter's ideal point—another case of mandate balancing. Our results indicate that nonpartisan voters are more likely than partisans to switch their vote to the loser as the margin of victory increases. While it is possible that this reflects an antipartisan stance by nonpartisans, this is unlikely since only those nonpartisans who believe in responsive parties exhibit a tendency to vote strategically. If nonpartisans tend to prefer moderate policies, then these results are supportive of the mandate-balancing theory and the formal models in Chapters 2, 4, and 5 that generated this theory.

Chapter 7 draws attention to the fact that the costs of turnout are borne on Election Day and before, whereas benefits related to the outcome of the election are not reaped until much later. This suggests that patience plays an important role in the turnout decision, especially if voters are influenced by a signaling motivation to vote as hypothesized in Chapter 5. Patient citizens who are willing to wait for future benefits should be more likely to vote because they place a greater value on the impact of the election on *future* policy changes. Impatient citizens should be less likely to vote because they are more influenced by the immediate burdens of decision-making and physical participation.

Evidence from the laboratory supports this hypothesis. Subjects were given a series of choices between an earlier, smaller prize and a later, larger prize. Those who consistently choose the later prize are significantly more likely to vote than those who consistently choose the earlier prize. The statistical relationship between patience and turnout remains even when we control for numerous other factors thought to affect the decision to vote. Patience is also found to correlate with political interest and church attendance, which suggests that variation in patience may be able to explain other relationships with turnout.

In Chapter 8, we look outside the electoral system for evidence of the importance of mandates. We utilize rational partisan and policy risk theories to show that presidential mandates (margins of victory) have an effect on interest rate expectations. If people expect parties to adjust the policies they offer in response to the margin of victory (or loss) in the last election, then rational partisan theory implies that people should expect higher inflation as expected vote share for the Left increases. Similarly, policy risk theory suggests that people should expect greater policy uncertainty as the margin of victory for *either* party increases since a larger margin of victory may give the winning party more leeway to implement the more extreme version of its policies. The empirical model confirms both expectations, showing that nominal interest rates rise when Democrats become more likely to win either branch of government.

In addition, the results are suggestive of new lines of research that could make contributions to several existing literatures. For example, the policy risk theory is an important complement to the rational partisan theory because it helps to make sharper predictions about interest rate expectations. Previous work that did not control for vote margin and incumbency (e.g., Cohen 1993) may have underestimated the partisan effect since both Democratic Party incumbents and Republican Party challengers may have an ambiguous effect on nominal interest rates. Future tests of partisan theory should, therefore, control for incumbency, the institutional division of power, and margins of victory.

The last chapter offers an overview of the theory of electoral mandates, substantive and methodological lessons the reader may have learned from this work, and the most important implications of our analysis for the study of electoral politics and democratic processes in general.

WHO IS THIS BOOK FOR?

This work should appeal to a wide range of scholars in its breadth of methods and data employed. First, we hope to appeal to game theorists who study political competition. Our work has certain parallels with previously published books by Roemer (2001) and Conley (2001). Roemer presents a more rigorous and abstract treatment of the subject intended for scholars with advanced formal training. Conley's work, on the other hand, is more applied and focused. Our theoretical analysis fits somewhere in between. Additionally, we build upon both of these efforts by creating a model that is dynamic and by using an agent-based model to relax some of the stricter assumptions associated with the closed-form model.

Second, the models we employ should appeal to political scientists who are increasingly interested in bounded rationality, alternative formal models, and interdisciplinary approaches to the study of politics. In this respect, our formal models are influenced by recent developments in other disciplines: sociology, experimental economics, evolutionary psychology, and computational modeling in social sciences (see in particular Chapters 4–7).

Third, the extensive empirical analysis in the book should appeal broadly to scholars with substantive interests in the American party system and voter behavior. We draw on an unusually broad range of data sources, and utilize experimental data from TESS and the Iowa Electronic Markets (IEM) to complement more standard analyses based on National Election Survey and candidate position data.

Finally, several scholars now emphasize the value of combining formal theoretic and empirical approaches in a single work (known as empirical implications of theoretical models movement, or EITM). We hope to appeal to these readers, as well, with the variety of theoretical and empirical tools that we employ in our analysis.

## TWO

Moving with the Mandate: Policy-Motivated Parties in Dynamic Political Competition*

How do electoral outcomes affect policy? The most obvious answer to this question is that elections determine *who* gets to make policy. But elections also determine *what* kind of policy winners can enact. After a landslide victory, winners may claim a "mandate" to govern, arguing that the size of the victory shows that the public is eager to support their policies (Kramer 1977; Kelly 1983). After a close election, losers may claim that there is no mandate—the public's ambivalence should be interpreted as a sign that support for the winners' policies is qualified at best. Dahl (1990) points out that both of these arguments are self-serving and notes that even if the margin of victory is large it is unclear whether overwhelming support for the winner translates into support for a particular policy. However, recent empirical evidence indicates that mandates do have an effect on policies and candidates (Conley 2001; Peterson et al. 2003). In this chapter, we develop a formal theoretical model that shows how and why electoral margins affect the policies and candidates offered by the two major parties.

To understand how parties use mandates, we return to the literature on spatial political competition between two parties. Traditional models assume that parties care *only* about winning elections (Downs 1957; Davis, Hinich,

* From Oleg Smirnov and James H. Fowler. 2007. Moving with the Mandate: Policy-Motivated Parties in Dynamic Political Competition. *Journal of Theoretical Politics* 19(1): 9–31. Reprinted by permission of Sage Publications Ltd., ©2007; in production.

and Ordeshook 1970). Wittman (1977) extends these models by assuming that parties also care about policy outcomes (see also Wittman 1983; Calvert 1985; Duggan and Fey 2005; Roemer 1997, 2001). Under this assumption, parties face a dilemma. By moving *toward* the median voter's preferences, they increase their likelihood of winning. By moving *away* from the median voter's preferences toward their own preferred policy, they increase the desirability of the policy they implement should they win the election. As a result, policy-motivated parties offer policies that diverge when there is uncertainty about the preferences of the median voter.

The Wittman model is based on a very simple concept: parties must balance the fear of losing the election against the greed of proposing the policies they most prefer. Unfortunately, this simplicity quickly disappears in formal settings. As the two parties simultaneously maximize their expected utilities, analytical solutions become very complicated. Roemer (1997) provides a rigorous and not trivial proof that a unique equilibrium exists in the Wittman model. However, this model is usually too complicated to yield closed-form solutions for comparative statics analysis (Roemer 2001). The few models that can be solved in closed form rely on the assumption that the median voter's preference is exactly equidistant between the preferences of the two parties (symmetry). Without the symmetry assumption, however, the Wittman model *cannot* be solved in closed form. As a result, there have been very few attempts to build on the Wittman model.[1]

To analyze the effect of electoral outcomes on policy, we extend the Wittman model by placing it in a dynamic setting and relaxing the crucial symmetry assumption. We introduce a model of Bayesian learning in the traditional spatial context, which allows policy-motivated parties to use information about the past to update their beliefs about the state of electorate. We then analyze the effect of information gained in previous elections on policies offered by the two parties. Unfortunately, incorporating Bayesian inference in the Wittman framework causes it to become analytically intractable. However, instead of abandoning the model, we analyze it using *numerical comparative statics*. A special section in this chapter is devoted to the proper methodology for conducting such an analysis.

The model yields a number of novel hypotheses that can be tested empirically (see Table 2.1 for a complete summary). The most important of these (and the one on which we focus in this book) is that mandates matter—equilibrium policies are affected not only by *who* wins the election but by *how much*. Larger margins of victory cause both parties to move the policies they offer toward the winner's preferred policy. Moreover, the losing

TABLE 2.1   Summary of the Effects of Electoral Outcomes of Policy

	Exogenous Change				
Effect	*Winning Party's Vote Share Increases*	*Winning Party's Ideal Point Becomes More Extreme*	*Electoral Volatility Increases*	*Confidence in Prior Beliefs Decreases*	*Electoral Polarization Increases*
Winning party's platform becomes	Somewhat more extreme	Much more extreme	More extreme for close elections; more moderate for landslides	More extreme	More extreme
Losing party's platform becomes	Much more moderate	Somewhat more moderate	More extreme	More extreme for close elections; more moderate for landslides	More moderate
Result #	1, 2	3	4	5	6

party tends to shift more than the winning party. This dynamic yields an interesting result. Contrary to the common view that close elections imply compromise and moderation, the model suggests that close elections may lead to the *largest* divergence (smallest convergence) in policies offered by the two parties. This might help to explain the coincidence of close elections and divisive partisanship that has recently occurred in national politics of the United States.

A THEORY OF DYNAMIC RESPONSIVENESS

Parties have access to a lot of information about the electorate (Alvarez 1997). However, they probably do not have perfect information about the precise voter distribution because preferences change over time (Stimson, Mackuen, and Erikson 1995), variable turnout generates uncertainty about who will actually vote (Calvert 1985; Morton 1993), and pre-election polls are not precise. Previous election results may help parties find the median voter in two ways. First, elections produce a winner and a loser. Assuming that voters choose the candidate closest to them in a single-dimension issue space, a candidate who wins an election will be ideologically closer to the median voter than a candidate who loses. Second, elections also produce a margin of victory. A candidate who wins in a landslide is likely to be located closer to the median voter than one who only barely wins against the same opponent.

Figure 2.1 illustrates this point. Imagine a hypothetical election between a Democratic candidate and a Republican candidate in which the voter distribution is not known. Under proximity voting, voters choose the closest candidate, so we can draw a cutpoint that is exactly halfway between the two candidates. All voters on the left of the cutpoint choose the Democratic candidate and all voters on the right choose the Republican candidate. The vote share for the Republican (Democrat) is simply the area under the voter distribution to the right (left) of the cutpoint. When the election is very close (top of Figure 2.1), it implies that the median voter is centered near the cutpoint as the median divides the electorate in half. A moderate Democratic victory (middle of Figure 2.1) suggests that the voter distribution is centered

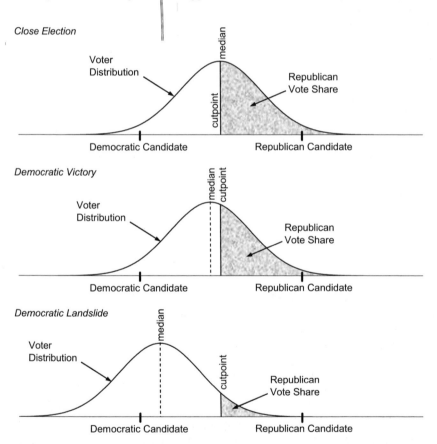

FIGURE 2.1   Relationship between the margin of victory and the voter distribution. The top figure shows the voter distribution implied by a close election. The middle figure shows the location of the voter distribution implied by a slight Democratic victory. The bottom figure shows the voter distribution implied by a Democratic landslide.

slightly to the left of the cutpoint. This is because some voters to the right of the median voter must have chosen the Democrat and are therefore to the left of the cutpoint. Thus, the median voter must lie slightly closer to the Democrat than the Republican. If the Democrat wins in a landslide (bottom of Figure 2.1), then the voter distribution is centered far to the left of the cutpoint, implying that the Democratic candidate lies much closer to the median voter than the Republican.

How do these changes in beliefs about the median voter affect party behavior? If parties are policy-motivated and uncertain about the voter distribution, then they face a trade-off that ties their actions to the location of the median voter (Wittman 1977; Calvert 1985; Osborne 1995; Roemer 2001). These parties want to implement their preferred policy, but they also want to win the election. Their beliefs about the voter distribution influence their choice because it affects their beliefs about the probability of winning.

In the next section, we show formally that when beliefs about the location of the median voter shift, the equilibrium candidates chosen by policy-motivated parties also shift in the direction of the winning party's position and monotonically in the size of the shift. However, the reasoning that underlies our hypothesis is intuitive. Consider the following thought experiment.

Suppose a liberal Democrat beats a conservative Republican. As shown before, both parties can use the election results to infer that the median voter was closer to the Democrat than to the Republican. The Democrats know they could have supported a more liberal candidate and still could have won the election. Similarly, the Republicans know that their candidate was too far from the median voter and would only have been competitive if he or she were more liberal. The lesson both parties draw is that they should have chosen more liberal candidates. If the parties apply this lesson to the next election, then the candidates of both parties will tend to be more liberal.

Of course, the vote share matters, too. If the Democrats won in a landslide, they could have proposed a much more liberal candidate. If the Republicans lost in a landslide, they would have needed to be much more liberal to compete. Thus, any change in candidates due to updated beliefs about the location of the median voter is likely to be increasing in the margin of victory. One might argue that this reasoning is nonstrategic. After all, if the Republicans know that the Democrats are going to shift left, then they might be able to win the next election by merely staying put. However, knowing that the Republicans know that, the Democrats would have an incentive to shift closer to their own preferences but not so much that they dramatically decrease the probability of winning the next election. Even when strategic reasoning is extended to full common knowledge, the formal model shows that both parties tend to shift in the direction of the median voter.

THE FORMAL MODEL

Two parties engaged in political competition, L and R, choose platforms (y_L, y_R) in a one-dimensional policy space such that $-\infty < y_L \leq y_R < \infty$. Parties are policy-motivated with exogenous ideal points, $-\infty < p_L < 0 < p_R < \infty$, and gain utility according to a Euclidian utility function $U_i = -(y_w - p_i)^2$, $i = L, R$, where $y_w \in \{y_L, y_R\}$ is the platform of the winning party.[2] When choosing platforms, parties have full information about the previous election. This includes the location of platforms in the previous election (x_L, x_R), and the previous election results as reflected in the vote share for the left party, $0 \leq s \leq 1$.

To introduce uncertainty, we assume that parties have prior beliefs about the location of the median voter, M. These beliefs are subject to a continuous distribution

$$M \sim \psi(M; \mu, \beta), \tag{1}$$

with mean μ and variance $\beta > 0$. The mean can be interpreted as a party's *best guess* about the location of the median voter, whereas the variance denotes its *confidence in prior beliefs*. Small values of β imply that the parties are confident in their prior guess about the location of the median voter; large values suggest that the prior information is less reliable.

Parties use information from the previous election to update their estimate of the location of the median voter. Elections, however, may not provide perfect information about the location of the median voter due to fluctuating turnout, idiosyncratic platforms, changing "policy moods" (Stimson, Mackuen, and Erikson 1995) and a variety of other random shocks (Londregan and Romer 1993; Adams and Merrill 2003). Therefore, for any single election the median voter, m, can be thought of as the outcome of a random variable with mean M. These election outcomes are distributed according to the continuous distribution

$$m \sim \gamma(m; M, b), \tag{2}$$

where mean M is the location of the median voter and variance $b > 0$ can be thought of as *electoral volatility*, or how much the parties trust that the results of the previous election reflect the true location of the median voter. Small values of b indicate that the parties think the election provides very accurate information about the location of the median voter; conversely, large values of b imply that they think election results are more random and may contain little information about the location of the median voter.

Suppose that parties use Bayes' rule to incorporate information from the previous election into their estimate of the location of the median voter.[3] Specifically, parties must update their *beliefs* about the location of the median voter, M, given an *observation*, m, which is the location of the median voter implied in the previous election. If we assume that the distributions (1) and (2) are normal, then the posterior mean μ' and posterior variance β' are

$$\mu' = \frac{\mu b + m\beta}{b + \beta}, \; \beta' = \frac{b\beta}{b + \beta}.$$

PROOF: *See Box and Tiao (1973, pp. 74–75).*

Notice that the updated estimate of the location of the median voter is simply a weighted average of the prior belief and the new information obtained in the previous election.[4] The weights on these beliefs are the variances. If prior information is unreliable, then more weight is given to the new information yielded in the election. If electoral volatility is high, then more weight is given to the prior belief.

This updating process assumes that the location of the median voter for the previous election, m, can be observed. However, it is not possible to use the vote share to infer the location of the median voter without also having a belief about the voter distribution. Therefore, we assume that parties believe that voters are distributed according to a symmetric continuous distribution

$$v \sim \emptyset(v; M, B). \tag{3}$$

Since the distribution is continuous and symmetric, the mean of the voter distribution, M, coincides with the location of the median voter. See Table 2.2 for an overview of the distributions of M, m, and v and the rationale why all three are necessary in the model. The variance of the voter distribution, B, represents how widely voter preferences spread across the policy space. For simplicity, we call it *electoral polarization*.[5] Small values of B suggest that most voters have similar preferences in the middle of the policy space; large values imply that there are more extremists in the electorate and voter preferences are spread more broadly across the policy space.

TABLE 2.2 Summary of the Three Distributions in the Formal Model

Distribution	Description	Mean	Variance	Purpose/Necessity
$M \sim \psi(M;\mu,\beta)$	M is the true and unknown location of the median voter. Parties believe that it is distributed according to $\psi(\mu,\beta)$.	μ describes the parties' initial best guess about the location of the median voter.	β describes how certain the parties are about their initial best guess.	The distribution is essential in the model as it describes the uncertainty about the location of the median voter as reflected in the parties' prior beliefs.
$m \sim \gamma(m;M,b)$	m is the location of the median voter in the previous election (which can be inferred from the previous election; Lemma 1).	M is the true and unknown location of the median voter; a median voter in a particular election is most *likely* to be located at the mean M.	b describes how much the parties trust that the results of the previous election reflect the true location of the median voter.	The distribution makes the model dynamic: It describes the new information about the location of the median voter that the parties receive as the previous election results become known. The parties' posterior beliefs are a Bayesian product of the prior beliefs and the newly acquired information.
$v \sim \phi(v;M,B)$	v is the density of the voter distribution; the area under the density function corresponds to the total number of voters.	M is the true and unknown location of the median voter *and* it is also the mean of the voters' distribution.	B is assumed to be known and it describes the spread of the voters' distribution which we call "electoral polarization."	The distribution is necessary because it allows the parties to use the results of the previous election to calculate m, the true location of the median voter in the previous election (Lemma 1).

Specifying the voter distribution leads us to the following lemma:

LEMMA 1: *If parties have beliefs about the degree of electoral polarization, then they can infer the location of the median voter in the previous election by observing the platforms and the margin of victory.*

PROOF: *See Appendix 2.1.*

Conforming to the intuition illustrated in Figure 2.1, Lemma 1 shows that parties can use election results to make an educated guess about the location of the median voter. This allows us to connect party behavior in one election to the next election.

Most previous models of party competition focus on a single election, but our model focuses on the *dynamics* of party competition from one election to another. Parties choose platforms, an election is held, parties observe the outcome, and then they choose platforms for the next election. To model this process, we need only use the Wittman model to find equilibrium platforms in the first election, Lemma 1 to see how parties update their beliefs given the election outcome, and then the Wittman model again to find equilibrium platforms in the second section. One might object that in this setup we do not consider the possibility that parties might use their platforms to manipulate future inferences about the location of the median voter. However, given the posited beliefs about the voter distribution and common knowledge of the platforms, notice that *it is not possible to manipulate future inferences*. Under proximity voting there is a fixed relationship between the voter distribution and the election outcome given a set of platforms. Changing those platforms will change the vote share, but it also changes the cutpoint between them. As a result, the inference about the location of the median voter will always be the same *regardless of the choice of platforms*. Thus, our model accounts for the behavior of parties that optimize dynamically over a series of elections because this behavior will be exactly the same as the behavior of parties that optimize separately in each period.

Although we have characterized the conditions for equilibrium in Appendix 2.1, we do not have a closed-form expression for the equilibrium posterior platforms. This is because an analytical solution is usually not available in the Wittman model. Even when there is a closed-form solution, analytical comparative statics always rely on an assumption of preferences that are symmetric around the mean of the median voter distribution. It is not possible to make this assumption if beliefs about the median voter change from one election to the next—parties can have symmetric preferences either in the prior election or the posterior election but not both. How then should we proceed? Roemer (2001: 89) notes that "although the Wittman model is, in most cases, too complex to permit solving for the political equilibrium by hand, solutions are easily computable by machine." Therefore, to study the effect of beliefs on the equilibrium behavior of policy-motivated parties we turn to computational simulation.

COMPARATIVE STATICS IN
COMPUTATIONAL MODELS

There is a perception among formal theorists that computational results are unreliable because they are sensitive to human error. However, mathematical proofs are also subject to error. Moreover, although programs are sometimes more complicated than proofs, the computer enforces a consistency on the programmer that may be missing for the analytical theorist. Mistakes in coding often cause a program not to run. Mistakes in proofs, however, must be discovered by the author or human referees and colleagues. Another major criticism of computational results deals with inability to cover all possible values of the parameter space. We show how this problem can be addressed and substantially alleviated as follows.

Although it is obviously difficult to quantify uncertainty related to errors in proofs and programming, we can estimate uncertainty in comparative statics results given there are no errors in these methods. Suppose we claim that for a given parameter space, a value of interest $f(a, b)$ is always increasing in one of the parameters, a. If an analytical solution is available, we can prove this claim with certainty by showing that the derivative $df(a, b)/da$ is positive in this space. What the derivative tells us is that for each very small change in the parameter a we get a positive increase in $f(a, b)$. The equivalent procedure for a computational model is to *sample* parameters from the space. For a given set of parameters, we find $f(a, b)$. Then we increase a by a very small amount ε and find $f(a + \varepsilon, b)$. If $f(a + \varepsilon, b) \leq f(a, b)$, then we have contradicted the claim and it is false. If not, the claim may be true.

Each draw from the sample space decreases uncertainty about the claim. If the parameters are drawn equally from all parts of the space and each point in the space has an equal chance of contradicting the claim, then we can use conventional probability calculations to estimate the uncertainty. Suppose that in n draws we do not contradict the claim. If the portion of the space that would contradict the claim is p, then the probability of not contradicting the claim is $(1-p)^n$. To estimate the maximum value of p consistent with 0 observations of a contradiction we can set this probability equal to 0.05 (to establish 95% confidence). Then $(1-p)^n = 0.05$, which implies $p = 1 - 0.05^{\frac{1}{n}}$. It is easy to compute this threshold exactly for any n, but a well-known rule of thumb is $p \approx 3/n$ (Hanley and Lippmanhand 1983). Although analytical results are always more certain ($p = 0$), when they are not available we can ensure that p is very small for computational results by relying on a large n number of draws.

In this chapter, we are interested in how the parameters *vote share, party preferences, electoral volatility, confidence in prior beliefs,* and *electoral polarization* affect the dynamic choice of party platforms. Party preferences are held constant at -1 and 1 to model parties with divergent interests. However, for one of the results we relax this assumption and vary the right preference between 0 and 1 to see how preference change affects party platforms. We allow vote share for the left to vary between 0 and 1, but we restrict the belief about the mean location of the median voter to the interval between the party preferences. Substantively, this means the parties always think they are on opposite sides of the median voter. Finally, we allow each of the three variance parameters (electoral volatility, confidence in prior beliefs, and electoral polarization) to range from 0 to 1. To search this parameter space, we draw each parameter from an independent uniform distribution on the defined interval.

Each of the results we present later is accompanied by figures that illustrate the relationships in question with a single set of parameter values. However, to test the general validity of each result, we sample the parameter space 1,000 times and evaluate the claim for each set of parameters. To do this, we find posterior equilibrium platforms for a given set of parameters, then increase one parameter by 0.001, and repeat the procedure to see how a small change in one of the parameters affects the model. *Not one of the draws contradicts any of the results.* According to the above analysis, that means we can be 95% confident that less than 0.3% of the parameter space contradicts the findings. Thus, these results are *robust* for a wide array of possible real-world elections in almost the same way as an analytically solved model.

VOTE SHARE: MOVING WITH THE MANDATE

The intuitive idea behind the notion of electoral mandates is that, depending on the margin of victory, the winning party adopts a platform closer to its ideal preference point. In the model, we indeed observe that as the vote share of the winning party increases, the winner moves its platform closer to its most preferred policy.

Result 1: Increasing the vote share of one party in the previous election causes both parties to shift their platforms toward the ideal policies of the party with increased vote share.

Figure 2.2 illustrates how both parties react to the outcome of the previous election represented as a vote share for the left party.[6] The left plot

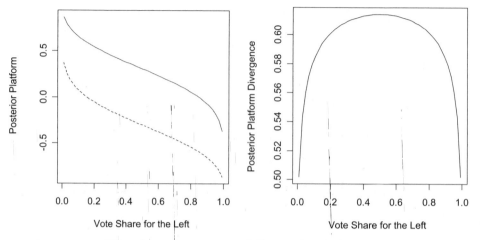

FIGURE 2.2   Effect of vote share on party platforms. The solid line designates the
right party; the dashed line designates the left party.

shows the effect of vote share on the equilibrium platforms of both parties
when everything else in the model is held fixed. Higher values in this figure
indicate more conservative platforms. The top line represents the platform
for the right party whereas the bottom is the platform for the left party.
Notice that *both* platforms become more liberal as vote share for the left
party increases. The higher left vote share indicates the median voter is farther to the left, so the left party has more leeway to move platforms toward
its own preferences, whereas the right feels more pressure to move its
platforms toward the center. In other words, *both* parties move with the
mandate.

The right plot in Figure 2.2 shows the effect of vote share on divergence.
Notice first of all that, regardless of the size of the vote share, parties do not
converge. This confirms a well-known result that policy-motivated parties
offer divergent platforms when the location of the median voter is not known
with certainty (Wittman 1983, Hansson and Stuart 1984, Calvert 1985, Roemer 1997). In addition, the degree of divergence varies with the margin of
victory. The right platform is farthest away from the left platform when the
previous election was very close ($s = 0.5$). Conversely, when one party wins
in a landslide (e.g., $s = 0.1$ or $s = 0.9$), the platforms end up closer together.

Result 2: Close elections yield the largest platform divergence if the perceived
location of the median voter is close enough[7] to the midpoint between the
preferences of the two parties.

How can we explain such a puzzling result? Under certainty, the margin of victory would have no effect: the candidates will converge to the known location of the median voter. Under uncertainty, however, the divergence is persistent and its magnitude is *inversely* related to the margin of victory. This may seem counterintuitive. For example, Robertson (1976) argues that close elections indicate the electorate is evenly divided and, therefore, parties will compromise and offer centrist platforms. However, recent empirical evidence suggests the contrary: electoral margins in the 2000 and 2004 U.S. presidential elections were just 0.5% and 2.4%, yet there is widespread agreement that partisan divisions between Democrats and Republicans have increased. Moreover, this argument does not take into account the asymmetric forces that affect the equilibrium platforms of the winning and losing party. Election results suggest that the location of the median voter is closer to the party that won the election. *In addition*, they decrease uncertainty about the location of the median voter. For the losing party, both forces work in the same direction—toward the center. The party not only learns that the median voter is located father away from its own ideal point, it also becomes more confident about this location. For the winning party, the two forces oppose each other. Winning the election allows a party to move away from the center toward its own ideal point. At the same time, the party becomes more confident about the location of the median voter, which drives its new equilibrium platform toward the center.

It is important to note here one limitation of this model. In the limit, absent shocks to the voters' distribution, the two parties will learn the location of the median voter to which they will eventually converge. The convergence will be slow if the electoral margins are small, that is, under close elections (or if the voters' distribution changes over time). Conversely, convergence will be fast if there are landslide elections and if the preferences of the electorate are fixed. In the real world we do not expect such convergence because there will be new sources of variance at each election. Moreover, it is unlikely that parties know the exact variance of the voter distribution. In Chapter 4, we relax this assumption and show that parties do converge, but not all the way to the median voter. Instead, they converge to a set of divergent platforms and the size of the divergence is increasing in the steady state variance. Alternatively, Dew-Becker (2006) explicitly models random shocks to the voter distribution and shows that they contribute to the steady state variance with much the same effect on divergence and implications for policy choices.

ASYMMETRIC PREFERENCES

Another potentially important implication of the model is the effect that increased extremism of one party has on the platform of the other party. Figure 2.3 shows how changing the preference of the right party from 0 to 1 affects equilibrium platforms. Notice that as the preferences of the right party become more extreme, it tends to choose platforms farther to the right. This may not be surprising, but it does provoke an interesting reaction from the left: the left party reacts to a more extreme opponent by choosing a platform *closer* to the center.

Result 3: As one party's ideal point becomes more extreme, the equilibrium platforms of both parties move in the direction of the more extreme party.

This dynamic may surprise formal theorists and scholars who study party behavior. First, a more extreme platform has a lower probability of winning the election. Second, a more extreme platform can be viewed as an aggressive challenge to the other party. Both factors might warrant a tit-for-tat–type response: the other party could similarly choose a more extreme platform closer to its preference point. Nevertheless, the other party chooses a more moderate platform in equilibrium.

This has to do with risk aversion in the utilities. Although more extreme platforms are less likely to win elections, when they do it is much more

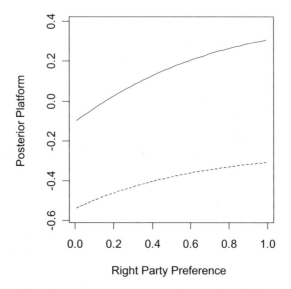

FIGURE 2.3   Effect of party preferences on platforms. The solid line designates the right party; the dashed line designates the left party.

painful to the opposing party. In equilibrium, offering a moderate platform is the best response to increased extremism in one's opponent. This may help to explain why in the United States the recent movement of the Republican Party to the right has been accompanied by the Democratic Party moving to the center rather than to the left.

ELECTORAL VOLATILITY: WINNER'S FOE, LOSER'S ALLY

Recall that electoral volatility is the variance in the distribution of the median voter. Lower values of electoral volatility indicate that parties believe election results provide reliable information that can be used to infer the location of the median voter. Higher values mean parties believe there is a noisier relationship between election outcomes and the voter distribution. Turnout may be one of the more important determinants of electoral volatility. For example, ceteris paribus high turnout would provide more reliable information about preferences of the electorate and, therefore, would correspond to a smaller variance.

In our model, the effect of electoral volatility on future platforms is intuitive. If the volatility is high and the election results are not very informative about the true preferences of electorate, then parties have not learned much about the possible location of the median voter. As a result, both the winner and the loser have freedom to adopt platforms that substantially diverge. However, there is one exception. Consider the plots in Figure 2.4. The left figure shows how electoral volatility affects platforms when the right party wins a close election whereas the right figure shows the effect when it wins in a landslide.

Regardless of the margin of victory, increasing the belief that the election results do not reflect the opinion of the electorate causes the left party to discount the election and move toward its own preference in choosing a new platform. The effect on the right party depends on the margin of victory. When the right wins a close election, greater electoral volatility leads to a more extreme platform. When the right wins in a landslide, greater electoral volatility makes the party choose a more moderate platform. This is a counterintuitive result:

Result 4: If the margin of victory is large enough, greater electoral variance causes the winning party to choose a more moderate platform.

The explanation, however, is straightforward. We know that uncertainty is necessary for divergence, but it also decreases the importance of the

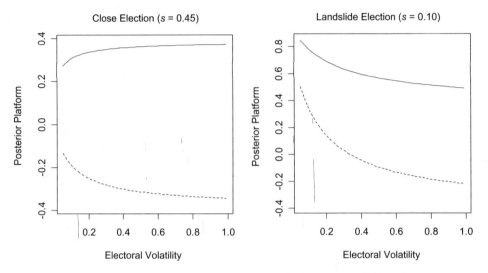

FIGURE 2.4   Effect of electoral volatility on party platforms. The solid line designates the right party; the dashed line designates the left party.

margin of victory. Higher electoral volatility makes it more difficult to tell who the electorate actually prefers when the election is close, which causes both the winner and the loser to offer more extreme platforms. However, higher volatility also increases the chance that a landslide victory might have been a fluke, weakening the inference that the landslide winner is much closer to the median voter. This pushes the winner back toward the center and at a high enough margin of victory reverses the relationship between electoral volatility and the winner's platform.

PRIOR INFORMATION: CONFIDENCE
YIELDS DIVERGENCE

Confidence in prior information is defined as the party's prior belief about the variance of the location of the median voter. High variance means that parties have little certainty about their prior beliefs. Low variance means that prior information is thought to be reliable. In the extreme case when the variance is zero (perfect certainty), the parties think they know the exact location of the median voter to which they converge.

Higher uncertainty about prior beliefs increases the relative importance of new information obtained from the election outcome, which makes winning more meaningful for estimating the location of the median voter. This increases the ability of the winning party to shift platforms toward its own preference by claiming a mandate after an election. Thus, the effect on future platforms is less straightforward. Consider the figures in Figure 2.5.

The left figure shows how uncertainty about prior beliefs affects platforms after the right party wins a close election, whereas the right figure shows the effect after it wins in a landslide. Regardless of the margin of victory, increasing uncertainty (decreasing confidence) in prior beliefs causes the right party to propose a platform closer to its own ideal point. The effect on the left party depends on the margin of victory. When the left loses in a landslide, increasing uncertainty causes the left to shift toward the right. Otherwise, when the left loses a close election, increasing uncertainty causes the left to shift toward its own ideal point. This implication of the model is symmetric to the implication regarding electoral volatility:

Result 5: If the margin of victory is large enough, decreasing confidence in prior beliefs causes the losing party to choose a more moderate platform.

Decreasing confidence in prior information increases posterior uncertainty about the location of the median voter, which pushes both parties toward the extreme. However, reduced confidence in prior beliefs also increases the relative importance of new information obtained from election results and makes both parties more sensitive to the winner's claim of

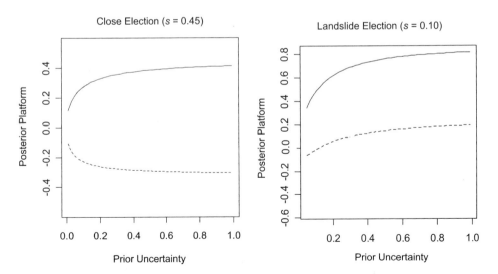

FIGURE 2.5   The effect of prior uncertainty on party platforms. The solid line designates the right party; the dashed line designates the left party.

a mandate. Thus, at a high enough margin of victory the relationship between confidence and the loser's platform reverses.

An important implication of these dynamics is that greater *prior* uncertainty *increases* the likelihood that both parties will move toward the center. This result may seem at odds with what we have learned from the literature on policy-motivated parties under uncertainty. Static models of party competition suggest that uncertainty about the location of the median voter increases *divergence*. However, when parties are less certain about their *prior* beliefs they are more likely to *converge*. The explanation for this paradox is straightforward. Parties are most likely to move toward the center when the election is close because there is no mandate effect to push parties left or right and the reduced uncertainty from observing the election causes the parties to converge toward the center. As the prior uncertainty *increases*, it improves the informative value of the observed election for *reducing* posterior uncertainty. This increases the strength of the pull toward the center and counteracts the mandate effect for a wider range of election outcomes.

ELECTORAL POLARIZATION: MANDATE AMPLIFIER

Party leaders, activists, and even rank-and-file members are known to have polarized preferences that diverge significantly from those of the median voter (Iversen 1994; DiMaggio et al. 1996; Abramowitz and Saunders 1998; Hetherington 2001; Layman and Carsey 2002). Our model suggests how the magnitude of divergence in *voter* preferences might affect political equilibrium. Recall that the degree of polarization of the electorate is related to the variance of the voter distribution. A small variance indicates that voters have similar preferences. A large variance suggests that there are more extremists and voters are spread more broadly across the policy space. Figure 2.6 shows what happens to platforms after a victory by the right party as we increase electoral polarization. Notice that increasing polarization causes both parties to shift toward the right.

Result 6: Increasing electoral polarization causes the winning party to propose a more extreme platform and the losing party to propose a more moderate platform.

The effect of electoral polarization on platforms is straightforward. A fixed margin of victory implies a shift in the location of the median voter from the prior belief about its location. As voters become more polarized,

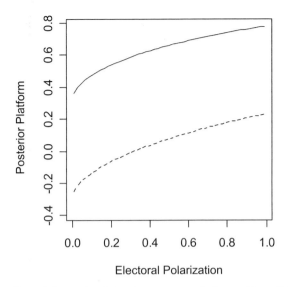

FIGURE 2.6   Effect of electoral polarization on party platforms. The solid line designates the right party; the dashed line designates the left party. A vote share of $s = 0.10$ is assumed.

the size of this shift increases because the same number of voters is spread over a larger region of the policy space. Thus, electoral polarization magnifies the importance of the mandate on future platforms.

CONCLUSION

Our analysis of dynamic political competition is based on a unidimensional spatial model, in which we assume that the location of the median voter is unknown and that the parties competing for office are policy-motivated. Past election results serve the same function as a very good opinion poll (cf., Adams et al. 2003). By introducing Bayesian learning into the well-known spatial context, we allow policy-motivated parties to use their past experience to estimate the location of the median voter in the present. This setup allows us to examine how the margin of victory, party ideal points, electoral volatility, confidence in prior information, and electoral polarization affect equilibrium behavior (Table 2.1).

The most important implication of the model is that *mandates matter*. An increase in the winning party's vote share in the previous election helps the winner and hurts the loser because it causes *both* parties to shift their platforms for the next election in the direction of the winner's ideal point.

This result can be tested empirically. For example, in Chapter 3 we show that U.S. Senate candidates from winning parties tend to become more extreme and candidates from losing parties tend to become more moderate in proportion to the previous margin of victory. The model also suggests that the losing party tends to shift more than the winning party and the size of the difference is increasing in the margin of victory. Thus, contrary to the conventional wisdom, close elections yield the greatest amount of divergence in the parties. Thus, our model may help to explain the recent coincidence of close elections and increasing polarization in U.S. politics.

In contrast to past analytical efforts that assume party ideal points are symmetric about the median voter, we analyze the effect of asymmetric ideal points on party behavior. Scholars have typically assumed that extremity provokes extremity, but our model shows that when one party becomes more extreme in its ideal point the other party responds by offering a more *moderate* platform. This suggests a perverse incentive. If activists with extreme ideal points can manipulate the ideal point of their party they can pull not only their *own* party's platform, *but also the opponent party's platform* toward their ideal point. This may help to explain the extremity of preferences known to exist among party leaders, activists, and rank-and-file party members (Iversen 1994; DiMaggio, Evans, and Bryson 1996; Abramowitz and Saunders 1998; Hetherington 2001; Layman and Carsey 2002).

We also analyze the effect of two different kinds of uncertainty on the model, electoral volatility and confidence in prior beliefs. The impact of electoral volatility is well known (Roemer 2001). More volatile elections yield greater uncertainty about the location of the median voter causing both parties to offer more extreme platforms. Our model reproduces this result with one exception. A party that wins the previous election in a landslide will actually offer a more *moderate* platform as electoral volatility increases because the greater uncertainty decreases the credibility of claiming a mandate. The second kind of uncertainty, confidence in prior beliefs, has not been studied previously but we show it also has an important impact on equilibrium platforms. Decreasing confidence in prior beliefs means parties have *greater* prior uncertainty about the location of the median voter and this causes both parties to offer more extreme platforms. Once again there is an exception relating to the vote share. A party that *loses* the previous election in a landslide will actually offer a more *moderate* platform as confidence in prior beliefs decreases because this increases the information value of the loss, which makes the loser more sensitive to the mandate.

Finally, electoral polarization has an important effect on the choice of equilibrium platforms. A more polarized electorate allows the winning party to choose a platform closer to its ideal point, but it also makes the losing party choose a more moderate platform. Again, this suggests a perverse incentive. If parties can influence the relative polarization of the electorate, then winners may try to divide the public whereas losers try to unite it. Since winners end up with control of the policy apparatus, this may help to explain why polarization in the electorate persists. However, these results are merely suggestive—future analytical efforts should endogenize electoral preferences to study whether or not such incentives exist in a richer model. In Chapter 4, we take one step toward such a model by exploring the effect of local information and retrospection on voter behavior in the context of the Wittman model.

To conclude, we note that we are surprised that this work has not been conducted already. The Wittman model is very simple and has been around for about 30 years. Roemer (2001: 71) notes that the fact that it produces policy divergence means that it is probably a better model than the traditional models of office-motivated parties. However, very little work has been done to extend the Wittman model, probably because of its analytical intractability. This is unfortunate because the model is extremely easy to solve and analyze with the use of simulation. We hope these results will encourage further analytical exploration of the Wittman model and further efforts to test empirically some of its implications. We also hope that the guidelines we provide for deriving numerical comparative statics will be used by other scholars when they think they have the right model but cannot solve it in closed form.

THREE

Dynamic Responsiveness in the U.S. Senate*

I n theory, elections allow voters to choose candidates who will respond to their desires. This is the core feature of democratic government. For example, Miller and Stokes (1963) find that members of Congress are ideologically predisposed to agree with voters in their districts and Mayhew (1974) and Fenno (1978) note that they frequently abandon their party positions in order to appeal to their constituents. More recently, several authors find that the government is responsive to general shifts in public opinion (Jackson and King 1989; Bartels 1991; Page and Shapiro 1992; Stimson, Mackuen, and Erikson 1995) and specific district interests (Fiorina 1977; King 1997; Ansolabehere, Snyder, and Stewart 2001a). These authors carefully establish the relationship between constituent interests and politician behavior and assert that the incentive to gain or retain office drives the relationship. Yet if elections are the key to responsiveness, it raises interesting empirical questions. Do parties pay attention to election outcomes? If so, how do they respond?

The theoretical model in Chapter 2 suggests that parties respond dynamically to past elections in the following way: winning parties move toward the extremes to satisfy their own preferences, whereas losers move toward the center in order to improve their chances of winning the next election.[1]

* From James H. Fowler. 2005. Dynamic Responsiveness in the U.S. Senate. *American Journal of Political* Science 49(2):299–312. Reprinted courtesy of Blackwell Publishing.

This is because previous election results give parties district-specific information about the location of the median voter. In a two-party contest on a single-issue dimension with proximity voters, parties know that the median voter is closer to the winning candidate than the losing candidate. They also know that the median voter is closer to the candidate who wins by a wide margin than a candidate who only barely wins against the same opponent. Therefore, when parties observe an election outcome they should update their beliefs in the direction of the winning party's preference and the magnitude of the change should be increasing in the margin of victory. As we have already seen, these updated beliefs will change the ideology of candidates offered by both parties in the next election. For example, if the left wins a close election, both parties will update their beliefs about the location of the voter slightly to the left and will offer slightly more liberal candidates in the next election. If the left wins in a landslide, candidates from both parties will be noticeably more liberal in the next election.

In this chapter, we test this theory of dynamic responsiveness by analyzing the relationship between Republican vote share in U.S. Senate elections and the ideology of candidates offered in the subsequent election. The results show that Republican (Democratic) victories in past elections yield candidates who are more (less) conservative in subsequent elections, and the effect is proportional to the margin of victory. This suggests that parties and/or candidates pay attention to past election returns and change their behavior in a way that privileges winning party candidates who are more extreme and losing party candidates who are more moderate in the next election.

One major implication of these dynamics is that parties may remain polarized in spite of their sensitivity to the preferences of the median voter. This might help to explain an important puzzle in American politics. Several scholars argue that politicians are responsive to the views of their constituents (Miller and Stokes 1963; Mayhew 1974; Fiorina 1977; Fenno 1978; King 1997; Ansolabehere, Snyder, and Stewart 2001a) and this ought to imply convergence toward the median voter (Stokes 1999). However, parties and candidates tend to remain ideologically polarized (Iversen 1994; Hetherington 2001; Layman and Carsey 2002). The theory of dynamic responsiveness suggests a reason for this. If candidates from losing parties adjust by moving toward the center, whereas candidates from winning parties adjust by moving toward the extremes, then as a district becomes more conservative (liberal) it will tend to be represented by more conservative (liberal) politicians. This will also produce a cross-sectional relationship— more conservative (liberal) districts will tend to be represented by more conservative (liberal) politicians. However, this process does not necessarily yield convergence. The fact that both parties tend to shift in the same direction means that they may or may not get any closer to one another. Thus, polarization may persist indefinitely.

The analysis up to this point has been based on the simplifying assumption that parties are unitary actors who choose candidates to represent the best trade-off between their preferred policies and their probability of winning the election.[2] However, we can relax this assumption. Suppose instead that each party is an aggregation of ideologically similar individuals and potential candidates from their ranks self-select by deciding whether or not to vie for nomination (Jacobson and Kernell 1981). A party victory in the previous contest means that potential candidates from that party think they are more likely to win the next general election because the median voter has shifted in their direction. However, these candidates must also win their party's nomination. If they think that the previous victory means party members will support a candidate more faithful to their preferences, then extreme candidates are more likely and moderate candidates are less likely to vie for and win the nomination. Symmetrically, candidates from the party that lost the previous election are now more likely to lose the general election because the median voter has shifted away from them. If they think the party will support a candidate who is more electable, then moderate candidates are more likely, and extreme candidates are less likely, to vie for and win nomination. Thus, relaxing the assumption of parties as unitary actors still yields the same result. Candidates from the party that won the previous election will tend to become more extreme, whereas candidates from the losing party will tend to become more moderate.

DATA AND ANALYSIS

To test the theory of dynamic responsiveness, we need ideology scores for party candidates in a two-party system. Many scholars have used interest group assessments of candidates like ADA (Americans for Democratic Action) scores. These scores may have good internal validity for a specific congress, but comparisons across congresses are problematic (Groseclose, Levitt, and Snyder 1999). Therefore, several authors have turned to roll-call records to impute ideology positions across legislatures (e.g., Poole and Rosenthal 1997; Ansolabehere, Snyder, and Stewart 2001b). Poole (1998) specifically addresses not only the problem of longitudinal comparability, but also the problem of comparability across branches of government. We use the first dimension[3] of his "Common Space" scores (based on the NOMINATE methodology), which rank candidates from most liberal to most conservative. An additional advantage of using ideology scores based on voting records is that it implicitly controls for candidate quality—every candidate in the data set has held office at least once. This is important since some studies have shown a relationship between candidate quality and election results (Jacobson and Kernell 1981).

Common Space scores are available for the House and Senate for candidates with voting records from 1937–2000. Those with voting records are those who won, so the availability of scores for candidates who did not win in the House is limited to losers who later won House elections. However, candidates who lose elections for the Senate frequently have voting records from their service in the House. We, therefore, focus our attention on elections in the Senate.[4] We also need a source for election results, so we match Common Space scores to Senate candidates in the "Candidate Name and Constituency Totals, 1788–1990" file (ICPSR 0002) and Federal Election Commission election results for 1992–2000. Election results are used to calculate Republican vote share as a percent of the vote gained by Republicans and Democrats.[5]

Of 2,295 Democrat and Republican candidates, only 1,285 have Common Space scores. Moreover, in order to measure the change in candidate ideology between elections, we must have the Common Space score of the party's previous candidate in the state. Only 1,233 of these have Common Space scores. Because missing data in each of these variables overlap, there are only 968 cases where the Common Space scores of both the current and previous party candidates are observed.[6] The number of cases is further reduced when we introduce controls (see Table 3.1 for a comparison of descriptive statistics when data are completely and incompletely observed).

Most authors ignore problems related to missing data (King et al. 2001), but it can cause bias in model estimates if the data are not missing completely at random. Pairwise correlations between model variables and a missing data indicator are insignificant with two notable exceptions. First, there is an incumbency bias—challengers in the current and previous election are underrepresented in the data since they frequently do not have voting records, whereas incumbents nearly always do. Second, there is a slight partisan bias—Democrats are slightly overrepresented as are Republican losses in the previous election. Interaction terms in the models that follow show that the relationship between change in ideology and previous

TABLE 3.1 Summary Statistics Where the Common Space Scores of Both the Current and Previous Party Candidates Are Observed

Variable	Model	Completely Observed Cases					Incompletely Observed Cases				
		N	Mean	SD	Min	Max	N	Mean	SD	Min	Max
Change in ideology	All	424	0.01	0.20	-0.69	0.73	544	0.02	0.20	-0.66	0.73
(Magnitude of change in ideology)		424	0.14	0.14	0.00	0.73	544	0.15	0.14	0.00	0.73
Republican vote share	All	424	0.47	0.12	0.10	0.80	1,450	0.48	0.13	0.10	0.80
(Magnitude of change in Republican vote share)*		424	0.17	0.14	0.00	0.75	1,450	0.16	0.17	0.00	0.77
Candidate's party lost previous election†	1c	424	0.22	0.41	0	1	2,146	0.63	0.48	0	1
Challenger†	2a	424	0.45	0.50	0	1	2,146	0.74	0.44	0	1
Previous challenger†	2b	424	0.41	0.49	0	1	1,812	0.75	0.43	0	1
Previous Republican loss†	2c	424	0.59	0.49	0	1	2,146	0.35	0.48	0	1
Democrat†	2d	424	0.55	0.50	0	1	2,146	0.50	0.50	0	1
Northeast Republican	2e, 3a–3f	424	0.08	0.27	0	1	2,146	0.06	0.23	0	1
Southern Democrat	2e, 3a–3f	424	0.10	0.30	0	1	2,146	0.10	0.30	0	1
RDI growth if candidate is from President's Party	3a–3f	420	0.01	0.03	-0.15	0.11	1,612	0.01	0.04	-0.15	0.11
Democratic President	3b–3f	424	0.54	0.50	0	1	2,146	0.55	0.50	0	1
Mean Senate ideology	3c	395	-0.02	0.06	-0.10	0.09	1,396	-0.02	0.06	-0.10	0.09
Public mood	3d	308	0.60	0.05	0.51	0.69	1,081	0.61	0.05	0.51	0.70
Republican vote share for President	3e	350	0.52	0.10	0.13	0.77	1,187	0.50	0.12	0.03	0.80

* This variable is the *absolute value* of the within-state change in Republican vote share between the previous election and the current election. In other words, what is the size (not direction) of change in vote share from one election to the next?

† Dependent variable is not missing completely at random with respect to these variables.

Republican vote share is not different for the overrepresented and under-represented groups. Thus, missing data should not be a cause for concern.

RESULTS

Table 3.2 shows the first three versions of the model. The dependent variable for all models is change in ideology for U.S. Senate candidates running in elections from 1936–2000. This is the Common Space score of the current candidate minus the Common Space score for the candidate from the same party in the previous election. Each model also includes the vote share for the Republican candidate in the previous election. Recall that Common Space scores increase with the conservatism of the candidate. If parties use information about past elections to update their beliefs about the location of the median voter, then there should be a positive relationship between Republican vote share in the last election and the change in candidate ideology. Large wins for the Republicans should push candidates to the right and large losses for the Republicans should push candidates to the left.

TABLE 3.2   Effect of Previous Elections on Candidate Ideology in U.S. Senate Elections, 1936–2000

	Dependent Variable Change in Candidate Ideology		
Independent variables (models)	*(1a)*	*(1b)*	*(1c)*
Previous Republican vote share from election two years ago	0.21† (0.07)	— —	0.21† (0.07)
Previous Republican vote share from election four years ago	— —	−0.05 (0.08)	— —
Candidate's party lost previous election	— —	— —	−0.04 (0.15)
Candidate's party lost previous election* Previous Republican vote share	— —	— —	0.13 (0.31)
Intercept	−0.11† (0.03)	−0.07* (0.04)	−0.11* (0.03)
Adjusted R^2	0.02	0.01	0.02
N	424	384	424

Note: Dependent variable is change in ideology of U.S. Senate candidates, 1936–2000. Ideology is measured using the first dimension of Poole's (1998) Common Space scores. Coefficient estimates are from ordinary least squares with heteroskedastic-consistent standard errors (in parentheses).
*$p < .05.$ $^\dagger p < .01.$

Model 1a is the most basic version of the model with no controls. Notice that the coefficient on the previous Republican vote share is positive and significant. This coefficient indicates that higher Republican vote share in the previous election yields more conservative candidates in the next election. To interpret the coefficient, we simulate first differences (see King, Tomz, and Wittenberg 2000) by estimating the expected change in candidate ideology when other variables are held at their means and the vote share is increased by the average magnitude observed in the data (see Table 3.1). The ideology variable is somewhat abstract (What does it mean to become 0.1 more conservative?), so we express the change in ideology as a percent of the average magnitude of change in ideology observed in the data. In other words, how much of the average change in ideology will be caused by the average change in vote share from one election to the next? Simulations from model 1a suggest that an average increase in Republican vote share yields a shift to the right that is 28% ($\pm$17%) the size of the average shift in ideology. To make the point qualitatively, this would be like switching from Christopher Dodd to John Edwards, from Dianne Feinstein to Charles Robb, from John McCain to Orin Hatch, or from Paul Coverdell to Strom Thurmond.

An alternative explanation for these results is regression to the mean. Suppose parties do not respond to past vote share. Instead, Democratic candidates are drawn randomly from a distributin with a mean at the moderate left and Republican candidates are drawn randomly from a distribution with a mean at the moderate right. Suppose further that an extreme liberal candidate is drawn for the Democratic Party. Simple regression to the mean suggests that the next candidate will be more conservative. At the same time, an extreme liberal Democrat is more likely than a moderate Democrat to lose in a landslide. Thus, a landslide conservative victory would be associated with a shift to the right. Similarly, suppose a very centrist Democrat is drawn. A centrist is likely to win a large share of the vote and regression to the mean suggests the next candidate would be more liberal. Thus, a big liberal victory would be associated with a shift to the left. By symmetry, regression to the mean might explain the association for Republicans, too.

Fortunately, we can use the data to determine whether dynamic responsiveness or regression to the mean is driving the results. In the U.S. Senate, each state's two senators have terms that normally overlap by two or four years. Thus, in some states the most recent election took place two years ago, whereas in others it took place four years ago. If the regression to the mean argument is true, then there should be an association between vote share in the previous election and ideology in the current election, regardless of how long ago it took place. An extremist in an election four years ago should lose just as badly as an extremist in an election two years ago, and reversion to the mean should be just as strong. In contrast, the dynamic responsiveness argument suggests that the relationship might be stronger for more recent elections. If the voter distribution tends to change over time, then newer information about it will be more relevant than older information. Moreover, as time passes, there are more sources of information that affect party estimates of the voter distribution, which decreases the relative contribution of information gleaned from the most recent Senate election. In particular, major elections occur every two years and give parties a lot of information even if there is no U.S. Senate election in a given state.

Model 1a in Table 3.2 shows the effect of vote share on candidate ideology when the previous election took place two years ago, whereas model 1b shows the effect when the most recent election occurred four years ago. Notice that the effect of vote share from two years ago is significant but the vote share from four years ago is not. These results suggest that regression to the mean is not driving the relationship. Otherwise, there would be a similar relationship between vote share and ideology for both elections. These results also suggest that candidates only respond to the previous election if it was very recent. Thus, in the models that follow, we will focus only on cases where the most recent election was held two years ago.

Notice that the basic model does not distinguish between candidates from parties that won the previous election and candidates from parties that lost. This is problematic because it is possible that winning and losing parties react differently to the previous margin of victory. For example, Macy (1995) argues that people use a "win-stay/lose-shift" heuristic to adapt to a changing environment. When a strategy works, they repeat it. When it does not work, they search for a new strategy. If parties use such a heuristic then they should respond to vote share in previous elections when they lose, but not when they win. Model 1c tests the difference between winners and losers by including a variable that indicates when a candidate's party lost the previous election and an interaction term with the vote share. The coefficient for the interaction term is positive, indicating that losing parties react more strongly to the mandate than winning parties as hypothesized in Chapter 2. However, this coefficient is not strongly significant, suggesting that there is no statistically meaningful difference between winners and losers. Winners move toward their extremes and losers move toward the center.

DYNAMIC RESPONSIVENESS
AND INCUMBENCY

So far this has been a simple story about parties. One aspect that is notably missing is the effect of incumbency. In theory, incumbency should not affect dynamic responsiveness—incumbents should be under pressure to shift with the margin of victory just like challengers. An incumbent who stays put, while his or her constituency moves to the extreme, risks facing a primary challenge from a more extreme candidate. However, Fiorina (1977) and Jacobson (1991) have noted that incumbents are relatively insulated from their constituents and several other scholars argue that they do not change their behavior over time, in spite of changes in district interests (Stone 1980; Arnold 1990; Poole and Rosenthal 1997; Poole 2003). If so, then this implies that incumbents might not respond to election results.

To test the effect of incumbency on dynamic responsiveness, model 2a in Table 3.3 includes a dummy variable for challengers. The challenger variable is also interacted with past Republican vote share to see if incumbents and challengers respond differently to past election results. Notice that the coefficients on the challenger dummy and the interaction term are not significant, suggesting that challengers and incumbents react similarly to the previous election.

Another important feature among incumbents is their ability to retain office. Several authors have written on the incumbency advantage (e.g., Gelman and King 1990), noting that it is very difficult for challengers to beat incumbents. Moreover, voters in races between incumbents and challengers may be focused on a variety of other factors relating to the incumbent's performance besides ideology.[7] If so, then parties and candidates might discount information obtained from previous elections in which incumbents stood for office. After all, the incumbent might be able to win in spite of his or her ideology, meaning that an election between a challenger and an incumbent is less relevant for providing information about the voter distribution than an open-seat election.

To test the importance of incumbency in the previous election, model 2b in Table 3.3 includes a dummy variable indicating when the previous election was for an open seat. This variable is also interacted with past Republican vote share to see if incumbency affects the way candidates use information from the previous election. The coefficients on the open-seat dummy and the interaction term are not significant. These results suggest that ideology is thought to be an important factor in all elections, even in races with incumbents.

TABLE 3.3   Effect of Previous Elections, Incumbency, and Partisanship on
Candidate Ideology in U.S. Senate Elections, 1936–2000

	Dependent Variable Change in Candidate Ideology				
Independent variables (models)	(2a)	(2b)	(2c)	(2d)	(2e)
Previous Republican vote share	0.21*	0.27†	0.41*	0.28*	0.32†
	(0.09)	(0.10)	(0.18)	(0.12)	(0.08)
Challenger	−0.02	—	—	—	—
	(0.07)	—	—	—	—
Challenger* Previous Republican vote share	0.03	—	—	—	—
	(0.14)	—	—	—	—
Open seat in previous election	—	−0.17	—	—	—
	—	(0.15)	—	—	—
Open seat in previous election* Previous Republican vote share	—	0.06	—	—	—
	—	(0.07)	—	—	—
Democrat won previous election	—	—	0.12	—	—
	—	—	(0.12)	—	—
Democrat won previous election* Previous Republican vote share	—	—	−0.20	—	—
	—	—	(0.22)	—	—
Democrat	—	—	—	0.04	—
	—	—	—	(0.08)	—
Democrat* Previous Republican vote share	—	—	—	−0.08	—
	—	—	—	(0.16)	—
Northeast Republican	—	—	—	—	−0.11†
	—	—	—	—	(0.03)
Southern Democrat	—	—	—	—	0.08*
	—	—	—	—	(0.03)
Intercept	−0.10†	−0.12†	−0.23†	−0.14*	−0.16†
	(0.04)	(0.04)	(0.11)	(0.07)	(0.04)
Adjusted R^2	0.02	0.03	0.02	0.02	0.05
N	424	424	424	424	424

Note: Dependent variable is change in the ideology of candidates for the U.S. Senate, 1936–2000. Ideology is measured using the first dimension of Poole's (1998) Common Space scores. Coefficient estimates are from ordinary least squares with heteroskedastic-consistent standard errors (in parentheses).
*$p < .05$. †$p < .01$.

DYNAMIC RESPONSIVENESS
AND PARTISANSHIP

Another important variable to consider is partisanship. For example, it is possible that the ideology of candidates is simply affected by the party who won the previous election but not the vote share. If so, then a past

Democratic victory would cause a fixed shift to the left, a past Republican victory would cause a fixed shift to the right, and ideology would be invariant with the size of the victory. Model 2c introduces a dummy variable for a Democratic victory in the previous election to control for this possibility. It also includes an interaction term to see if the partisan identity of the previous winner affects how candidates react to vote share. Notice that the coefficient on vote share is large and significant but the coefficients on the dummy and interaction term are not. This suggests that winning and losing have no independent effect on change in ideology. Apparently, size matters in electoral competition.

In the previous models, Democrats and Republicans are lumped together, but what if they respond to vote share differently? Perhaps one party is responsive to the vote share, whereas the other is not. For example, we show in Chapter 6 that voters believe the Republican Party is less responsive than the Democratic Party. Model 2d introduces a dummy variable for Democratic candidates and interacts it with previous Republican vote share to see if Democrats and Republicans respond differently to the previous election. The coefficients on these additional variables are insignificant, suggesting that candidates from both parties respond similarly to the previous election.

Thus, partisanship in general does not seem to affect change in ideology. However, students of American politics are keen to point out that candidate ideology within the parties often varies by region. In particular, models frequently control for the independent effect that southern Democrats and northeast Republicans have on the relationship in question. Model 2e includes these combinations of region and party and finds both to be significant. However, they do not affect the main result that candidates respond to the previous election outcome. In fact, model 2e suggests an even stronger result: an average increase in Republican vote share yields a shift to the right that is 45% ($\pm 18\%$) the size of the average shift in ideology.

DYNAMIC RESPONSIVENESS AND INSTITUTIONAL FACTORS

Incumbency and partisanship are not the only factors that may influence change in ideology. Parties must also consider the institutional context in which they are competing. For example, the state of the economy has a strong effect on the likelihood that the incumbent party will win the presidency (Bartels and Zaller 2001). Incumbent senators from the President's party may be similarly affected. However, it is unclear whether a bad economy causes candidates to moderate toward the center or shift toward the left or right. Model 3a in Table 3.4 includes a variable for real disposable income (RDI) growth for senatorial candidates who belong to the current President's party and an interaction term to separate the effect for Democrats and Republicans. The sign on both variables is negative and the coefficient on the interaction term is insignificant. The combined effect, however, is significant and suggests that candidates from the incumbent party shift left when the economy is bad, regardless of partisan orientation. Notice that even with this control, the effect of vote share remains significant.

Senate candidates may also be affected by the partisanship of the President. Alesina and Rosenthal (1995) suggest that voters attempt to balance the outcome of elections for President and the Senate. If so, then parties may choose Senate candidates in order to counteract the ideology of the President. Model 3b includes te partisanship of the President and an interaction term to separate the effect for presidential and midterm elections. The coefficient on the partisanship variable is positive and significant, indicating that candidates shift more to the right when the President is a Democrat than when he is a Republican. Thus, there does appear to be some balancing activity, but the coefficient on the interaction term is insignificant suggesting the effect does not change much for midterm elections. Adding these controls does not change the significant relationship between vote share and candidate ideology.

DYNAMIC RESPONSIVENESS AND IDEOLOGY

Another important set of controls relates to broader trends in ideology. For example, recently the nation has become more conservative at the same time the Republican Party has been winning more elections. This might cause a spurious correlation between change in ideology and vote share at the state level if we do not control for the broader trends. Thus, model 3c includes a variable for the mean ideology of the Senate and model 3d includes Stimson's measure of the "public policy mood."[8] The results show that neither of these measures is significantly related to change in ideology. Nor does including them in the model change the effect of previous Republican vote share.

Another possibility is that other factors have been omitted that are relevant to the location of the median voter. We control for this by including the contemporaneous vote share of the Republican President in each state.

TABLE 3.4   Effect of Previous Elections, Public Ideology, and Institutional Factors on Candidate Ideology in U.S. Senate Elections, 1936–2000

Independent variables (models)	Dependent Variable Change in Candidate Ideology					
	(3a)	(3b)	(3c)	(3d)	(3e)	(3f)
Previous Republican vote share	0.27†	0.27†	0.27†	0.25†	0.30†	0.23†
	(0.07)	(0.07)	(0.07)	(0.07)	(0.10)	(0.09)
Northeast Republican	−0.11†	−0.12†	−0.13†	−0.11†	−0.11†	−0.10†
	(0.03)	(0.03)	(0.03)	(0.03)	(0.03)	(0.03)
Southern Democrat	0.06	0.06	0.07*	0.05	0.07	0.00
	(0.03)	(0.03)	(0.03)	(0.04)	(0.04)	(0.06)
Real disposable income growth if candidate is from president's party	−0.94	−1.55†	−1.26†	−1.42†	−1.80†	−1.36†
	(0.49)	(0.37)	(0.40)	(0.59)	(0.39)	(0.44)
RDI growth if candidate is from president's party* Democrat	−0.68	—	—	—	—	—
	(0.53)	—	—	—	—	—
Democratic president	—	0.04*	0.03	0.04	0.02	0.06
	—	(0.02)	(0.02)	(0.02)	(0.02)	(0.13)
Democratic president* nonpresidential election year	—	−0.01	—	—	—	—
	—	(0.03)	—	—	—	—
Mean Senate ideology	—	—	0.13	—	—	—
	—	—	(0.16)	—	—	—
Public mood	—	—	—	0.09	—	—
	—	—	—	(0.19)	—	—
Republican vote share for president	—	—	—	—	0.01	—
	—	—	—	—	(0.14)	—
State and year dummies	—	—	—	—	—	(omitted)
Intercept	−0.11†	−0.13*	−0.13*	−0.17	−0.14*	−0.07
	(0.03)	(0.03)	(0.03)	(0.12)	(0.06)	(0.07)
Adjusted R²	0.11	0.11	0.09	0.17	0.18	0.38
N	420	420	395	308	350	420

Note: Dependent variable is change in ideology of U.S. Senate candidates, 1936–2000. Ideology is measured using the first dimension of Poole's (1998) Common Space scores. Coefficient estimates are from ordinary least squares with heteroskedastic-consistent standard errors (in parentheses). Model (3f) includes state and year dummies (coefficient estimates for 80 state and year variables not shown).
*$p < .05$. †$p < .01$.

This variable has frequently been used as a proxy for state ideology (e.g., Ansolabehere, Snyder, and Stewart 2001a)—thus, one might expect it to diminish the impact of the vote-share variable since it may also be correlated with the location of the median voter. Model 3e shows that the President's vote share has no effect on change in ideology. Even more importantly, including the President's vote share in the model does not noticeably diminish the size or the significance of the coefficient on the Senate candidate's vote share. An average increase in Republican vote share yields a shift to the right that is 38% ($\pm 24\%$) the size of the average shift in ideology.

Finally, there may be other region-specific or temporal factors not considered here that affect ideology. For example, some states tend to be more conservative, whereas others tend to be more liberal. We control for this by including a dummy variable for each state. Or perhaps there is a cross-state push to the left or right in response to some idiosyncratic event or the national strategic institutional context in certain years. We control for this by including a dummy variable for each year. Model 3f shows that when these controls are added, the coefficient on previous Republican vote share remains large and significant.[9]

CONCLUSION

Using national policy mood measures and aggregate seat totals, Stimson et al. (1995) show that the U.S. Senate "works like a textbook representation mechanism: Senate elections are responsive to public opinion, and then new membership produces expected policy outcomes" (Stimson et al. 1995:54). However, they do not analyze the electoral mechanism that produces such an outcome. This chapter elaborates on this mechanism by testing our theory about the link between election results and candidate ideology. Parties use past election results to update their beliefs about the location of the median voter and then adjust the candidates they offer accordingly. If the median moves right (left), Republican vote share increases (decreases) and causes both parties to move proportionally to the right (left).

We find that past elections have a dynamic impact on the ideology of future political candidates. Winning parties tend to offer candidates who are more extreme in the next election and losing parties tend to offer candidates who are more moderate. Moreover, the size of the victory matters. Close elections yield small changes in the ideology of future candidates, whereas landslides yield larger changes. Figure 3.1 summarizes the estimated effect sizes from all models presented. It shows that an average

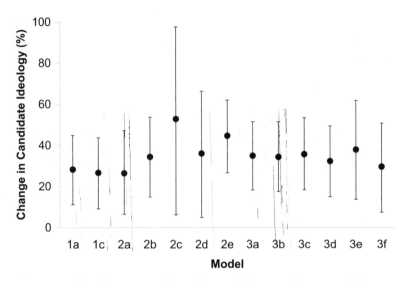

FIGURE 3.1   Effect of an average change in Republican vote share on candidate ideology in U.S. Senate elections. Values show the effect of an average-sized change in vote share (as observed in the data) on the magnitude of change in candidate ideology (as a percent of the average-sized change in ideology observed in the data). Estimates are based on simulated first differences (see King et al. 2001). The model number refers to the models shown in Tables 3.2–3.4. Error bars show 95% confidence intervals.

increase in Republican vote share yields a shift to the right that is about one-quarter to one-half the size of the average shift in ideology.

Note that the estimates in Figure 3.1 are relatively consistent for a variety of specifications. Model 1c shows that winners and losers do not differ much in how they react to previous vote share. Model 2a compares the effect of previous elections on incumbents and challengers. Both are equally responsive to previous vote share. Model 2b further suggests that candidates do not discount the importance of previous elections in which an incumbent stood for office. Model 2c shows that size matters: vote share remains important even when a dummy for victory is included. Models 2d and 2e indicate that partisan orientation does not affect the way parties respond to vote share, even when controlling for significant regional changes in the parties. Finally, models 3a–3f show that previous election results remain important even when controlling for the economy, institutional balancing, mean ideology in the Senate, national shifts in public mood, and omitted variables related to state ideology.

These results suggest a potential cause for persistent polarization in American politics. The literature on responsiveness has typically been somewhat puzzled by polarization. If politicians are responsive to the views of their constituents (Miller and Stokes 1963; Mayhew 1974; Fiorina 1977; Fenno 1978; King 1997; Ansolabehere, Snyder, and Stewart 2001a), then, informally, this ought to imply convergence (Stokes 1999). Yet parties and candidates remain polarized (Iversen 1994; Hetherington 2001; Layman and Carsey 2002). Our theory of dynamic responsiveness suggests a solution. Losing parties adjust by moving toward the center, but winners move toward the extremes. Thus, as a district becomes more conservative (liberal) it will tend to be represented by more conservative (liberal) politicians, producing the relationship between district and politician ideology that has been noted in the literature on responsiveness. However, this process does not yield convergence. If both parties shift with the median voter rather than toward the median voter, then they may or may not get any closer to one another. The model we presented in Chapter 2 implies that parties converge to the location of the median voter in the limit because the losing party shifts more than the winning party in response to shifts in the voter distribution. However, in Chapter 4, we show that divergence persists when we relax assumptions about the information that parties have about the median voter. Thus, the tendency to move with the mandate may cause party polarization to persist indefinitely.

Although the results in this chapter lend support to a theory of dynamic responsiveness, they do not identify the agents responsible for reacting to previous elections. We have described the process as one in which parties observe past election results and then choose new candidates based on information they provide about the location of the median voter. However, it is also possible that control of the process may be more dispersed—candidates themselves may exhibit self-selection by avoiding contests they think they will lose. For example, if past election results indicate the median has shifted to the right, candidates in the left wing of the right party may be less likely to run because they believe they have a lower probability of winning their primary. Future work should focus on identifying whether party leaders or potential candidates are conscious of a relationship between past electoral margins and the ideology of future candidates.

Finally, future work should also develop the formal aspects of dynamic responsiveness. It is not obvious that a shift in the median voter should cause both parties to shift. After all, if the losing party knows that the winning party is going to shift to its extreme then it may simply stay put to increase its own probability of winning without sacrificing its own preferences. In Chapters 2 and 4, we show that both parties do shift in the direction of the winner's preferences. However, this effort may not necessarily apply in contexts where divergence is caused by other factors like the threat of entry (Palfrey 1984; Greenberg and Shepsle 1987). The empirical results in this chapter should motivate formal theorists to extend their models to explore the relationship between updated beliefs implied by past vote shares and the positions parties choose to take.

## FOUR

Dynamic Parties and Social Turnout: An Agent-Based Model*

C hapters 1 and 2 are devoted to the development of our argument about the link between election results and candidate ideology. In Chapter 3, we also tested the theory empirically using data from the U.S. Senate. However, these theoretical and empirical results are based on the assumption that citizens always choose to vote. What if we relax this assumption? The fact that people choose to vote may not seem to be puzzling. However, given standard assumptions about rationality, voter turnout cannot be easily explained. Numerous formal attempts to explain the decision to vote predict vanishingly small turnout since the probability of affecting the outcome of an election approaches zero in large populations (Palfrey and Rosenthal 1985; Aldrich 1993; Myerson 1998). In fact, people going to polls have a much higher chance of getting into a car accident on the way to the polls. This has led many scholars to infer that rational explanations of turnout must rely on an additional benefit derived from fulfilling a sense of duty or a general taste for voting (Riker and Ordeshook 1968).

In Chapters 5 and 6, we examine whether our main substantive results from Chapters 2 and 3 hold if we endogenize individual turnout decisions. Because of the complexity involved in modeling both parties and voters,

*From James H. Fowler and Oleg Smirnov. 2005. Dynamic Parties and Social Turnout: An Agent-Based Model. American Journal of Sociology. 110(4):1070–1094. Reprinted courtesy of the University of Chicago Press. Copyright ©2005 by the University of Chicago. All rights reserved.

there have only been limited efforts to combine the two elements (Osborne 1995). Models of voter turnout have usually relied on assumptions of fixed party platforms, whereas models of platform choice have assumed a fixed level of voter turnout (usually 100%). The interdependence between people and politicians also has a dynamic character that is missing from many models because they consider a single election in isolation. Most elections are, in fact, part of a longer process of party competition and take place in a context of information about previous elections. In Chapter 2, we show that this dynamic process has specific effects on party behavior. Do these effects also have implications for voter behavior?

Economists and political scientists have frequently abstracted away from elements that sociologists and psychologists believe to be critical for determining electoral behavior. For example, many models of elections have avoided situating voters in social networks, or social context in general. Voters are often assumed to exist independently of one another in spite of a growing body of sociological evidence suggesting that how they are situated in relation to one another plays a critical role in the decision to vote (Lazarsfeld, Berelson, and Gaudet 1948; Berelson, Lazarsfeld, and McPhee 1954; Campbell, Gurin, and Miller 1954; Glaser 1959; Straits 1990; Kenny 1992; Knack 1992; Huckfeldt and Sprague 1995; Beck et al. 2002; Fowler 2005). Most models of elections also make typical cognitive assumptions about information and individual rationality, in spite of evidence from psychology that both may be severely limited (e.g., Simon 1982; Quattrone and Tversky 1988). Instead, people might use "fast and frugal heuristics" to deal with informational limitations and strategic complexities but still achieve relatively good results (cf., Cosmides and Tooby 1996; Lupia and McCubbins 1998; Gigerenzer et al. 1999).

The complexity of including all these features in a formal analytical model would overwhelm it. A closed-form solution would probably not be tractable. However, leaving some or all of these features out may yield incomplete inferences about voter and party behavior. Therefore, in this chapter we develop a formal model using an alternative methodology: agent-based modeling (ABM) (Axelrod 1997; Tesfatsion and Judd 2006). Like analytical models, ABMs are built on formal assumptions about agents (players in games) and how they interact. Similar to the standard analytical models, the assumptions are clearly defined, the results are stated in precise terms, and are typically easy to replicate (Gilbert and Troitzsch 1999). Unlike most analytical models, however, ABMs are usually analyzed computationally, which means they are less elegant but also less susceptible to problems of tractability. Computational models generate data to show the relationships between variables of interest. Moreover, ABMs may make it easier to analyze paths to equilibrium, to recognize emergent patterns of interaction, and to quickly generate models where interaction is especially complicated (Johnson 1998; Durlauf 2001; Skvoretz 2002). In other words, computational models provide insights into not only the outcome of a process, but also the dynamics of the process itself without sacrificing the rigor of formal modeling (Nelson and Winter 2002). In political science, ABM is not yet widely accepted although it has been established as a viable methodology (e.g., Taber and Timpone 1996; Axelrod 1997; Kollman, Miller, and Page 2003; De Marchi 2005).

In this chapter, we describe and analyze an ABM of repeated elections in which voters and parties behave simultaneously. We place voters in a social context and let them interact with one another when choosing whether or not to vote. We also let parties choose the platforms they offer much as they did in Chapter 2, and these choices may change from election to election depending on feedback from the electorate. This allows us to explore the endogenous interaction of dynamic platforms and costly turnout. In the process, we relax standard assumptions of unlimited information-processing capacities and individual hyperrationality. Citizens are limited to information they can get from their immediate neighbors. They are boundedly rational agents who use simple heuristics to make the turnout decision. Parties are assumed to be more sophisticated optimizing their choices, given their beliefs about the expected behavior of voters and their opponents. However, they form these beliefs based on limited information—they only know the results of past elections.

The computational model that we analyze generates a number of results for voter behavior. First, the average level of aggregate turnout is empirically realistic and it varies from election to election within a stable range. Second, we show that the model is consistent with much of the empirical evidence generated to test the rational calculus of voting. Turnout increases as the cost of voting decreases, the stakes of the election increase, and the margin of victory declines. Although citizens have very limited information and use a very simple learning rule, they are able to respond as though they were prospectively rational to variation in the incentive to vote. Third, the model is consistent with empirical results from the literature on the social context of voting. In particular, turnout correlates highly between neighbors, and citizens who discuss politics with more neighbors are more likely to vote. Fourth, the model also generates a surprising result: when citizens are situated near people with similar preferences, they are less likely to vote. In short, segregation depresses turnout. Finally, we explain why a local imitation structure inherently yields dynamics that encourage positive turnout.

The model also generates a number of results for party behavior. First, consistent with our findings in Chapter 2, policy-motivated parties offer divergent platforms. In this setting, citizens who are free to vote or abstain serve as an endogenous source of uncertainty since the location of the median voter is changing all the time. Second, parties adjust their platforms in direct response to the vote share in the previous election. Both parties move in the direction of the previous winner and in proportion to the previous margin of victory. Third, parties are drawn not only to the median voter, but also to the median citizen since he or she represents the median of the pool of potential future voters. Finally, the model generates another surprising result: electorates with higher local correlation of preferences lead to a greater divergence of party platforms. This suggests that parties polarize as neighborhoods become more segregated.

In the following section, we describe the general structure and most important elements of the agent-based model of elections: how voters make their decisions and how parties choose their platforms. Then, we proceed with analysis of the main results of our model: most notably, why people vote despite the cost of voting, and what electoral aspects influence party platforms. In the final section, we summarize our findings and discuss application of computational models of elections in future research.

THE MODEL

In this section, we describe a simplified version of our computational model (code for the model can be found in Chapter 4 Appendix). As in the standard political science model of elections, we assume that each citizen in a population has some preferred policy point on a one-dimensional left–right scale, which one can think of as liberal–conservative issue space. Two parties compete in elections, and these parties have fixed left and right preferences. The parties choose electoral platforms (see later) and each citizen chooses to vote or abstain. If a citizen turns out, he or she chooses the party offering the platform closest to the voter's own preference. Votes for the left and right are counted and the election winner is determined by majority rule. After each election, a citizen's utility is simply the negative squared distance between his or her preferred policy and the platform implemented by the winning party, minus the cost of voting.[1] Parties are assumed to be policy-motivated: they have the same preferences and utility over the policy space as voters (a party prefers to win the election with a policy closer to its ideal point).

Parties only know their own preference point and the results of past elections. They do not know the distribution of voter preferences and, therefore, they do not know the exact location of the median voter. Moreover, some of the former voters may abstain and some of the former abstainers may vote, meaning that the location of the median voter may change from election to election (Brody and Page 1973). To deal with this uncertainty, we assume that parties use previous election results to learn about the voter distribution, just as they did in Chapter 2. First, they use the results of the past election to estimate the location of the median voter.[2] For example, if the left party wins in a landslide, both parties can infer that the median voter was located closer to the left platform than the right platform. Second, they use Bayesian inference to update their beliefs about the expected median voter in the coming election.[3] Given these beliefs about the electorate, the parties choose platforms by simultaneously optimizing their expected payoffs.[4]

Unlike parties, citizens employ a less-sophisticated decision-making mechanism. We model citizens as boundedly rational agents with access to limited information. In the model, they only know the utility and turnout behavior of their immediate neighbors. This means they also do not know the true preferences of any other citizens or parties. One might argue that this is unnecessarily naïve. However, we know from much of the empirical literature on contextual effects that local information has a powerful influence on individual voter behavior (Beck et al. 2002; Fotos and Franklin 2002). Imitation has been shown to be an extremely cost-effective strategy in complex environments, even if it does not necessarily lead to the best possible outcome (e.g., Tesfatsion 1980, 1984; Boyd and Richerson 1985).

To model local interaction, we endow citizens with preferences and place them randomly on a grid.[5] We then allow them to have political discussions with other people in their neighborhood.[6] Given the constraints on information and the enormous complexity of maximizing utility over some set of future elections, citizens adopt the most successful strategies from past elections. We assume that information flows between immediate neighbors with respect to the past election—in particular, whether or not they voted and how satisfied they were with the results. Since voters can learn about the turnout behavior and relative satisfaction of their neighbors, they can use this information to decide whether to vote in the next election. Specifically, they divide people in their neighborhood between voters and abstainers, decide

which type is more satisfied, and then imitate the behavior of the most satisfied group.[7]

RESULTS: GENERAL DYNAMICS

To analyze computational results from the model, we employ three strategies. First, we develop a graphical user interface (GUI) for the model so we
can watch what happens to voter utilities, turnout, platforms, and other
variables of interest. Computational modeling is unique in this respect
because it allows us to inspect visually what is happening to our model as it
progresses. This sometimes leads to hypotheses about the dynamic processes
that might not otherwise have been obvious using different methodologies
(Gilbert and Troitzsch 1999). Second, we produce graphs of several runs of
consecutive elections. These graphs are snapshots of the dynamic behavior
of one or two variables from the model, and they are useful for character-
izing typical boundaries and changes in the values for a given set of model
assumptions. Third, we conduct multiple runs and collect data at the end of
each run. This allows us to do robustness checks and see how changes in
assumptions affect the way the model behaves on average.

In Figure 4.1, we present some results from a typical run of 100 elections. The lower left graph shows that turnout varies between 35% and
55%. When we let the simulation run for thousands of elections, turnout
never jumps out of this range: turnout seems to be significant and stable
even when it is costly. The upper right graph shows how the model generates instability in the location of the median voter. Although the preference
of the median citizen remains fixed for a given run (represented by the
straight horizontal line in the graph), the preference of the median voter
depends on who decides to vote and changes from election to election.
Notice especially that the median voter can remain to the left or right of the
median citizen for several elections, indicating a period when one party's
supporters are more active than the other's.

The upper left graph shows how party platforms change over time to
adapt to these circumstances. After a brief convergence from initial conditions and a period of instability, the platforms tend to oscillate in a stable
range that remains significantly far from the center. This oscillation seems
to vary with the location of the median voter as parties attempt to adjust
their platforms in the median voter's direction. Constant adjustment by the
parties also generates variation in the margin of victory in the lower right
graph as parties alternate winning and losing elections.

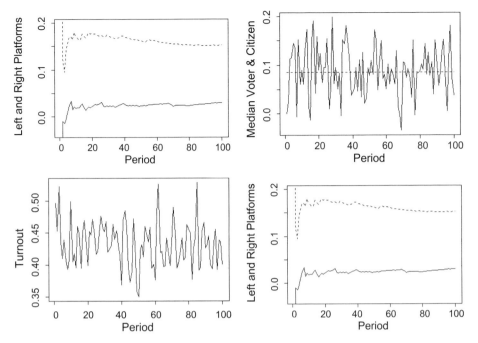

FIGURE 4.1   Results of a single run of 100 elections. For this run, we test a population of 1,024 voters with independent preferences drawn from a standard normal distribution, party preferences at −1 and 1, cost of voting of 0.1, and initial probability
of turnout of 0.5. In the upper left graph, the solid line is the left party and the dotted
line is the right party. In the upper right graph, the solid line is the median voter and
the dotted line is the median citizen. In the lower right graph, the dotted line marks
the location of a tie (right vote share = 0.50).

WHY SO MUCH TURNOUT?

Bendor, Diermeier, and Ting (2003) and Fowler (2006) describe models
that generate significant turnout in which voters update their behavior using
simple reinforcement learning rules. However, these models also assume
that voters are socially isolated. In contrast, the main source of turnout in
our model has to do with imitation in a social context. Here, we assume that
citizens are boundedly rational, acquiring information only from their
neighbors in order to decide whether to vote in the next election. In the
extreme cases in which everyone votes or everyone abstains, the citizen simply repeats his or her prior action. In other cases, we can derive the expected
probability that the voters in a randomly sampled neighborhood will happen to do better than the abstainers because of the random location of their

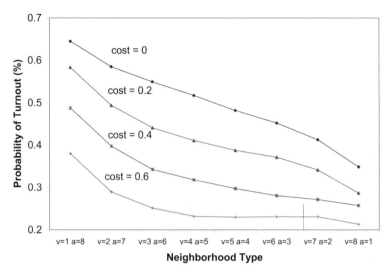

FIGURE 4.2   Theoretical impact of cost and neighborhood type on turnout.
a = number of abstainers in a neighborhood in previous election; v = number of
voters in previous election (e.g., v = 1 a = 8 is a neighborhood with one voter and
eight abstainers in the previous election. Citizens in a neighborhood like this have a
65% chance of voting if the cost of voting is 0, 58% if the cost is 0.2, 49% if the cost is
0.4, and 38% if the cost is 0.6). Probabilities are based on assumption that neighbors
have preferences that are randomly drawn from a standard normal distribution.

preferences.[8] Figure 4.2 shows the probability that a randomly sampled citizen will vote given the number of his or her neighbors who voted in the
previous election and the cost of voting.

From top to bottom, each curve in Figure 4.2 represents a higher cost
of voting. Note that increasing the cost of voting decreases the probability
of voting for all neighborhood types. This is because the cost of voting
directly decreases the average satisfaction of voters in all neighborhoods.
This effect is intuitive and conforms to other theoretical and empirical models. Note also that when voting is costless (the top curve), the probability of
voting is about 0.5 when about half the neighborhood votes and half
abstains (between 4 and 5 voters in a 9-person neighborhood). The expected
utility to voters and nonvoters is the same if there is no cost to voting, so
the odds that one group does better than another should be the same for
both at 0.5. However, this is only true when the number of voters and
abstainers is about the same. The downward slope in the curves in Figure
4.2 indicates that citizens with *fewer* voters in their neighborhood are *more*
likely to vote and citizens with *more* voters in their neighborhood are *less*

likely to vote. This suggests a negative reinforcement effect that encourages turnout. As the probability of turnout declines, so do the expected number of voters in a given neighborhood, but the probability of turnout for these neighborhoods increases as the number of voters in the neighborhood decreases.

Negative reinforcement may seem counterintuitive, but consider the fact that each citizen is essentially sampling from the population. When one sampled group is substantially larger, it is more likely to yield an average satisfaction level that is close to the population average. The smaller group is privileged because there is a better chance that they will happen to have preferences very close to the winning platform. For example, suppose that half the citizens in a neighborhood vote in the first election and voting is costly. After that, citizens decide whether or not to vote by comparing average utilities of voters and abstainers. It is likely that eventually the number of voters in the neighborhood will decrease to one or two since the cost of voting is positive. However, if one of the few remaining voters happens to have a preference that is relatively close to the platform of the winning party, the voter will be more satisfied than the abstainers. Since the number of voters in the neighborhood is small, the voter's satisfaction will dominate the average satisfaction of turnout. As a result, the neighbors will imitate the voter's turnout behavior. Of course, the local surge of voting will be quickly suppressed by the cost of voting and, thus, we have a local turnout-abstention cycle. The global dynamic is a combination of all the overlapping local neighborhoods, all of which experience periods of turnout and abstentions at different moments of the time. Hence, a local imitation structure inherently yields dynamics that encourage turnout.[9]

THE RATIONAL CALCULUS OF VOTING

The rational calculus of voting model assumes that voters think *prospectively* about the impact of their actions on their own utility. Advocates of this model cite several empirical regularities predicted by the model as evidence that these assumptions are correct. In contrast, our model assumes that voters *adapt* to past outcomes. In Figure 4.3, we see that our model generates the same empirical regularities.

For example, turnout is sensitive to the cost of voting. An increase from nothing to 0.1 depresses turnout by about 4 percentage points on average.[10] The tendency of voters to respond to higher costs with lower turnout is consistent with a broad empirical literature on the subject. For example,

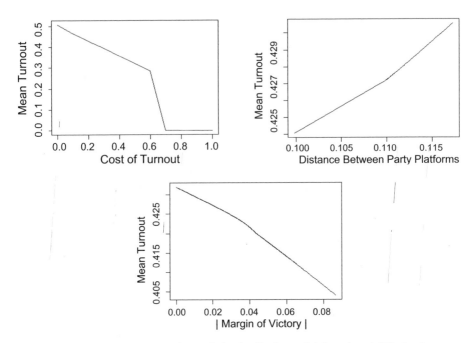

FIGURE 4.3   Determinants of voter behavior. Each graph is based on 1,000 simulations of a population of 1,024 voters with independent preferences drawn from a
standard normal distribution, party preferences at −1 and 1, and initial probability of
turnout of 0.5. Upper right and lower graphs assume a cost of voting of 0.1. Cost of
turnout was varied from 0 to 1 in the upper left graph. Means were calculated using
full-bandwidth Lowess.

restrictive registration laws clearly discourage voting (Rosenstone and
Wolfinger 1978; Squire, Wolfinger, and Glass 1987; Nagler 1991; Fenster
1994; Rhine 1995; Franklin and Grier 1997; Highton 1997, 2000; Knack
1997, 2001; Knack and White 2000; Huang and Shields 2000), whereas
liberal absentee ballot laws and all-mail elections encourage it (Oliver 1996;
Karp and Banducci 2000; Southwell and Burchett 2000).

   The rational calculus of voting literature also posits that voters should
be influenced by the expected benefits from voting expressed as a function
of the distance between the parties and the probability of influencing the
outcome of the election. Our model produces both of these relationships.
In the upper right graph of Figure 4.3, turnout increases with the distance
between party platforms, consistent with empirical work that suggests that
turnout is somewhat higher in elections with higher stakes (Wolfinger and
Rosenstone 1980; Hansen, Palfrey, and Rosenthal 1987; Boyd 1989; Forgette

and Sala 1999; Jackson 2000) and a larger distance between the parties (Kaempfer and Lowenberg 1993).

In the lower graph, turnout varies inversely with the closeness of the election: participation decreases as the margin of victory increases by one of the parties. This effect is consistent with an empirical literature that has tried to use the closeness of an election as a proxy for how voters perceive the likelihood of affecting the outcome. Though some have questioned the relationship (Key 1949; Matsusaka 1993; Kirchgassner and Himmern 1997; Kunce 2001), the weight of the evidence seems to point to a small but significant correlation between closeness and turnout (Jackson 1983; Cox and Munger 1989; Berch 1993; Grofman, Collet, and Griffin 1998; Hanks and Grofman 1998; Shachar and Nalebuff 1999; Alvarez and Nagler 2000).

The fact that the model produces results consistent with the rational calculus of voting suggests that the adaptation model for citizens is sufficiently sophisticated so that they are able to learn to vote more often when it would make them better off—that is, when costs are low, stakes are high, and elections are close. However, turnout is still quite high relative to a model in which citizens are perfectly informed and strictly utility-maximizing. To see if this discrepancy is associated with limited information, we alter our model slightly by endowing citizens with memory.

Memory permits citizens to combine information from previous elections with new information about the merits of voting and not voting. Specifically, a memory parameter governs how new information is weighed relative to previous information.[11] If this parameter is set to zero, then citizens only remember the results of the past election. As the parameter increases toward one, they remember more and more of the past and, consequnctly, the relevance of the current election decreases. The graph in Figure 4.4 shows the effect of increasing citizen memory. As voters acquire more information about the relative merits of voting and abstaining, they choose to abstain in greater numbers.

The negative relationship between memory and turnout suggests that limited information about the costs and benefits of voting plays an important role in supporting high levels of participation. To make sense of this, think of the extreme case. Without memory, the only information citizens have is the relative satisfaction levels of their neighbors and themselves for the most recent election. With memory, citizens have access to all this information, plus some of the information they acquired in previous elections. As memories lengthen, the number of individual satisfaction levels that go into the average satisfaction level increases, improving the estimate

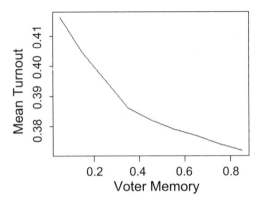

FIGURE 4.4 Effect of memory on turnout. *Note:* The graph is based on 1,000 simulations of a population of 1,024 voters with independent preferences drawn from a standard normal distribution, party preferences at −1 and 1, and initial probability of turnout of 0.5. Voter memory was varied from 0 (least weight on past information) to 0.9 (most weight on past information). Means were calculated using full-bandwidth Lowess.

of the relative costs and benefits of participation and increasing the likelihood that citizens will realize that voting is not net beneficial.

SOCIAL NETWORKS AND TURNOUT

Our model produces results that are consistent with findings related to social networks. At the level of the individual voter, we find correlation in vote strategies between neighbors. For the baseline simulation, this correlation is about $\rho = 0.29$ and it does not change much when we try different combinations of parameters. This result conforms to the finding that turnout is correlated between friends, family, and co-workers (Lazarsfeld, Berelson, and Gaudet 1948; Berelson, Lazarsfeld, and McPhee 1954; Campbell, Gurin, and Miller 1954; Glaser 1959; Straits 1990; Kenny 1992; Knack 1992; Huckfeldt and Sprague 1995). One might argue that this is a trivial result. After all, the model assumes that voters imitate their neighbors, so we should expect to find some correlation in turnout behavior. However, we emphasize that this is the only theoretical model we are aware of that generates correlated turnout. Other computational models of adaptive voters like those in Fowler (2006) and Bendor, Diermeier, and Ting (2003) typically assume voters make decisions in a vacuum that bear no relation to the decisions of their neighbors. What the model here suggests is that models that do not embed their citizens in a social network context may be omitting an important feature of the real world that is relevant to turnout behavior.

The social network context that we have supposed so far is artificial in a very important way. We assume that individual preferences are not correlated. The probability of a liberal speaking to another liberal in our model is the same as the probability of a liberal speaking to a conservative. However, a consistent finding in the social voting literature is that people tend to segregate themselves into like-minded groups. As a result, most social ties are between people who share the same interests. Even when people with ideological or class-based interests are not surrounded by like-minded individuals in their *physical* neighborhoods and workplaces, they tend to withdraw and form relationships *outside* those environments (Berger 1960; Huckfeldt and Sprague 1987). Thus, preferences between acquaintances tend to be highly correlated. For example, in the Indianapolis–St. Louis Election Study the correlation in liberal–conservative ideology is $\rho = 0.66$, whereas the correlation in party preference is $\rho = 0.54$.

What effect does the concentration of shared interests have on our model? Figure 4.5 shows that preference correlation has a dramatically negative effect on turnout. When a citizen has discussions with a diverse group, it is more difficult to discern the costs and benefits of voting. However, when all of the neighbors are just like the citizen, the voter is more likely to free ride. To see why, suppose an extreme case in which everyone in a

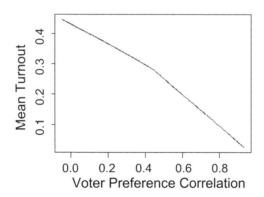

FIGURE 4.5   The effect of preference correlation on turnout. The graph is based on 1,000 simulations of a population of 1,024 voters with independent preferences drawn from a standard normal distribution, party preferences at -1 and 1, cost of voting of 0.1, and initial probability of turnout of 0.5. Preference correlation was varied from 0 to 0.95. Means were calculated using full-bandwidth Lowess.

citizen's neighborhood has the same preference. When comparing the average satisfaction level of voters and abstainers, the benefits will be the same for everyone. The only thing that differentiates the voters from the abstainers is the cost of voting. Thus, it will be easy to figure out that free riding makes sense. Now suppose the opposite case in which neighbors have heterogeneous preferences. Although all voters pay a cost of voting, some voters will be very satisfied because they happen to be located close to the winning candidate. Conversely, although abstainers do not pay a cost of voting, some will be very dissatisfied because they have preferences that are far away from the winning candidate. Thus, as preference correlation decreases, the relationship between satisfaction level and turnout behavior breaks down and it becomes more difficult to discern the advantage of free riding. In short, social segregation hurts participation.

PARTY BEHAVIOR

Turning to party behavior, we note that the model generates a substantial degree of platform divergence (see Figure 4.1). The game-theoretic literature suggests that uncertainty is a necessary condition for platform divergence (Wittman 1977; Calvert 1985). These models introduce an exogenous source of uncertainty, but in our model, uncertainty is generated endogenously by variation in voter turnout. The location of the median voter changes from election to election as new sets of voters show up to the polls. Figure 4.6 compares results when we fix voter turnout to those when we

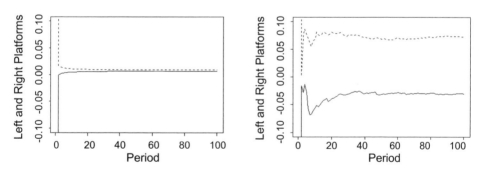

FIGURE 4.6   Effect of fixed and variable turnout on party behavior. The examples are based on a population of 1,024 voters with independent preferences drawn from a standard normal distribution, party preferences at −1 and 1, and cost of voting of 0.1. Solid lines are the left party and dotted lines are the right party. The left graph assumes fixed voter turnout and the right graph assumes variable voter turnout.

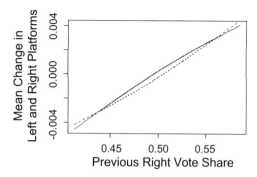

FIGURE 4.7   Effect of vote share on party behavior. The graph is based on 1,000 simulations of a population of 1,024 voters with independent preferences drawn from a standard normal distribution, party preferences at −1 and 1, cost of voting of 0.1, and initial probability of turnout of 0.5. The solid line is the left party and the dotted line is the right party. Means were calculated using full-bandwidth Lowess.

allow it to vary. When we fix turnout and the location of the median voter is constant, the parties quickly infer its location and converge. When we allow voters to choose whether to vote, the platforms diverge. Clearly, parties behave differently when turnout behavior is allowed to vary, suggesting that it may be important to model both voters and parties simultaneously as we do here.

The model also suggests that platform divergence may result from parties choosing strategies that react positively to the margin of victory. Figure 4.7 shows that both parties typically move their platforms in the direction of the winning candidate and in proportion to the margin of victory. For example, if the left wins a close election, both parties will shift slightly to the left. If the left wins in a landslide, both parties will shift a lot to the left. This is because a landslide victory causes the winning party to infer that it can win with a platform that is closer to its own preferences. It also causes the losing party to learn that it must moderate in order to be competitive in the next election. The relationship between platforms and vote share is consistent with the simpler model we present in Chapter 2, the literature on Presidential mandates (Kingdon 1966; Conley 2001), and evidence we presented in Chapter 3 that shows past vote share affects the ideology of U.S. Senate candidates.

The effect of these strategic interactions is that parties try to adapt to the (unknown) positions of the median voter and the median citizen.

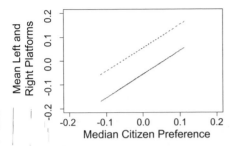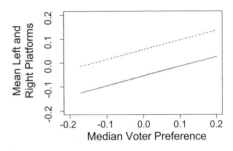

FIGURE 4.8   The effect of median citizen and median voter preferences on party behavior. *Note:* The graphs are based on 1,000 simulations of a population of 1,024 voters with independent preferences drawn from a standard normal distribution, party preferences at −1 and 1, cost of voting of 0.1, and initial probability of turnout of 0.5. The solid lines are the left party and the dotted lines are the right party. Means were calculated using full-bandwidth Lowess.

In Figure 4.1, we show that in a given run the median voter changes frequently, whereas the median citizen remains constant. Parties have a short-term incentive to exploit the former if there tends to be some persistence in the set of voters who turn out from one election to the next. However, they also have a long-term incentive to stay close to the median citizen since this represents the pool of all possible voters in future elections. Figure 4.8 shows that platforms tend to track *both* changes in the location of the median voter and the fixed location of the median citizen. Interestingly, the parties are more sensitive to the location of the median citizen than the median voter, which implies that parties pay more attention to the long-term shape of the electorate rather than short-term changes.

Finally, we highlight a surprising interaction between parties and voters. Figure 4.9 shows that increasing preference correlation among voters dramatically increases platform divergence. This is because preference correlation tends to increase variance in the vote share. Heterogeneous neighborhoods will have one or two citizens switching their behavior when the parties adjust slightly to the left or right, but homogeneous neighborhoods will have several citizens switching together—small changes in the location of the parties can quickly lead to waves of imitation among supporters of one of the parties. Whole neighborhoods teeter on the brink of voting or not and the result is to increase swings in electoral outcomes. This increases uncertainty about the location of the median voter and has a corresponding effect on the parties. In short, self-segregation yields party polarization.

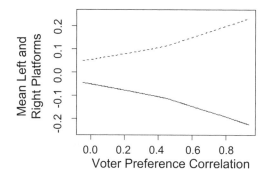

FIGURE 4.9   The effect of preference correlation on party behavior. *Note:* The graph is based on 1,000 simulations of a population of 1,024 voters with correlated preferences drawn from a standard normal distribution, party preferences at −1 and 1, cost of voting of 0.1, and initial probability of turnout of 0.5. Voter preference correlation was varied from 0 to 0.95. The solid line is the left party and the dotted line is the right party. Means were calculated using full-bandwidth Lowess.

CONCLUSION

The subject of elections, including turnout and platforms dynamics, is challenging for all social scientists. One of the main reasons for this difficulty lies in the fact that various elements of the electoral process are easier to study separately. We believe that an interdisciplinary approach, based on contributions from several social science disciplines, will lead us to a better understanding of the subject. The agent-based model we propose in this chapter is built upon a number of important contributions by sociologists (social context of voters), psychologists (bounded rationality and use of heuristics), economists (platforms dynamics and turnout decision), anthropologists (cultural influence exemplified by imitation), and last, but not least, political scientists (interdependence of voters and candidates, dynamic nature of the electoral competition).

Our model yields several findings consistent with the empirical literature on parties and voters and suggests some relationships that have not yet been tested (see Table 4.1 for a summary).

The central result is that turnout is significant, platforms diverge, and they both vary over time in an empirically realistic way. These phenomena emerge when we allow both turnout and platform strategies to adapt to one another over time. Making citizens boundedly rational and placing them in a social context turns out to be important. A closer look at the model neighborhoods shows that local imitation in a social network inherently yields negative

TABLE 4.1 Summary of the Dynamic Parties and Social Turnout Chapter Results

Result	Consistent with
Turnout is significant and stable	Mackie and Rose 1997
Turnout depends negatively on voting costs	Rosenstone and Wolfinger 1978; Squire, Wolfinger, and Glass 1987; Nagler 1991; Fenster 1994; Rhine 1995; Oliver 1996; Franklin and Grier 1997; Highton 1997, 2000; Knack 1997, 2001; Huang and Shields 2000; Karp and Banducci 2000; Knack and White 2000; Southwell and Burchett 2000
Party divergence increases turnout	Wolfinger and Rosenstone 1980; Hansen, Palfrey, and Rosenthal 1987; Boyd 1989; Kaempfer and Lowenberg 1993; Jackson 2000
Turnout increases with the closeness of the election	Jackson 1983; Cox and Munger 1989; Berch 1993; Grofman, Collet, and Griffin 1998; Hanks and Grofman 1998; Alvarez and Nagler 2000
Longer voter memories reduce turnout	Original result
Decision to vote depends on turnout behavior of socially-connected peers	Lazarsfeld, Berelson, and Gaudet 1948; Berelson, Lazarsfeld, and McPhee 1954; Campbell, Gurin, and Miller 1954; Glaser 1959; Huckfeldt and Sprague 1995; Straits 1990; Knack 1992
Local imitation yields positive feedback for turnout	Original result
Ideological segregation reduces turnout	Original result
Parties diverge	Wittman 1977; Hansson and Stuart 1984; Peltzman 1984; Poole and Rosenthal 1984; Grofman, Griffin, and Glazer 1990; Lindbeck and Weibull 1993
Parties respond to past margins of victory	Conley 2001; Kingdon 1966; Fowler 2002; Smirnov and Fowler 2007
Parties respond both to median voter and median citizen	Original result
Ideological segregation yields polarized parties	Original result

feedback dynamics that encourage turnout. The effect is further amplified by the natural limits on the information-processing capacities of the citizens such as the length of memory. On the other hand, local correlation of preferences appears to decrease the individual propensity to turn out, which implies that ideologically homogeneous communities are least likely to vote. The model also conforms to findings from the social voting literature. Citizens appear to be affected by the turnout decisions of their neighbors.

Turning to parties, the model yields several empirical implications. Allowing turnout to vary endogenously generates uncertainty about the location of the median voter and causes party platforms to diverge. We also note that parties pay attention to electoral mandates as they try to estimate the location of the median voter to remain competitive. This could help to explain the empirical work we present in Chapters 3 and 8 that shows the ideology of U.S. Senate candidates and expectations of economic policy tend to move in the direction of and in proportion to the mandate. The model also shows that party platforms tend to correlate with changes in the position of both the median voter and the median citizen, with parties being more sensitive to the latter. Finally, we find that a higher degree of local preference correlation among voters leads to greater platform divergence. Voter segregation yields party polarization.

Though our model generates relationships that correspond to much of what we know about turnout and platforms, it is important not to read too much into the results. There are many factors that we have not included here that may affect turnout and platforms such as socioeconomic status, endogenous voter and party preferences, multidimensional issue space, multiple parties, multiple districts, different electoral institutions, political institutions like legislatures, and so on. ABM makes it easy to add such factors quickly to see if and how they are relevant, but we believe that initial modeling efforts for problems like these should remain simple to provide a bridge to what may already be an extensive analytical effort. Our hope is that this approach will not only provide good predictive models of electoral politics—we hope it will also generate hypotheses that inspire future analytical efforts to find related closed-form solutions and empirical efforts to test relationships suggested by the model.

In conclusion, we observe that our main substantive result from Chapters 2 and 3 holds if we endogenize *both* politicians and voters. Candidates choose new platforms in the direction of the previously winning party's preference and the size of the shift is increasing in the margin of victory in the previous election. One of the limitations of the model in Chapter 2 is the fact that the voter distribution is exogenously fixed, which in the limit leads to certainty about the location of the median voter and convergence of the parties (Dew-Becker 2006). However, uncertainty in the model in this chapter results from endogenous turnout decisions that yield a constant source of uncertainty—as a result, platform divergence endures indefinitely as parties move back and forth with the mandate.

## FIVE

A Dynamic Calculus of Voting

As we have already noted in Chapter 4, an explanation for why people vote in large electorates has been a difficult problem for rational choice theory. Rational choice scholars have primarily focused on models of turnout that rely on the pivotal motivation to vote in a single election (Downs 1957; Riker and Ordeshook 1968; Ferejohn and Fiorina 1974; Palfrey and Rosenthal 1983, 1985; Ledyard 1984). This motivation stems from the belief that there is a small chance that a single vote will decide the outcome of the election. Although the probability of being the pivotal voter is extremely small even in highly contested elections, one can still resort to the subjective nature of beliefs and argue that people may overestimate the probability of casting the pivotal vote. However, sometimes people actually know that their votes cannot be pivotal (Jackson 1983; Aldrich 1993), and yet they vote in large numbers despite widespread knowledge that there is a clear election favorite.

In Chapter 4, we show how turnout may be sustained if citizens are *adaptively* influenced by their neighbors' turnout decisions in a dynamic model of voters and parties. However, in the full model, it is difficult to discern the precise effect party dynamics have on the turnout decision. To simplify the analysis, we focus, in this chapter, on individual turnout incentives using the concept of electoral mandates as an explanatory variable. In particular, we show that an individual may have a rational incentive to vote if he or she believes that politicians behave according to our theory of mandates, with each party moving in the direction of the winner.

We construct, building on insights from previous chapters, a decision-theoretic model of turnout in which individuals maximize their subjective expected utility in a context of repeated elections. We assume that the perceived probability of being pivotal is strictly zero—no one believes that there is a chance of being decisive. Instead, the turnout decision is driven by what we call the *signaling motivation*.[1] Suppose that parties are policy-motivated (Wittman 1977) and that they adjust their platforms in response to the margin of victory in the previous election. The theoretical models that we present in Chapters 2, 3, and 4 suggest that parties will move with the mandate. Winning parties shift their platform toward the extremes to satisfy their own preferences, whereas losers shift toward the median voter in order to improve their chances of winning the next election. The size of the shift in platforms depends on the size of the victory—landslides yield big changes, whereas close elections yield little if any change (Bernhard, Sala, and Nokken 2002). If parties do move with the mandate, then citizens may have a signaling motivation to vote because they can change the margin of victory in the current election. A vote for the expected winner signals a tolerance for even more extreme platforms, whereas a vote for the expected loser signals a preference for platforms closer to the center.

The model we present in this chapter indicates that a signaling motivation exists for all possible beliefs about the closeness of the election. The size of this signaling motivation is proportional to a citizen's *external efficacy, patience,* and *electoral pessimism.* (1) External efficacy describes the "belief in the influence of one's actions on the decision of the government" (Rosenstone and Hansen 1993: 143). Voters with high external efficacy believe that parties pay attention to the electorate (and, presumably, election results) when they are deciding what policies to offer. The stronger this belief, the more likely citizens will vote because they believe parties will respond to the vote share they receive. (2) Patient citizens who are willing to wait for future gains will place a higher value on the outcome of future elections. We, therefore, expect citizens with higher discount factors to be more likely to vote. (3) Electoral pessimists are those who expect their favorite party to lose the current election. An extra vote for a party expected to lose will have a small impact on the margin of victory, but an extra vote for a party expected to win 100% of the vote will not change the margin of victory at all—it will still win by 100%. We show that the impact of a single vote on the margin of victory decreases as the expected margin of victory increases. Thus, the worse a voter expects his or her favorite party to do in the election, the greater the incentive to balance the outcome by voting.

An empirical analysis of National Election Studies (NES) data on U.S. presidential elections from 1976 to 1988 confirms all three hypotheses generated by the model. Many studies have established a relationship between turnout and external efficacy. We extend this research and suggest both theoretically and empirically that turnout depends on subjective rates of time preference and subjective beliefs about the probability that one's favorite party will win the election. The model may also provide an explanation for the relationship between the closeness of the election and turnout. When we include variables for the signaling motivation, closeness is no longer a significant factor for turnout.

Finally, the model generates additional results regarding differences between voters with extreme and moderate preferences. In the model, a voter with extreme preferences always chooses the nearest party as that will tend to move both party platforms in the voter's preferred direction. Moderates, on the other hand, must also consider electoral probabilities. Voting for the winner would cause the winning platform to be adjusted further *away* from the center. Thus, even if a moderate prefers such a party, there may be an incentive to choose the party that is more likely to lose in order to keep the favorite party from straying too far away from the voter's own preference. We call this counterintuitive phenomenon *mandate balancing*, and we note that it may help to explain why moderates are more likely than extremists to vote for their least-preferred party. This phenomenon is in contrast with the theory of directional voting (Rabinowitz and MacDonald 1989). A moderate Republican would prefer an extreme Republican over a moderate Democrat under the Rabinowitz-MacDonald theory but might prefer the Democrat under mandate balancing. We test this later in the book. Mandate balancing also complements institutional balancing literatures (Fiorina 1988; Alesina and Rosenthal 1995) and may help explain why midterm elections in the United States usually penalize the party of the President (Campbell 1960) and "second-order" elections penalize the ruling party in parliamentary systems (Reif and Schmitt 1980).

Before proceeding, we emphasize the limitations of the approach in this chapter. Fully informed and rational voters in large electorates would probably not be willing to vote if the signaling motivation were the only incentive because the impact of a single vote on the margin of victory would be minimal. But we do not argue in this book that the signaling motivation is the only incentive to vote. Nor do we argue that all voters are fully informed and rational. Nor do we argue that our theory should supplant other theories of turnout. Instead, we concur with Rosenstone and Hansen (1993) and Verba, Schlozman, and Brady (1995) who argue that there are many factors that contribute to the decision to vote. Classic pivotal models of turnout have yielded a number of comparative statics results that have been confirmed empirically (Aldrich 1993). More importantly, other authors have used these comparative statics to establish a rational basis for turnout behavior, even if it is not fully rational. For example, resource mobilization theory (see Verba, Schlozman, and Brady 1995) suggests that people with better resources (such as education and experience working in groups) are more likely to vote because the costs of gathering information and engaging in action are lower. This is a comparative static that results from the simple Downsian model. Similarly, our model's main contribution is to suggest comparative statics that might provide a rational basis for behavioral results such as the relationship between turnout and external efficacy.

A DYNAMIC MODEL OF THE
CALCULUS OF VOTING

In this section, we develop a formal model of turnout in which there is no pivotal motivation to vote. For simplicity, we assume that, in the voter's perception, the probability of casting a decisive vote is strictly zero. We also focus our attention only on the "economic and political goals of an individual" (Downs 1957: 6), specifically setting aside arguments about the duty motivation or a taste for voting because we are interested in exploring how individual self-interest in the outcome of the political process might affect one's decision to vote. We also focus on the importance of political efficacy. As Abramson (1983) notes, "Next to party identification, no political attitude has been studied more extensively than feelings of political efficacy." Our model suggests a reason for the relationship between external efficacy and electoral involvement. We hope it will reduce the gap between formal modeling and decades of qualitative and empirical research on a concept that "lies at the heart of many explanations of citizen activity and involvement" (Verba, Schlozman, and Brady 1995: 346).

We start with a conventional spatial model of electoral competition (discussion of the mathematical features of the model is presented in the Chapter 4 Appendix). Citizens have ideal points that are located on a one-dimensional issue space and two parties compete for their votes in a winner-take-all election by proposing platforms located somewhere in the issue space. Each citizen prefers the party whose platform is located closer to her ideal point. In a static model, potential voters care only about the outcome of the current election; in the dynamic model, they also care about the future.

How does the outcome of the current election affect future elections? In Chapters 2 and 4, we show how and why parties use the margin of victory from the past election to adjust the platform they offer in the next election. Both winners and losers update their beliefs about the voter distribution and move the policies they offer toward the winner's preferred set of policies. Here we abstract away from the complex interactions that would result if voters were perfectly informed and perfectly rational, and we assume that voters have a simple rule in mind when they consider party behavior. Specifically, they think both parties move with the mandate:

$$F_{t+1}^J = F_t^J + \mu E \text{ (see Chapter 5 Appendix for derivation)} \qquad (1)$$

where F_{t+1}^J is party J's platform for the election at time $t + 1$ and F_t^J is the platform for the election at time t. The variable μ denotes the margin of victory for party J in the election at time t, and is positive for a victory and negative for a loss. The variable E is an *efficacy* parameter indicating the magnitude of a party's response to an electoral victory. The sign on E indicates the preferred direction of movement for party J (negative if J is the left party and positive if J is the right party). The size of a platform shift is proportional to the margin of victory μ and the magnitude of E, which is how much a citizen believes parties pay attention to the views of the electorate.

In Chapter 6, we will show evidence from a nationally representative sample of Americans that indicates the average voter does use this heuristic, although there is significant variation in expectations about the magnitude of party responsiveness. Citizens with low external efficacy may not think the parties adjust their platforms much in response to electoral outcomes, corresponding to low values of E. Citizens with high external efficacy believe that parties do react to the electorate, but only in proportion to the margin of victory. The importance of external efficacy for political participation has been documented in a rich literature (Lane 1959; Iyengar 1980; Craig and Maggiotto 1982; Finkel 1987; Cassel and Luskin 1988; Huckfeldt and Sprague 1992; Rosenstone and Hansen 1993; Timpone 1998).

Given these beliefs, why would a citizen choose to vote? The answer may be in a desire to make sure that his or her "voice" is heard by the government

(Pateman 1970; Thompson 1970; Verba and Nie 1972; Mason 1982). If we assume that citizens believe their votes are not decisive in the current election, then there is only one variable that they can influence: by voting instead of abstaining, they can change μ, the margin of victory. This in turn changes the platforms offered by *both parties* in the next election. Hence, citizens have an incentive to vote that is independent of the *closeness* and *outcome* of the current election. Each voter in every election has the capacity to signal to parties whether they should move their platforms left or right.[2]

Obviously, this signaling motivation depends critically on subjective beliefs about how much a single vote can change the margin of victory ($\Delta\mu$). This is, in turn, a function of the number N of people voting, and the expected proportion p of voters choosing the citizen's *preferred* party in the current election:

$$\Delta\mu = \frac{2(1-p)}{N+1} \text{ (see Chapter 5 Appendix for derivation).} \qquad (2)$$

The role of N is straightforward: the more people vote, the less important is a single "voice." The role of p requires a bit more explanation. As defined here, it contrasts with pivotal models where p can represent the probability of *either* party winning since it is only used to estimate how close the election will be. Why is this distinction important? Equation (3) shows that the effect of a single vote on the margin of victory declines as one expects one's favorite party to win a larger portion of the vote. In fact, when the margin of victory is expected to be 100%, giving one more vote to one's preferred candidate would not change the 100% margin of victory at all. Thus, citizens who expect their favorite party to lose should believe they have a *greater* impact on the margin of victory than those who expect their favorite party to win.

The size of this signaling motivation might seem relatively small in large populations since a citizen can only change the margin of victory by a single vote. However, the *perceived* importance of a vote also depends on E, how responsive one thinks the government is. Moreover, if voters believe that parties update their platforms as shown before, then the effect of any decision made in the current election will persist since platforms in this election become the basis for platforms in the next election, the election after that, and so on.[3] Citizens who choose to vote in the current election thus capture a discounted stream of benefits for moving platforms in their preferred direction for *all future elections*. This means that the signaling motivation will be sensitive to an individual's discount factor δ.

Finally, suppose each citizen has a subjective belief about the likelihood q that the citizen's preferred party will win in future elections. This allows us to derive the following two propositions.

PROPOSITION 1: *All citizens have a nonnegative signaling motivation to vote. Specifically, extremists with preferences to the left or right of both party platforms have a signaling motivation to vote* $(\delta / (1-\delta))\Delta\mu|E| \geq 0$. *Moderates with preferences between both party platforms have a signaling motivation to vote* $(\delta / (1-\delta))\Delta\mu|E||1-2q| \geq 0$.

PROOF: *See Chapter 5 Appendix.*[4]

Notice that the first variable that determines the subjective value of a vote is the citizen's discount factor (δ). Those with higher discount factors care more about the future and thus receive greater benefits if they believe they can affect future elections. Thus, patience is a virtue for turnout—the more you are willing to wait, the more likely you are to vote.

The next variable is $\Delta\mu$, or how much a single vote changes the margin of victory. Recall from before that $\Delta\mu$ is decreasing in the expected proportion of votes received by one's preferred party (p). This means that those who are more pessimistic about their favorite party's performance in the upcoming election think their single vote will have a relatively larger impact on the margin of victory and future platforms. Thus, electoral pessimism is actually good for turnout—the worse that one expects the favorite party to do in the election, the more likely he or she is to vote.

The efficacy parameter E is also very important. Even if other factors make voting utility significant, the citizen who believes that parties do not care about election margins will not believe that any number of votes can have an impact on future party platforms, let alone his or her own. For these citizens, a victory is a victory and a loss is a loss, regardless of how close or lopsided the election is. On the other hand, if a citizen has a strong sense of external efficacy, he or she is more likely to believe that every vote helps parties shape the platforms they offer in the future. The more responsive one thinks parties are to the "voice" of the people as expressed in elections, the more likely one is to vote.

The variable q, the likelihood of your favorite party winning *in the future*, decreases the signaling motivation for moderates. This is because moderates, whose preferences lie between the party platforms, want to keep the platforms close to the center. If they expect their favorite party to win the next election, then voting for it now will cause the party to move the platform toward its own preferences and away from the center. Thus, the signaling motivation to vote for one's favorite party actually becomes negative when $q > 0.5$! Meanwhile, notice that q is not present in the equation for extremists, whose signaling motivation is always weakly positive. This is because one's vote moves platforms of both parties in the voter's preferred direction *regardless* of expected future probabilities. Therefore, a single vote always matters regardless of the outcome of the current and all future elections. This distinction between extremists and moderates generates differences not only in the utility of turnout, but in the choice of party, as shown in the following proposition:

PROPOSITION 2: *If no other incentives exist, extremists vote for the party with the closest platform if $(\delta/(1-\delta))\Delta\mu|E| > c$, otherwise they abstain. Moderates vote for the party that is more likely to lose in the future elections if $(\delta/(1-\delta))\Delta\mu|E||1-2q| > c$, otherwise they abstain.*

PROOF: *See Chapter 5 Appendix.*

   Since an extremist always votes for his or her first choice, the decision-making problem that is faced is clear: vote if the benefit from voting is greater than the associated cost. A moderate has to make a more difficult turnout decision. Given the citizen's belief about how parties respond to elections (equation 5), he or she knows that a higher margin of victory would lead the preferred party to move to its extreme, further from his or her preference point. The same logic applies for the other party. Obviously, a moderate voter is interested in moderate outcomes. By voting for the party that the voter expects to lose more often in future elections, he or she decreases the margin of victory for the winner and thus discourages the adoption of extreme platforms. Hence, moderates may not vote for their first choice—they might instead balance future platforms by engaging in *mandate balancing*, voting for the party they expect to lose future elections.

   Two recent models generate results that are closely related to our own. First, a phenomenon related to mandate balancing in multiparty systems can be found in Kedar (2005). In Kedar's model, voters often support parties whose positions differ from their own in order to affect the final policy outcome to their advantage. However, this only happens when the supported parties pull policy in the voters' preferred direction and it is unclear what happens in a dynamic context. Second, our model generates results like those in a pivotal voting model developed by Feddersen and Pesendorfer (1996). They argue that *less informed* moderates prefer to abstain. Similarly, moderates in our model who have no information about future electoral probabilities might assume the two parties are equally likely to win ($q = 0.5$), which would drive the signaling motivation to vote to zero. More informed moderates, on the other hand, might have some intuition about the future. For example, a moderate who prefers the Democratic Party in the United States and believes that demographic factors favor the Democratic Party may strategically vote for Republicans in order to make future platforms by the former less extreme. However, this belief would have to be strong enough to overcome the cost of voting. Since less certainty yields beliefs closer to $q = 0.5$, moderates with less information have a smaller signaling motivation to vote. This might not exceed the cost, yielding abstention by uninformed moderates. Thus, our model is also consistent with the finding that moderates tend to vote less often than extremists (Keith et al. 1992).

EMPIRICAL IMPLICATIONS

Our model makes at least three predictions about turnout that we can test using data from the American National Election Studies (NES). If the signaling motivation exists for voters, then turnout should be positively associated with external efficacy (E) and the discount factor (δ) and negatively associated with expectations about how well one's favorite party will do (p).[5] The strongly positive impact of external efficacy on turnout has already been widely documented (Iyengar 1980; Craig and Maggiotto 1982; Finkel 1987; Cassel and Luskin 1988; Huckfeldt and Sprague 1992; Rosenstone and Hansen 1993; Timpone 1998), but we are not aware of any empirical tests of the other two variables. To measure p, we index respondents according to whether or not they think the election will be close, which presidential candidate they think will win, and which candidate they prefer.[6] We code $p = 0$ for respondents who think their favorite candidate will lose in an election that is not close, $p = 1/3$ if the candidate is expected to lose a close election, $p = 2/3$ if the candidate is expected to win a close election, and $p = 1$ if the candidate is expected to win an election that is not close.[7]

To measure δ, we note that the NES has asked two questions related to subjective time preferences: (1) "Do you think it's better to plan your life a good way ahead, or would you say life is too much a matter of luck to plan ahead very far?" (2) "When you do make plans ahead, do you usually get to carry out things the way you expected, or do things usually come up to make you change your plans?" Respondents who answer yes to the first question have a *normative* preference for future planning, indicating that in principle it would be good to think about the future effects of current actions. Those who say yes to the second question have an *experiential* preference for future planning, indicating that past efforts to incorporate the future effects of current actions have yielded successful results. It seems reasonable to assume that a preference for future planning correlates with subjective time preferences. However, the correlation may be weak and the binary nature of allowable responses means that we can only coarsely divide respondents into two groups: those with higher discount factors and those with lower discount factors. To mitigate this problem somewhat, we create a discount factor index that is the average of the two responses.

Since we are comparing the signaling model of turnout to other rational models, we include variables related to the pivotal motivation to vote (see Chapter 5 Appendix for coding specifications). These include the benefit of voting as measured by the perceived difference between the two candidates, and the probability of being pivotal as measured by the perceived closeness of the election. We also add a variable for civic duty. This addition is especially challenging for testing our theory about the signaling motivation because it is based on the following question: "If a person doesn't care how an election comes out, then that person shouldn't vote in it." A negative answer to this question has often been interpreted to mean that respondents believe there is an obligation to vote that transcends individual incentives. However, we note that respondents might also answer negatively to this question if they consider that the impact on future elections is important enough to warrant a vote regardless of their incentives to vote in the current election. Nonetheless, we include it in our model to be sure that we have controlled for those respondents who answered negatively because they believe in a civic duty of voting.

We include several other variables related to turnout as controls (see Chapter 5 Appendix). Verba, Schlozman, and Brady (1995) argue that *socioeconomic status* (SES) variables like education and income are related to turnout because they affect the costs of acquiring information about politics—higher status individuals are more likely to vote because their costs are lower. They also note the importance of *institutional affiliation*. In particular, people acquire civic skills in organizations (writing letters, public speaking, and so on) that may make it easier for them to participate in politics. Verba, Schlozman, and Brady point out that *psychological* variables are important for turnout as well. The more informed people are about politics and the more they feel that they can understand political issues (internal efficacy), the more likely it is that they will be able to make a choice at the polls. Moreover, interest in politics and strength of partisan identification indicate how politically engaged potential voters are, which tends to correlate with turnout. Turnout has been shown to depend on these three factors in a wide variety of studies besides Verba, Schlozman, and Brady (e.g., Timpone 1998).

Each additional control reduces the efficiency of estimation, so we follow King, Keohane, and Verba (1994) in restricting our attention to variables that are correlated with, and causally prior to, our variables of interest. Several SES, institutional affiliation, and psychological factors correlate with our variables of interest and might also be causally prior to them. For example, a taste for future planning might be affected by feelings of personal security, which could be a function of SES. Similarly, perceptions of government responsiveness and the likelihood one's favorite candidate will win might be related to one's institutional experience and psychological factors related to politics. We, therefore, include them as controls.

Granberg and Holmberg (1991) note that self-reported turnout is significantly higher than aggregate turnout percentages would imply, so we focus on elections in which turnout was validated in the NES (1976, 1980, 1984, 1988). We model validated turnout using probit with heteroskedastic-consistent standard errors, but first we must address the problem of missing data. Listwise deletion restricts the observations to 1976 since this is the only year in which votes were validated and questions about subjective rates of time preferences were asked. We report these results because this is the default method of dealing with missing data in political science analyses. However, listwise deletion inefficiently wastes much of the information available in the NES, and, even worse, it may produce biased estimates since several independent variables are correlated with missingness in our dependent variable.[8] We, therefore, also report results based on multiple imputation of missing data. Details of this procedure and a discussion are provided in Chapter 5 Appendix.

In addition to predictions about turnout, our model also makes predictions about vote choice. In Proposition 2, we show that when no other incentives exist, extremist voters should always choose the closest party. However, moderates will only choose the closest party if they think it will lose future elections. We do not have a good empirical proxy for expectations of future electoral performance, but if we assume that at least some moderates believe their favorite party is likely to win future elections, then moderates should be more likely than extremists to abandon their first choice. We create a dichotomous dependent variable that is 0 if a respondent says he or she will vote for the candidate placed closest to the voter on a seven-point liberal-conservative scale, and 1 if he or she says they will vote for the candidate placed farther away. We then define moderates as those who place themselves in between the Democratic and Republican candidates on the liberal-conservative scale, and all others as extremists.

There are three major controls included in our vote choice analysis (see Chapter 5 data appendix for precise specifications). First, the directional voting literature (Rabinowitz and MacDonald 1989) suggests that voters may choose the candidate who is spatially further away because he or she is on the same side of the center of the issue space. In other words, it might be easier for a moderate liberal to vote for an extreme liberal who is farther away than for a moderate conservative who is closer. We, therefore, include a control that indicates when a voter has chosen a second-choice candidate who is on the same side of the liberal-conservative scale. Second, the institutional balancing literature (Fiorina 1988; Alesina and Rosenthal 1995) points out that some voters who prefer moderate outcomes may split their ticket between the Congress and the President by voting for candidates from different parties. This would also cause some voters to abandon their first choice, so we include a control for split-ticket voting. Third, certain psychological factors may make it more difficult for some voters to choose a candidate who is further away even if they know it is in their best interests. We, therefore, include controls for the ability to discern a strategic option (internal efficacy, political information, and interest in the campaign), and the level of attachment to the sincere option (strength of party identification). As in the turnout model, we use both listwise deletion and multiple imputation for missing data and for our analysis we use probit with heteroskedastic-consistent standard errors.

RESULTS

Table 5.1 shows estimates of the effect of pivotal, signaling, and civic duty variables on the probability of voting. Only one variable related to the pivotal motivation is significant—the candidate differential has a significant effect on turnout, but the perceived closeness of the election does not. Meanwhile, all three variables related to the signaling motivation are significant. In particular, respondents with high levels of external efficacy are 12% more likely to vote than those with low levels. Those who value future planning are 8% more likely to vote than those who do not. In addition, those who think their favorite candidate will surely win are 7% *less* likely

TABLE 5.1   Effects on the Probability of Voter Turnout

Variable	Pooled Model Using Multiple Imputation		Model for 1976 Using Listwise Deletion	
Pivotal motivation				
Candidate differential (B)	8	(±6)	—	
Closeness of election (P)	—		—	
Signaling motivation				
External efficacy (E)	12	(±5)	11	(±10)
Discount factor (δ)	8	(±5)	8	(±4)
Probability favorite party wins (p)	−7	(±5)	−16	(±14)
Duty motivation				
Civic duty (D)	8	(±3)	7	(±7)

Note: Probabilities are based on model in Table A-4.1 in the Appendix and they reflect the difference in the probability of turnout when each variable is changed from its lowest to its highest observed value holding all other variables at their mean. Simulated coefficients are used to incorporate estimation uncertainty (for details see King, Tomz, and Wittenberg 2000). Ninety-five percent confidence intervals are shown in parenthesis and estimates not significantly different from zero are not shown.

to vote than those who think he will surely lose. The civic duty motivation is also significant at 8%, but recall from before those respondents who believe in a signaling motivation might answer the civic duty question in the same way as those who believe in a normative obligation to vote. Thus, part of the civic duty effect in the model could be capturing the signaling motivation, meaning the signaling estimates may be too small and the civic duty estimate too large.

Unlike several other statistical models of turnout (e.g., Cox and Munger 1989; Berch 1993; Hanks and Grofman 1998; Grofman, Collet, and Griffin 1998; Shachar and Nalebuff 1999; Alvarez and Nagler 2000), closeness in our model is insignificant. The closeness variable typically divides respondents between those who expect a close election and those who expect a landslide. The variable p further divides respondents who expect a landslide election into two groups—those who think their favorite candidate will lose (electoral pessimists) and those who think he or she will win (electoral optimists). The pivotal model predicts that pessimists will stay home because they cannot help their favorite candidate who is sure to lose. The signaling model, on the other hand, predicts that pessimists will be the most likely to vote because they think they will have the greatest impact on future platforms. The NES data confirm that electoral pessimists do vote more often (64%) than optimists (58%) and those who think the election will be close (60%).

This suggests that the finding that closeness encourages turnout may be spurious. NES respondents are much more likely to be electoral optimists (25%) than pessimists (6%), meaning four out of five of those expecting a landslide also expect their favorite candidate to win. The average p for this group is thus quite high (0.80 in our specification). The group expecting a close election has lower average expectations for their favorite candidate and a lower average value of p (0.58), and is, therefore, more likely to vote according to the signaling model. Thus, the closeness variable may be picking up the effect of p, which is supported by the fact that including p in our model causes the closeness variable to become insignificant.

Although this evidence suggests the importance of variables related to the signaling motivation, the socioeconomic status (SES) variables in the model are still doing much of the work for explaining turnout. A variety of explanations has been advanced for why this might be, but our model suggests another. We conjecture that SES variables are, in part, proxies for the discount factor. The discount factor index we use here is a coarse estimate of subjective time preferences that may be only weakly correlated with respondents' true discount factors. However, the experimental economics literature on subjective time preferences has recently made progress in measuring discount factors and relating them to SES variables. Table 5.2 shows how education, income, home ownership, age, marital status, and gender affect discount rates (Harrison, Lau, and Williams 2002). For example, homeowners are expected to have discount factors that are 3.7% higher

TABLE 5.2   Socioeconomic Effects on the Discount Factor and Voter Turnout

Change in Variable (from → to)	Difference in Discount Factor (%)	Rank	Difference in Turnout (%)	Rank
High school education or less → College education or more	+6.8[†]	1	+31[†]	1
Poor (lowest quartile) → Rich (highest quartile)	+6.4[†]	2	+29[†]	2
Not a Homeowner → Homeowner	+3.7[†]	3	+24[†]	4
Young (18–30) → Old (50–75)	+2.3[†]	4	+26[†]	3
Single → Married	+1.2[†]	5	+14[†]	5
Female → Male	+0.1	6	+3[†]	6

Note: Differences in discount factors are calculated from mean discount rates estimated in table 3 of Harrison, Lau, and Williams (2002). Differences in turnout are based on mean validated turnout rates in the NES data, 1976–1988.
[†]$p < .01$.
NES—National Electoral Studies

TABLE 5.3   Vote Choice Models for the National Election Studies, 1976–1988

Variable	Pooled Model Using Multiple Imputation		Pooled Model Using Listwise Deletion	
Moderate	0.35*	(0.05)	0.45*	(0.08)
Directional voter	0.12*	(0.04)	0.13	(0.09)
Split-ticket voter	0.14*	(0.07)	0.36*	(0.10)
Psychological variables				
Political interest	−0.20*	(0.07)	−0.35*	(0.13)
Political information	−0.29*	(0.05)	−0.03	(0.11)
Internal efficacy	−0.33*	(0.05)	−0.29*	(0.09)
Strength of party ID	−0.20*	(0.05)	−0.30*	(0.13)
Intercept	−0.08	(0.05)	−0.57*	(0.15)
Pseudo R^2	0.05		0.06	
N	8,158		1,420	

Note: Dependent variable is 0 if voter chooses most proximate party on the liberal-conservative scale, 1 otherwise. Coefficient estimates are from a probit model with heteroskedastic-consistent errors. Missing data are imputed using the Expectations Maximization algorithm (King et al. 2001).

*$p < .05$. Standard errors are in parentheses.

than nonhomeowners. Notice that the direction of SES effects on discount factors correlates perfectly with SES effects on turnout. Moreover, notice that the magnitude of the effects is also strongly correlated ($\rho = .88$). This suggests to us that the causal flow might be SES variables → discount factor → turnout. In Chapter 7, we use a method from experimental economics to measure discount factors directly and see whether they affect turnout.

In addition to predictions about turnout, our model also makes predictions about vote choice. Among those who position themselves closer to one party than the other on this scale in the raw NES data, moderates are indeed more likely (34.1%) to vote for their second choice than extremists (21.9%). When we control for other explanations like directional voting, institutional balancing, and psychological factors, both our models of vote choice (see Table 5.3) indicate that moderates are 13% more likely to vote for their second choice than extremists.[9] This evidence is consistent with the prediction that moderates engage in *mandate balancing*, but we admit it is not definitive. In Chapter 6, we conduct an experiment on a nationally representative sample of voters that asks specific questions about how they would behave under different electoral expectations. The evidence from this experiment will show that independent voters are more likely than partisans to vote for their second choice if they believe parties are responsive to elections.

CONCLUSION

Our decision-theoretic model focuses on a citizen's subjective but rational estimates of whether he or she is better off voting or abstaining. The model emphasizes the value of a vote as a signal of one's preferences. Three empirical implications of our theoretical model are that citizens with higher levels of *external efficacy, patience,* and *electoral pessimism* should be more likely to vote. We find limited empirical support for all three implications using validated turnout from NES data (1976–1988). Turnout is higher among citizens with higher external efficacy, higher discount factors, and lower expectations about the proportion of votes their favorite candidate will receive.

We draw several conclusions from our model. First, the analysis suggests why a citizen may vote when elections are *not* close and there is a clear favorite. In fact, the signaling incentive to vote is actually strongest for citizens who expect their favorite candidate to lose in a landslide. Second, *mandate balancing* may explain why a voter might rationally support a party that is farther from his or her ideal point. This happens when moderates support a party that is more likely to lose future elections in order to keep future winners from becoming too extreme. Third, as in Feddersen and Pesendorfer (1996), we provide a rational explanation for why less informed moderates may be more likely to abstain. Fourth, studies based on the NES that show civic duty is an important motivation for turnout may, in fact, be capturing the effect of the signaling motivation. The civic duty question asked in the NES does not distinguish between those who believe in an obligation to vote and those who believe voting is an important signal for future elections. Fifth, we also suggest that the empirical relationship between the closeness of an election and turnout is spurious. When we include the expected proportion of votes for one's favorite candidate in the empirical model, closeness ceases to be significant.

Furthermore, we conjecture that the discount factor may explain why SES variables are related to turnout. In this respect, our model bridges the gap between formal theory and the large literature on turnout that emerged in the 1950s and 1960s exemplified by such works as *Voting* (Berelson, Lazarsfeld, and McPhee 1954) and *The American Voter* (Campbell et al. 1960). Drawing on recent work in economics, we show that income, education, age, home ownership, marriage, and gender affect the discount factor in the same direction and magnitude as they affect turnout. We also speculate that other SES variables may have such an effect on the discount factor. For example, Becker and Mulligan (1997: 741) argue that religious people have higher discount factors because they believe in an afterlife and thus have longer time horizons. If so, this might help to explain the strong correlation between church activity and turnout. Also, blacks may have lower discount rates because of institutional discrimination (e.g., less access to credit markets), which in turn might drive their difference in turnout. These are speculative arguments, but they are meant to illustrate reasons why future studies of turnout should take discount factors seriously. In Chapter 7, we take one step in this direction by measuring individual discount factors with a choice game to see how they relate to turnout and its known correlates.

Our analysis may also contribute to literatures on political economy, spatial modeling, and institutional balancing. For example, unlike many existing political economy models, our model explains why citizens with extreme preferences may abstain. Extremists who think parties are not responsive to the electorate or who expect their favorite party to do well (electoral optimists) get less utility from signaling and are thus *less likely* to vote. In a spatial context, we also explain why party platforms might be more stable over time than otherwise expected. If supporters of the party expected to lose tend to be more motivated than supporters of the party expected to win, then the result will be *negative feedback* in an electoral system that keeps margins of victory closer to zero. Thus, parties would have less of an incentive to make dramatic changes in their platforms, making the system more stable and slower to change than one might otherwise expect.

Finally, we note that both the *negative feedback* effect and the tendency of moderates to engage in *mandate balancing* may help to explain party surge and decline. Suppose that a party wins a national election (surge). If this causes voters to increase their estimate of the probability that the party will win the next election, our model suggests two effects. First, supporters of the winning party will have less incentive to vote in the next election because they are more optimistic about their favorite party's chances. Similarly, supporters of the opposition will have a greater incentive to vote. As a result, the vote share for the winning party should be lower in the next election (decline). Second, some moderates may change their mind about who is likely to win the next election. Since moderates have an incentive to balance by voting for the party less likely to win future elections, this would increase the vote share for the opposition and decrease it for the party that recently won (again, decline). Citizens might be relatively more inclined to use their vote as a signal in lower stakes elections when the pivotal motivation is less important. Thus, this may be why midterm elections in the

United States usually penalize the party of the President (Campbell 1960; Fiorina 1988; Alesina and Rosenthal 1995) and "second-order" elections penalize the ruling party in parliamentary systems (Reif and Schmitt 1980). Future work should examine the impact of the signaling motivation on surge and decline by modeling change in voter beliefs about electoral probabilities in a context of alternating high-stakes and low-stakes elections.

In summary, we once again see how mandates affect not only party behavior but voter behavior as well. The simple assumption that voters anticipate parties will move with the mandate yields several predictions that are borne out by the data. In Chapters 6 and 7, we extend our empirical examination of voter behavior as an integral part of the phenomenon of electoral mandates. In Chapter 6, we examine whether voters actually believe that candidates react to the margins of victory and, if so, whether they engage in mandate balancing as a result. In Chapter 7, we measure individual discount factors to see if more citizens that are patient are more likely to vote. These chapters provide further evidence that electoral mandates play an important role in our political system.

## SIX

Party Responsiveness and
Mandate Balancing

I n this book, we present theoretical models and empirical evidence from a wide array of sources that suggests parties in the United States respond to elections by changing the candidates they choose and the policies they implement. Specifically, both the winning and losing parties become more liberal when the Democrats win, more conservative when the Republicans win, and the size of the change in ideology is increasing in the size of the margin of victory. However, the possible existence of these party dynamics begs an important question. Do voters believe that parties and politicians are responsive to elections? Moreover, how do these beliefs affect voter behavior?

A number of recent formal models depend on the assumption that voters believe parties adjust their post-electoral policies in response to the margin of victory. For example, our model in Chapter 5 and Razin (2003) show that under this assumption, moderate voters who must choose between two responsive and polarized parties have a signaling motivation to vote that is much stronger than the motivation to affect the outcome of the election. Shotts (2000) notes further that voters may have an incentive to signal their preferences for moderate policies through abstention, even when the act of voting is costless. Meirowitz and Tucker (2003) show that "voting to send a message" to responsive parties causes split ticket voting in sequential elections, especially if the sequence involves the alternation of low and high stakes elections (see also Alesina and Rosenthal 1995). Meirowitz (2004) further extends these results from elections to polls, showing that if voters believe parties respond to vote intention surveys by adjusting their policies, then polling results cannot be a reliable measure of public opinion.

The unifying message from these formal models is that a belief in responsive parties gives voters an incentive to behave strategically in contests between two alternatives. Specifically, we should expect different behavior from extremist and moderate voters. Both kinds of voters want their preferred candidate to win, and thus have an incentive to vote sincerely. However, they also have an incentive to move post-electoral policy as close to their own preferred outcome as possible. Extremists experience no conflict between these incentives. Each vote for the preferred party increases the probability of victory and moves post-electoral policy closer to their ideal point. Moderates, on the other hand, must consider a tradeoff. If they believe that larger margins of victory cause the winning party to offer more extreme policies, then they may signal their preference for more centrist policies by voting for the expected loser—even if it means voting for their second choice. In the previous chapter, we defined this type of strategic behavior as *mandate balancing*.

In this chapter, we report the results of experiments conducted on a nationally representative sample of respondents in the United States that were designed to assess voter beliefs about party responsiveness and the impact of these beliefs on voter behavior. We find that voters tend to think that the electoral margin of victory affects policies and candidates offered by both parties—larger margins cause the winner to become more extreme and the loser more moderate. Moreover, partisanship helps to explain variation in these beliefs. Republican voters tend to believe that Democratic policies and candidates are much more responsive to vote share than policies and candidates offered by the Republican Party. Meanwhile, voters from both parties tend to think that Republican candidates are less responsive than their Democratic counterparts are. Although these results might seem counterintuitive, they are consistent with the debate over "flip-flopping" in the 2004 presidential election, and they highlight the fact that responsiveness has two very different normative interpretations. Although the literature on responsiveness typically views responsive parties as more "democratic" (Stokes 1999), expectations of responsiveness may also reflect the view that a party is unprincipled (Fenno 1986), or primarily office-motivated, and willing to change dramatically to become more competitive.

We also find evidence that is consistent with predictions of strategic voting by moderates who focus on the future electoral consequences of their current vote choice. Subjects typically respond to expected vote share in our experiments by bandwagoning—larger margins of victory elicit greater support for the winning candidate. However, subjects who do not consider themselves Democrats or Republicans exhibit significantly different behavior. As predicted by the theory of mandate balancing, nonpartisans are more likely than partisans to vote against the winner as the margin of victory increases. One possible alternative interpretation of this finding is that nonpartisans always prefer to vote against the party in power. However, we show that only those who believe parties are responsive tend to vote against the party expected to win. Thus, these results conform to predictions from the formal theory literature that beliefs about party behavior in certain instances may yield strategic voting, even in two candidate elections. They also further support the central claim of this book that parties move with the mandate.

VOTE SHARE, ELECTORAL MANDATES, AND MANDATE BALANCING

In Chapters 2 and 4, we show that one result of dynamic competition between policy-motivated parties under uncertainty (Wittman 1977; Calvert 1985; Roemer 2001) is that winning parties should move toward the extremes to satisfy their own preferences, whereas losers should move toward the center in order to improve their chances of winning the next election. In support of this theory, Conley (2001) provides evidence that presidents try to implement more extreme policies after landslide elections. We also show in Chapter 3 that the ideology of U.S. Senate candidates is significantly related to previous election outcomes, and, in Chapter 8, we show that markets expect the government to enact larger policy changes when the President wins in a landslide.

Suppose voters believe that both parties are responsive to vote share, shifting left when the left wins and right when the right wins in proportion to the margin of victory. What impact would these beliefs have on voter behavior? A number of formal models, including our own model in Chapter 5, suggest that beliefs about party responsiveness will cause some voters to engage in strategic behavior (Alesina and Rosenthal 1995; Piketty 2000; Shotts 2000; Meirowitz and Tucker 2003; Razin 2003; Meirowitz 2004). Here, we consider a specific kind of strategic voting implied by several of these models. Suppose voters want to minimize the distance between their ideal policy and the policy offered by the party that wins the election. Consider, first, the incentives facing left extremists with ideal points located to the left of the policies offered by both of the parties. These individuals have an incentive to vote for the left party because it will improve their chance of winning. Moreover, each additional vote that party gets will cause the post-electoral policies of both parties to shift a small amount to the left. Thus, there is no conflict between the effect of the vote on the probability of winning and the "signaling" effect of the vote on the margin of victory. The same reasoning applies to right extremists—they will have both an electoral and a "signaling" motivation to vote for the right candidate.

The decision is not so simple for moderates with ideal points located between the policies offered by the two parties. These individuals will have the same incentive as extremists to vote for the closest party to improve the probability that the preferred party wins the election. However, each additional vote gained by the winning party also moves the winning post-electoral policy farther away from the moderate's ideal point. Thus, moderates may have an incentive to vote for their second choice if they think their first choice is likely to win the election by a wide margin. This is an example of mandate balancing that we describe in Chapter 5.

Mandate balancing is the mirror image of another widely noted discrepancy in the model of citizens as sincere proximity voters. The literature on "protest voting" suggests that some citizens vote for a party other than their first choice in order to send a signal to one or both parties (Niemi, Whitten, and Franklin 1992; Heath and Evans 1994). However, protest voting in the American context often refers to extremists choosing a more extreme third party in order to signal their frustration with the centrifugal tendencies of the closest mainstream party. Whereas protest voting is often about the attempt by extremists to pull the mainstream parties outwards, mandate balancing is about the attempt by moderates to pull them inwards.

PARTY DYNAMICS AND VOTER BEHAVIOR: AN EXPERIMENT

In order to assess voter beliefs about party responsiveness and the effect on their behavior, we conduct an experiment on a nationally representative sample of respondents provided by Time-Sharing Experiments in the Social Sciences (TESS). This experiment seeks to test two hypotheses. The first hypothesis is that voters believe that an increase in the margin of victory in an election causes (1) the winning party to support more extreme policies and candidates and (2) the losing party to support more moderate policies and candidates. If this hypothesis is true and if self-identified Democrats and

Republicans are more likely to have extreme ideal points than nonpartisans,[1] then we should expect to see an important difference in voting behavior between partisans and nonpartisans. Democrats and Republicans want their party to win by as much as possible, but nonpartisans who think their favorite candidate is likely to win may have an incentive to switch their vote in order to moderate the election outcome. This suggests a second hypothesis: that nonpartisans who believe that parties respond to vote share are more likely to support the candidate expected to lose as the margin of victory increases.

In each experiment, subjects are asked to imagine a hypothetical future U.S. presidential election. They are then given a stimulus that concerns the vote share they expect in that election. Some subjects are told to expect landslides. Others are told to expect a close election. To ensure variation in expectations, we draw each voter's belief about expected Democratic vote share from a uniform distribution between 35% and 65%. Subjects are asked who they would vote for in the election and then they are asked to predict how both parties will react to the election outcome. Will Republican or Democratic or the policies for both parties become more liberal or conservative? Will Republican or Democratic or candidates for both parties become more liberal or conservative? Answers to these questions will help to establish whether voters expect parties to shift in the direction of the winner and in proportion to the magnitude of victory, and whether those who have these expectations are more likely to vote strategically.

Randomization ensures that responses generate information about how the population as a whole perceives party dynamics and how it affects their behavior on average. However, it is possible that some subjects are more likely than others to perceive party dynamics and react to them. Therefore, the survey includes a within-subject component. Subjects are asked to imagine a second hypothetical U.S. presidential election with a different randomly drawn stimulus, and then all the previous questions are repeated. At the end of the session, subjects are asked a standard question to determine with which party they identify.

The experimental approach offers an important advantage. One of the difficulties in using a real election to study the effect of voter expectations on voter behavior is the tendency of partisans to overestimate the probability their preferred party will win. As we note in Chapter 5, 25% of respondents in the 1976, 1980, 1984, and 1988 National Election Study (NES) said they expected their preferred party to win easily, whereas only 6% expected the opponent to win easily. In contrast, randomization of the vote share stimulus ensures that expectations will not be correlated with partisanship and makes it possible to estimate the uncontaminated effect of these expectations on voter behavior. If voters change their response to the vote intention question when we change the vote share stimulus, it may indicate that the margin of victory affects voter behavior in the way posited above.

RESULTS: VOTER BELIEFS

In January 2005, TESS contracted Knowledge Networks to field a survey instrument (see Chapter 6 Appendix) by Internet to 1,226 adults, 820 of whom completed the survey. Random digit dialing was used to recruit subjects who were then offered free Internet service and equipment in exchange for participation in surveys. To achieve a nationally representative sample, Knowledge Networks calculates poststratification weights by comparing sample and census data on gender, age, race, region, and education. Overall, Internet surveys using this methodology have been shown to be somewhat more reliable than telephone surveys (Huggins and Eyerman 2001).

Figure 6.1 shows the within-subject relationship in the raw data between the vote share stimulus and the expected shift in policies and candidates by both parties. The horizontal axis represents the change in the expected vote share for the Republican candidate between the first experiment and the second experiment. For example, if the stimulus in the first experiment is to expect the Republican to win 40% of the vote and the stimulus in the second experiment is to expect the Republican to win 55%, then the difference would be +15. The vertical axis represents the change in the expected shift in policies or candidates for each of the parties. There are five increasing categories of shifts, "much more liberal," "somewhat more liberal," "about the same," "somewhat more conservative," and "much more conservative." The difference reflects the change in categories from one experiment to another, with positive numbers indicating a change in the conservative direction. For example, if in the first experiment the subject expects the Democratic party to offer "somewhat more liberal" policies and in the second he or she expects the Democratic party to offer "somewhat more conservative policies," then the difference would be +2.

The circles in each graph in Figure 6.1 are proportional in size to the number of data points at each location and the lines represent a smoothed local regression (Loader 1999) with 95% confidence intervals. If voters tend to expect parties to shift in the direction and magnitude of the vote share, we would expect a trend line in the data to slope up and to the

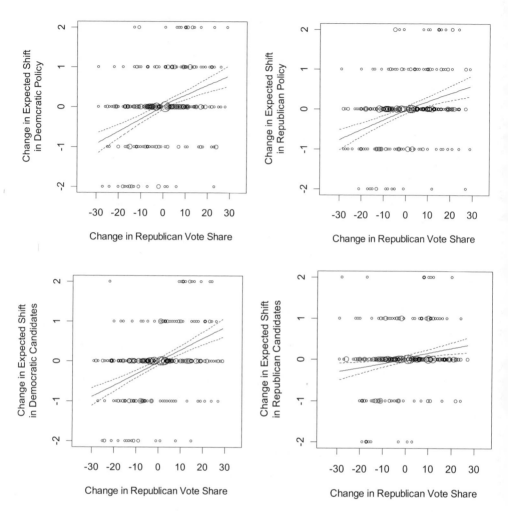

FIGURE 6.1   Impact of expected vote share on beliefs about party dynamics. Circle size is proportional to number of observations at a given point. Lines show mean effect of change in vote share on change in party behavior, calculated using local regression with 95% confidence intervals. Expected Shift in party behavior is coded as follows: 1 = much more liberal; 2 = somewhat more liberal; 3 = about the same; 4 = somewhat more conservative; 5 = much more conservative. Change in Expected Shift is the difference between respondent's expectation in experiment 1 and experiment 2.

right—Republican losses should increase the likelihood of liberal (down-ward) shifts and Republican gains should increase the likelihood of con-servative (upward) shifts. In fact, this is exactly what we see. The policies and candidates of both parties are expected to become more con-servative as vote share for the Republicans increases. The expectation appears to be weakest for Republican candidates (lower right of Figure 6.1) suggesting that voters think Republican politicians are less responsive than their Democratic peers.

Table 6.1 shows four within-subject statistical models of expectations of party behavior. In these models, the expectation of party behavior in the second experiment is regressed on the change in vote share and the party behavior expected in the first experiment. Although these models assume an ordinary least squares (OLS) form, other specifications using ordered logit form (not shown) yield substantively similar results and suggest that category thresholds are approximately equidistant as implied in the OLS model. The positive and strongly significant coefficient on change in expected Republican vote share across all four models indicates that sub-jects expect both Democrats and Republicans to offer more conservative candidates and more conservative policies as the Republican vote share increases. To provide a sense of the size of the effect, the first model in Table 6.1 suggests that a 25% increase in vote share for the Republicans

TABLE 6.1   Subject's Expectations of Party Behavior

Independent Variables	Dependent Variables			
	Democratic Policies	Republican Policies	Democratic Candidates	Republican Candidates
Expectation of party behavior in first experiment	0.52 (0.04)	0.51 (0.04)	0.48 (0.04)	0.57 (0.04)
Change in expected Republican vote share	2.01 (0.32)	1.37 (0.29)	1.91 (0.28)	0.73 (0.24)
Constant	−0.11 (0.04)	0.09 (0.04)	−0.10 (0.03)	0.04 (0.03)
Adjusted R^2	0.27	0.28	0.27	0.32
N	404	392	403	396

Note: Dependent variable is expectation of party behavior in experiment 2 (coded as follows: 1 = much more liberal; 2 = somewhat more liberal; 3 = about the same; 4 = somewhat more conservative; 5 = much more conservative). Coefficient estimates derived from weighted ordinary least squares with nationally representative sample weights. $p < 0.01$ for all variables in the model.

causes voters to expect Democratic policies to become about half a
category more conservative.

Although both parties are believed to be responsive, there appears to be
an expectation that Democrats are more responsive than Republicans are.
We take a closer look at this difference in Table 6.2 and find that the result
is largely driven by Republican respondents. In these models, we estimate
the separate expectations of Republicans, Democrats, and nonpartisans by
including a dummy variable for Republicans and nonpartisans and inter-
acting these with the vote share variable. The coefficients on the vote share
variable in Table 6.2 indicate Democratic voter beliefs and suggest that they
believe that the candidates and policies of both parties are responsive. However, the coefficients on the interactions suggest that Republican voters
expect Democratic policies and candidates to shift significantly more in
response to vote share.

TABLE 6.2   Expectations of Party Behavior by Partisan Identification

Independent Variables	Dependent Variables			
	Democratic Policies	Republican Policies	Democratic Candidates	Republican Candidates
Expectation of party behavior in first experiment	0.51 (0.04)	0.51 (0.04)	0.48 (0.04)	0.59 (0.05)
Change in expected Republican vote share	1.16 (0.49)	1.60 (0.49)	1.33 (0.43)	0.94 (0.40)
Change in expected Republican vote share nonpartisan	−0.04 (0.09)	−0.88 (0.69)	0.52 (0.64)	−0.47 (0.57)
Change in expected Republican vote share Republican	2.21 (0.73)	0.20 (0.79)	1.52 (0.67)	−0.06 (0.61)
Nonpartisan	−0.04 (0.09)	−0.20 (0.09)	−0.01 (0.08)	0.02 (0.07)
Republican	−0.06 (0.09)	−0.02 (0.10)	−0.03 (0.08)	−0.12 (0.07)
Constant	−0.09 (0.06)	0.15 (0.06)	−0.10 (0.05)	0.07 (0.04)
Adjusted R^2	0.28	0.29	0.27	0.32
N	404	392	403	396

Note: Dependent variable is expectation of party behavior in experiment 2 (coded as
follows: 1 = much more liberal; 2 = somewhat more liberal; 3 = about the same; 4 =
somewhat more conservative; 5 = much more conservative). Coefficient estimates derived
from weighted ordinary least squares with nationally representative sample weights. $p < 0.05$
for all coefficients in first two rows and first and third coefficients in fourth row.

One might expect voters to believe their own party is more responsive—after all, party responsiveness is often cited as a normatively advantageous feature of democratic government (Stokes 1999). However, parties are also frequently criticized for paying too much attention to the desires of the electorate. If politicians change their stance in response to public opinion, they may appear unprincipled (Fenno 1986) and willing to do or say anything in order to gain office. Our survey was in the field about two months after the 2004 presidential election. In the 2004 campaign, the Republican incumbent, George W. Bush, effectively exerted a great deal of effort in portraying the Democratic challenger, John Kerry, as a "flip-flopper" who changed his positions on issues (especially the Iraq war) when they became unpopular (Cave 2004). This portrayal may have continued to resonate among Republicans at the time of our survey, influencing their expectations of the behavior of future Democratic candidates.

RESULTS: VOTE CHOICE

Voters clearly expect parties to respond to elections, but to what extent does this affect their voting behavior? To answer this question, we divide subjects into those who believe parties are responsive and those who do not. About 28.2% of the subjects changed their expectations for shifts in party policy in the same direction as the change in vote share. This fraction probably represents a lower bound on the percentage of people who believe parties are responsive, since several subjects received two vote share stimuli that did not differ by much. However, we can use this distinction to test whether beliefs about party behavior influence vote choice.

Specifically, we would like to see if nonpartisans who believe parties are responsive are more likely than partisans to vote against the winner as their vote share increases. Model 1 in Table 6.3 shows how Republican vote share affects vote choice.

Here the subject's vote intention in the second experiment is regressed on vote intention in the first experiment and the interaction of change in expected Republican vote share and a dummy variable for nonpartisans who believe parties are responsive. The only thing that changes between the two experiments is the expected vote share for the Republicans, so if there is a significant relationship between the vote share stimulus and the vote intention response, then it suggests that expectations about the election influence vote choice. Notice first that the coefficient on change in vote share is positive and significant. Since subjects have very little information

TABLE 6.3   Effect of Vote Share on Vote Choice

Dependent Variable: Second Vote Choice	Model 1			Model 2		
	Coefficient	SE	p	Coefficient	SE	p
Responsive, nonpartisan change in vote share	−0.78	0.37	0.03	−0.75	0.37	0.05
Change in vote share	0.35	0.12	0.00	0.32	0.14	0.02
Responsive, nonpartisan	0.02	0.06	0.77	0.02	0.06	0.70
First vote choice	0.90	0.01	0.00	0.90	0.01	0.00
Nonresponsive, nonpartisan change in vote share				0.15	0.28	0.60
Nonresponsive, nonpartisan				0.02	0.04	0.49
Constant	0.20	0.03	0.00	0.20	0.04	0.00
R^2	0.86			0.86		

Note: Dependent variable is vote choice in second experiment (coded 1 if respondent "definitely" chooses the Democrat, 2 if "probably" chooses Democrat, 3 if "probably" chooses Republican, 4 if "definitely" chooses Republican). Coefficient estimates derived from weighted general linear model (GLM) with a logit link function using nationally representative sample weights.

about the candidates in these hypothetical elections, they may be using the vote share variable as a signal of candidate quality. If so, they would tend to bandwagon with the majority, becoming more likely to vote for the Republican as Republican vote share increases. However, the behavior of independents who believe parties are responsive is significantly different with respect to vote share. The coefficient on the interaction term is negative, suggesting that independents who believe parties are responsive become more likely than partisans to vote for the Democrat as the Republican gains more vote share. This indicates that independents are engaging in mandate balancing, voting strategically to reduce the winner's margin of victory.

One possible alternative hypothesis is that nonpartisans are not necessarily ideologically moderates and instead they just like to express opposition to the dominant party or parties. If this were true, then a belief in party responsiveness would make no difference—all independents would tend to vote against the winner. In contrast, the mandate-balancing hypothesis suggests that the only nonpartisans who have an incentive to vote against the winner are those who think parties will shift policies after the election in response to the vote share. Model 2 in Table 6.2 adds a second interaction dummy for vote share that identifies nonpartisans who do not believe parties are responsive. The coefficient on this interaction term is not significant and is actually weakly positive. This suggests that the strategic behavior of nonpartisans depends on their belief about party responsiveness as predicted by the mandate balancing theory presented in Chapter 5.

CONCLUSION

Political behavior is shaped by beliefs about how politics works. To understand political behavior, we need to know what people believe about the political process. In Chapters 2 and 4, we show two formal models that suggest parties have an incentive to respond to electoral margins, and in Chapter 5, we show how party responsiveness might specifically influence voter behavior. In this chapter, we provide evidence that voters do believe parties are responsive, and this influences how they vote.

These results have important implications for the study of party and candidate behavior. The assumption that voters believe in responsive politicians is vital for a number of recent formal models of electoral competition (Alesina and Rosenthal 1995; Piketty 2000; Shotts 2000; Meirowitz and Tucker 2003; Razin 2003; Meirowitz 2004). This chapter provides evidence that such an assumption can be supported empirically. Specifically, we find that voters tend to believe that the policies and candidates of *both* parties respond to past election results. However, Republican voters appear to believe even more strongly than Democratic voters do that the Democratic Party is responsive. This asymmetry may seem counterintuitive since responsiveness is often seen as a positive aspect of democratic government (Stokes 1999). However, responsiveness also implies a readiness to compromise one's positions in order to remain competitive in an election. Since the survey was conducted in January 2005, many Republican voters may have continued to be affected by an electoral campaign that described Democrats and John Kerry as "flip-floppers." Future work should thus revisit this effect to see if it endures.

We also test an important empirical implication of these models, which suggests that some voters may vote strategically. Voting for the winner causes the winning platform to be adjusted further away from the center. Thus, moderates may have a "signaling" incentive to choose the party that is more likely to lose in order to keep the winning party from straying too far away from the voter's ideal point (mandate balancing). Our results indicate that nonpartisan voters are more likely than partisans to switch their vote to the loser as the margin of victory increases. Whereas it is possible that this reflects an antipartisan stance by nonpartisans, this is unlikely since only those nonpartisans who believe in responsive parties exhibit a tendency to vote strategically. If nonpartisans tend to prefer moderate policies, then these results are supportive of the mandate-balancing theory and the formal models in previous chapters that generated this theory.

## SEVEN

Patience and Turnout

Among numerous attempts to explain why people vote, several empirical studies suggest that voter turnout is influenced by the costs of processing information and going to the polls, and the policy benefits associated with the outcome of the election (Hansen, Palfrey, and Rosenthal 1987; Nagler 1991; Kaempfer and Lowenberg 1993; Franklin and Grier 1997; Highton 1997; Knack 1997, 2001; Jackson 2000). However, none of these studies consider the fact that the costs of voting are paid on and before Election Day, whereas policy benefits may not materialize until several days, months, or even years later. The signaling motivation to vote that we identify in Chapters 5 and 6 amplifies the difference between the present and the future since it relies on voter concern for the outcome of several future elections and the policies that result. Thus, if people must bear the cost of participation long before they see its effects, then patience should also affect individual turnout decisions. Patient individuals who place greater value on the future benefits of participation should be more likely to vote, whereas impatient individuals who place greater value on the up-front costs of participation should be less likely to vote.

In Chapter 5, we use data from questions about future planning on the 1976 National Election Studies (NES) survey to suggest that citizens with higher discount factors (i.e., those who are least likely to discount the future) are more likely to vote because they care most about future policies, which are often a result of mandate declarations. However, this proxy is based on

attitudinal questions that only imprecisely measure subjective time preferences. In this chapter, we test the relationship between patience and voter
turnout in the laboratory by using a technique from experimental economics. Subjects are asked a number of standard questions regarding their
socioeconomic status, political beliefs, and turnout behavior. They then play
a "choice game" (Coller and Williams 1999; Harrison, Lau, and Williams
2002; Harrison et al. 2004) in which they are asked to make a series of
choices between a prize that will be awarded in 30 days and a larger prize
that will be awarded in 60 days. The choices they make reveal the degree to
which subjects are willing to wait for future benefits and can be used to estimate how much they discount future payoffs. In other words, this procedure yields a measure of the patience of each individual.

Regression analysis of the turnout behavior of the subjects in the experiment suggests that more patient individuals are significantly more likely to
vote. Moreover, patience is found to be positively related to two other widely
studied correlates of turnout—political interest and church attendance. The
results suggest that we may need to reevaluate theories that have been
advanced to explain the relationship between political interest, church attendance, and voter turnout.

PATIENCE AND THE COSTS AND BENEFITS
OF VOTING

A wide range of empirical studies of voting have shown that turnout is
influenced by the costs associated with making a decision and going to the
polls and the benefits associated with the outcome of the election (Aldrich
1993). For example, Verba, Schlozman, and Brady (1995) argue that socioeconomic status variables like education affect turnout because they influence the cost of obtaining and processing political information. Restrictive
registration laws that increase the cost of voting also discourage turnout
(Nagler 1991; Franklin and Grier 1997; Highton 1997; Knack 1997, 2001),
whereas liberal absentee ballot laws and all-mail elections encourage it
(Oliver 1996; Karp and Banducci 2000; Southwell and Burchett 2000). Even
rainfall on election day has been shown to depress turnout among some
voters (Knack 1994). Although less well documented, benefits related to the
election outcome also have an effect on turnout. For example, people are
more likely to vote in "high stakes" elections that have larger policy effects
(Wolfinger and Rosenstone 1980; Hansen, Palfrey, and Rosenthal 1987;

Jackson 2000) and when they think there is a larger difference in the policies offered by the competing parties (Kaempfer and Lowenberg 1993).[1]

An important oversight in this literature is that the costs of voting are paid on or before Election Day, but any benefits related to the outcome are not obtained until after the election. In fact, it may take several years for an election result to yield the policy outcomes that motivate citizens to go to the polls. Given that present costs are being compared to future benefits, subjective time preferences may have an impact on the decision to vote. Patient citizens might value future policy benefits more and be more likely to vote. Impatient citizens might focus more on the costs of voting and be less likely to vote. Thus, variation in patience may be an important factor in explaining individual turnout decisions. Furthermore, as we show in Chapter 5, the effect of patience on turnout should be even stronger for those who believe parties are dynamically responsive to the margin of victory.

PATIENCE AND THE DISCOUNT FACTOR

To test the effect of patience on turnout, we need a measure for how much people are willing to wait for future benefits. One way experimental economists have tackled this problem is by presenting subjects with a series of choices between two payoffs, a smaller amount paid now and a larger amount paid later. Each choice yields information about how much a subject discounts future payoffs, which allows us to estimate the subject's discount factor (δ). For example, if a subject chooses $90 now instead of $100 later, we know that he or she values the earlier payment more than the later payment. This implies a subjective inequality for his or her discount factor: $90 > \delta\,$100 or $\delta < 0.9$ for the period between the present and future payoff. If the same subject also chooses $100 later instead of $80 now for the same time period, then we know that $80 < \delta\,$100 and the discount factor must lie in the interval $0.8 < \delta < 0.9$. A series of choices with different values for the same time period allows us to identify the interval in which the discount factor falls for each subject. Those who more frequently choose the future payoff will have higher discount factors. Thus, there should be a positive relationship between the discount factor and patience.

One potential wrinkle in the procedure for measuring patience is that discount factors may be hyperbolic, meaning that people tend to value the present much more strongly than other periods (Laibson 1997). As a result, recent efforts by economists to elicit discount factors usually avoid choices with immediate payments and instead give subjects two future choices (Coller and Williams 1999; Harrison, Lau, and Williams 2002). This work suggests that beyond the immediate present the discount factor is approximately constant—people make consistent choices when they are faced with similar future time intervals. For example, subjects make the same choices between a smaller payment in 30 days and a larger payment in 60 days as they do when they must choose between a smaller payment in 90 days and a larger payment in 120 days.

RESEARCH DESIGN AND SUBJECT PROFILE

In May 2004, about 350 subjects were recruited from two introductory undergraduate political science courses to participate in a study administered by computer. Subjects were offered credit toward their course grade for their participation in the study, and 249 (about 70%) of them chose to participate. Of these, 235 were eligible to vote in the March 2004 California primary election. Each subject answered several standard socioeconomic and political attitude questions (exact question wording can be found in Chapter 7 Appendix).

Subjects ranged in age from 18 to 27 years, were evenly divided between women and men, and about 53% were minorities. They were asked whether or not they voted in the March 2004 California primary, which included nominations for national and local offices and four widely publicized ballot measures related to the California budget crisis. Typical for a younger population, about 21% of those eligible say they voted, compared to 31% in the population as a whole. The average subject leaned left and Democratic, with placement at 3.57 on the seven-point liberal conservative scale and 3.27 on the seven-point party identification scale. About 39% said they were very interested in the election campaign, but only 34% agreed that voting in elections is a duty. Finally, there was a wide range of religious observance, with the average subject attending services about once a month.

At the end of the survey, each subject was informed that he or she was eligible to win a prize and then asked to make a series of choices between a $100 prize in 30 days or a larger prize in 60 days (see Chapter 7 Appendix for a full description). Following Harrison, Lau, and Williams (2002), both a dollar amount and an effective annual interest rate were displayed in order to help subjects think about their choices. At the conclusion of the survey, a lottery was used to choose a single prizewinner and another lottery to decide which set of alternatives determined the payoff. It should be noted that just like previous experiments using this method (Coller and Williams 1999; Harrison, Lau, and Williams 2002), the expected value of the prize to each subject in this experiment is quite low (approximately $0.40 to each subject). However, Camerer and Hogarth (1999) show that stake size has only a small effect on average behavior in experiments like these and the biggest effect of stakes on behavior is changing from zero to positive stakes. Coller and Williams (1999) specifically show that discount factors elicited with a single prize are significantly different than discount factors implied by hypothetical choices, suggesting that even a small prize incentive causes subjects to take their decisions seriously.

If subjects are consistent and make no mistakes, they should always choose the earlier payoff, always choose the later payoff, or switch from the earlier payoff to the later payoff at exactly one point during their series of choices. The point at which they switch indicates the interval of the implied discount factor. For example, a subject may choose the earlier $100 prize when the later prize is less than or equal to $104.25 and then switch to the later prize for all values greater than or equal to $106.44. If so, then the implied discount factor is estimated to fall somewhere between $100/$106.44 ≈ 0.94 and $100/$104.25 ≈ 0.96. About 82% of the subjects in the experiment made consistent decisions across all twenty choices, whereas 15% made only one "mistake." Inconsistent choices are dropped from the data as in Harrison, Lau, and Williams (2002) and Coller and Williams (1999), but none of the analysis changes significantly when the first observed choice of the larger prize, the last observed choice of the smaller prize, or multiple imputation is used to estimate the remaining discount factors.

Figure 7.1 shows the distribution of monthly discount factors implied by subject responses in this experiment.[2] For subjects who always choose the earlier or later prize, discount factors are set to the value implied by maximum and minimum values, respectively. All other values are set to the midpoints of the estimated intervals. Notice that there are modes at the endpoints, suggesting that several subjects were either willing to wait for all future prizes (the patient), or not willing to wait for any of them (the impatient). There is another mode in the center where subjects chose the future prize once its value rose above $110. This is consistent with evidence from Harrison et al. (2004) showing that subjects sometimes focus on dollar values instead of rates of return and thus may be influenced by "focal points" in the dollar amount. The rest of the discount factor estimates span the distribution, ensuring a wide range of variation for evaluating the influence of patience on turnout.

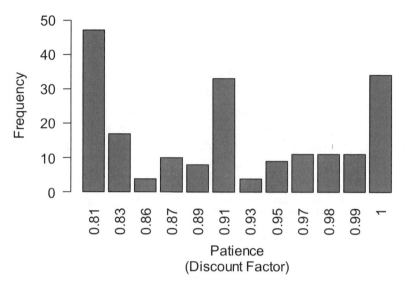

FIGURE 7.1   Distribution of patience in the discount factor experiment.

PATIENCE AND TURNOUT

To test the hypothesis that patient subjects are more likely to vote, we regress individual turnout on the discount factor measured in the experiment. Table 7.1 shows results from several logit models. Model 1 with no controls indicates that the relationship between patience and turnout is positive and significant. People who are more willing to wait for a larger prize in the choice game are more likely to vote, supporting the connection between patience and turnout.

A number of factors are added to Model 2, which are widely thought to affect turnout. Verba, Schlozman, and Brady (1995) argue that individuals with higher socioeconomic status (SES) are more likely to vote because their costs are lower, so we include variables like age, gender, race, and marital status. SES variables for parents (income and education) are also added because they have been shown to be important for the development of turnout behavior among young people (Plutzer 2002). Verba, Schlozman, and Brady (1995) suggest the inclusion of several other variables in turnout models. Interest in politics, the frequency of news reading or viewing, and the ability to answer basic questions about the government indicate political engagement, which tends to correlate with turnout. Moreover, if people feel that they can understand political issues (internal efficacy) and their government responds to them (external efficacy), then they are more

TABLE 7.1   Effect of Patience and Other Variables on Voter Turnout

	Dependent Variable: Did Subject Vote?					
	Model 1			Model 2		
	Coefficient	(SE)	95% Confidence Interval	Coefficient	(SE)	95% Confidence Interval
Patience	4.91	(2.54)	0.02 10.01	8.21	(3.49)	1.58 15.38
Age				0.27	(0.14)	−0.01 0.55
Female				−0.87	(0.52)	−1.92 0.13
Race				0.14	(1.32)	−3.06 2.53
Married				0.38	(4.17)	−5.66 6.14
Parents' income				0.27	(0.15)	−0.01 0.58
Parents' education				−0.10	(0.18)	−0.46 0.25
Strength of party ID				0.18	(0.28)	−0.37 0.74
Political interest				0.32	(0.45)	−0.55 1.23
Reads the news				0.32	(0.12)	0.09 0.56
Watches the news				0.19	(0.11)	−0.03 0.41
Political information				0.18	(0.17)	−0.15 0.52
External efficacy				0.17	(0.29)	−0.40 0.75
Internal efficacy				0.00	(0.18)	−0.37 0.36
Civic duty				−0.08	(0.17)	−0.41 0.24
Church attendance				−0.04	(0.18)	−0.40 0.31
Constant	−5.71	(2.34)	−10.45 −1.24	−18.84	(4.97)	−29.23 −9.62
IC	198.83			173.35		
N	186			170		

Note: Model estimated using the General Linear Model (GLM) with logit link function.
Standard errors in parentheses, 95% confidence intervals are from profile likelihood.
IC—information criterion; SE—standard error

likely to go to the polls. Church attendance has also been found to be significantly related to turnout in a number of studies (e.g., Timpone 1998). In particular, Verba, Schlozman, and Brady (1995) argue that church attendance is important because people acquire civic skills in religious organizations (writing letters, public speaking, and so on) that may make it easier for them to participate in politics. Finally, we include a variable for civic duty (Riker and Ordeshook 1968) to control for the possibility that the feeling that voting is an obligation causes subjects to turnout. Details on coding and question wording for all these controls can be found in Chapter 7 Appendix.

Even with the addition of numerous controls, Model 2 shows that patience continues to significantly affect turnout. Compare this with the fact that many variables related to conventional explanations of turnout such as

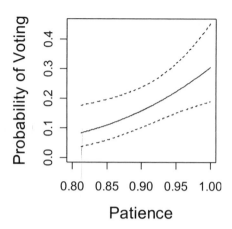

FIGURE 7.2   Effect of patience on turnout. Predicted turnout probabilities and
95% confidence intervals calculated from Model 2 in Table 7.1 by varying patience
and holding all other values at their means.

strength of party identification and political interest are not significant in
the model. The only variables that significantly affect turnout are patience,
parents' income, and news readership and viewership. To make the results
for patience concrete, Figure 7.2 shows the predicted effect of patience on
the probability of voting while holding all other values at their means. The
least-patient subjects vote at a rate of about 8% compared to 30% for the
most-patient subjects. These results suggest that subjective time preferences
have an important effect on the decision to vote.

PATIENCE AND THE DETERMINANTS
OF TURNOUT

How does patience directly relate to other variables thought to affect
turnout? Table 7.2 presents sufficient statistics and correlations with patience
for each of the control variables used above. Notice that patience is significantly correlated with both political interest and church attendance. These
correlations have two important implications for the literature on turnout.

First, the relationship between political interest and turnout may be
at least partially epiphenomenal. Although a number of studies show a
positive relationship between political interest and turnout (e.g., Verba,
Schlozman, and Brady 1995; Timpone 1998), none of these includes a control for patience. The data here indicate that patience is associated with both
political interest and turnout, but when patience and political interest are

TABLE 7.2   Study Variables and Their Correlations with Voter Patience

Variable	Sufficient Statistics Mean	SD	Minimum	Maximum	Correlation with Patience	p-value
Political interest	2.32	0.60	1	3	0.20	0.00
Church attendance	2.31	1.34	1	5	0.20	0.00
Civic duty	2.67	1.32	1	5	−0.12	0.08
Strength of party ID	2.99	0.84	1	4	0.08	0.25
Female	0.49	0.50	0	1	0.08	0.25
Internal efficacy	2.58	1.29	1	5	0.07	0.32
Parents' education	4.23	1.59	1	7	−0.06	0.37
Political information	4.76	1.60	1	8	0.03	0.71
Reads the news	3.29	2.24	0	7	0.02	0.73
Parents' income	5.73	2.19	1	8	−0.01	0.86
Married	0.01	0.09	0	1	−0.01	0.87
Age	19.77	1.62	18	27	−0.01	0.88
Race	0.02	0.15	0	1	0.01	0.90
External efficacy	2.37	0.83	0	4	0.00	0.93
Watches the news	2.89	2.21	0	7	0.00	0.99

included in a model of turnout only patience is significant. This suggests that the relationship between political interest and turnout is being driven by the effect of patience on both. In other words, political interest may not cause turnout—instead it might be a proxy for patience.

Second, the relationship between church attendance and turnout may also be partially epiphenomenal. A number of studies show that church attendance significantly increases the likelihood of turnout (e.g., Verba, Schlozman, and Brady 1995; Timpone 1998). Other studies suggest a link between patience and church attendance. For example, Iannaccone (1998) shows that those who believe in an afterlife are more likely to attend church, whereas Becker and Mulligan (1997: 741) argue that religious people have higher discount factors because they believe in an afterlife and thus have longer time horizons. The data in this study indicate that patience is associated with both church attendance and turnout, but when patience and church attendance are included in a model of turnout, only patience is significant. This suggests that the relationship between church attendance and turnout may be driven by the effect of patience on both. We should thus reevaluate theories that religious affiliation increases turnout because of the organizational effect it has on attendees (e.g., Verba, Schlozman, and Brady 1995). It may be the case that the relationship between church attendance and turnout is purely coincidental to the fact that religious groups tend to attract more patient individuals.

CONCLUSION

A number of scholars have demonstrated that individual decisions to vote depend on the costs of processing information and going to the polls, and the benefits associated with the outcome of the election. This chapter draws attention to the fact that the costs of turnout are borne on Election Day and before, whereas benefits related to the outcome of the election are not reaped until much later. This suggests that patience plays an important role in the turnout decision, especially if voters are influenced by a "signaling" motivation to vote as hypothesized in Chapter 5. Patient citizens who are willing to wait for future benefits should be more likely to vote because they place a greater value on the impact of the election on future policy changes. Impatient citizens should be less likely to vote because they are more influenced by the immediate burdens of decision-making and physical participation.

Evidence from the laboratory supports this hypothesis. Subjects were given a series of choices between an earlier, smaller prize and a later, larger prize. Those who consistently chose the later prize were significantly more likely to vote than those who consistently chose the earlier prize. The statistical relationship between patience and turnout remains even when we control for numerous other factors thought to affect the decision to vote. Patience is also found to correlate with political interest and church attendance, which suggests that variation in patience may be able to explain their relationship with turnout.

The results in this chapter further support our theory of electoral mandates. If voters believe that parties react to the margin of victory, then each vote gives them an opportunity to change policy in the future and an extra reward for those who are patient. If, on the other hand, voters do not believe parties are responsive, then it is unclear why there would be such an empirical relationship between turnout and the discount factor. Thus, both parties and voters behave in a way that is consistent with the idea that mandates matter in electoral competition. In Chapter 8, we see that third-party actors in financial markets also believe that mandates matter.

## EIGHT

Markets and Mandates: How Electoral Margins Affect the Economy*

I n this chapter, we turn away from parties and voters and toward the market. If parties and voters behave the way we suggest, how should we expect financial participants to behave? Partisan theory (Hibbs 1977) suggests that changes in the partisan orientation of the party in power affect the economy because parties of the Left are more likely than parties of the Right to choose fiscal and monetary policies that stimulate employment, inflation, and growth. Rational partisan theory (Alesina 1987) agrees but notes that if people rationally expect partisan differences then they adjust their economic behavior *prior to each election* in response to changes in the probability that each party will win. Extending the logic of Lucas (1977), this means that only *unexpected* electoral outcomes can have real effects on employment and growth, and these are transitory because there is no more uncertainty about future government policy once the result of the election is known.

In order to see the effect that electoral mandates have on the economy, we note in this chapter that rational partisan theory's focus on *electoral* uncertainty misses an important point about *policy* uncertainty. Even when the outcome of an election is known, there may still be uncertainty about

* From James H. Fowler. 2006. Elections and Markets: The Effect of Partisan Orientation, Policy Risk, and Mandates on the Economy. *Journal of Politics* 68(1):89–103. Reprinted courtesy of Blackwell Publishing.

what economic policy the victors will implement. For example, it may be easier to anticipate the policy of incumbents than challengers, since they have recently given direct evidence of their preferences and competence while in office. Similarly, people might be more certain about the future policies of a divided government than a unified government since they may be less able to implement large policy changes (which we elaborate below). These differences in policy risk directly affect inflation risk and nominal interest rates (Fischer 1975; Barro 1976; Benninga and Protopapadakis 1983; Cox, Ingersoll, and Ross 1985; Kandel, Ofer, and Sarig 1996), which indirectly affect consumption, investment, and growth (Harvey 1988; Estrella and Hardouvelis 1991; Kamara 1997; Estrella and Mishkin 1998). Therefore, it is important to understand not only potential differences in the *expected* policy outcome of the election, but also differences in the *uncertainty* surrounding that outcome.

Although market participants will clearly be concerned with *who* wins the election, our theory of electoral mandates suggests that they should also be concerned with *how much* the winner wins by. In earlier chapters of this book, we have already provided a wide array of theoretical and empirical evidence that suggests parties are more likely to propose and implement more extreme versions of their favorite policies after an election if they win by a wide margin. If people expect this, then rational partisan theory implies that inflation expectations rise as the expected vote share for the Left increases. Similarly, the theory of policy risk suggests that people should expect greater policy uncertainty as the absolute margin of victory for either party increases since a larger margin of victory may give the winning party leeway to implement the extreme version of its policies.

We formalize these arguments by specifying a model of nominal interest rates. We then develop a new way to measure expectations of partisan and policy-risk differences. Using election futures from Iowa Electronic Markets (IEM), we derive pre-electoral probabilities of various outcomes for U.S. presidential and congressional elections from 1988–2002 and analyze their impact on nominal interest rates implied by the futures market. As predicted by rational partisan theory, positive changes in the probability that Democrats win the presidency or the Congress are associated with increases in nominal interest rates, implying that expectations of inflation have increased. As predicted by the policy-risk theory, positive changes in the electoral probability of incumbent governments and divided governments are associated with declines in interest rates, implying that expectations of inflation risk have decreased. Furthermore, as an extension to both theories, we find that partisan and policy-risk effects depend not only on who controls political institutions, but how large their expected margin of victory is.

EXTENDING RATIONAL PARTISAN THEORY

Partisan theory (Hibbs 1977) suggests that different parties systematically choose different combinations of inflation, unemployment, and growth because they represent different interests in the electorate. Left-wing parties like the Democratic Party in the United States are more likely to use inflationary fiscal and monetary policies to stimulate employment because of their affiliation with labor. Right-wing parties like the Republican Party are more likely to use less inflationary fiscal and monetary policies because of their affiliation with capital. This difference in inflationary outcomes is denoted $\pi_D > \pi_R$.

Rational partisan theory (Alesina 1987) agrees that there should be observable changes in the inflation rate that last for the duration of each party's term in office. However, if workers have full information about and rationally expect different inflation rates under Democratic and Republican administrations, they will update their wage contracts as soon as a new party takes office, diminishing any real effects on the economy. In fact, this updating process takes place *prior* to the election in response to changes in the probability that each party will win. Therefore, expectations of post-electoral inflation in a two-party system are the sum of the product of the inflation rate associated with each party (π_D, π_R) and its corresponding probability $(p, 1-p)$ of winning the election, $E[\pi] = p\pi_D + (1-p)\pi_R$.

This theory applies generally to a unified government, but different branches of a government may have independent effects on economic policy. To address this issue, we extend rational partisan theory by assuming that new policies depend on a negotiation between the president and the Congress. Suppose this negotiation yields an outcome that is a simple linear combination of the outcomes associated with the policies preferred by the two branches of government (as in Mebane 2000 and Mebane and Sekhon 2002). If so, then the post-electoral inflation outcome can be written as

$$\pi = \alpha\pi_P + (1-\alpha)\pi_C \qquad (1)$$

where π_P, π_C are the inflation rates associated with policies proposed by the president and Congress, and $\alpha \in (0,1)$ represents the relative impact the president has on the inflation outcome.

This assumption complicates the model because we must now consider four possible electoral outcomes instead of just two. Let π_{ij} be the inflation associated with a government in which party $i \in \{D, R\}$ controls the presidency and party $j \in \{D, R\}$ controls the Congress, and let p_{ij} be the associated probabilities of each configuration of the government. Equation (1) suggests that the four outcomes for post-electoral inflation are:

$$\pi_{DD} = \pi_D \qquad\qquad \pi_{RD} = \alpha\pi_R + (1-\alpha)\pi_D$$
$$\pi_{DR} = \alpha\pi_D + (1-\alpha)\pi_R \quad \pi_{RR} = \pi_R \tag{2}$$

Suppose we observe separate measures of the probability that the Democrats win the presidency and the Congress (p_P, p_C). As in Alesina (1987), we will assume that these probabilities are commonly understood and shared by all individuals in the economy. However, random events during the course of a campaign affect movements in these probabilities, so we can think of these measures as outcomes of a random variable. To infer *joint probabilities* such as the probability of a unified Democratic government, it might be tempting to use the product of these two probabilities, but this assumes that the measures are independent. There are at least two reasons to be suspicious of such an assumption. One is that winning the presidency may create a "coattails" effect for the same party in Congress. If so, then measures of the probability that the Democrats win the presidency and the probability they win the Congress would covary *positively*. Alternatively, suppose that voters usually try to divide the government between the two parties. If so, then the probability that the Democrats win the presidency and the probability they win the Congress would covary *negatively* with the opposite effect on the joint probabilities. Thus, *inferences* regarding the joint probabilities p_{ij} should each include a covariance term $c_{PC} = Cov(p_P, p_C)$ such that $p_{DD} = p_P p_C + c_{PC}$, $p_{DR} = p_P(1-p_C) - c_{PC}$, $p_{RD} = (1-p_P)p_C - c_{PC}$, and $p_{RR} = (1-p_P)(1-p_C) + c_{PC}$. The expected inflation outcomes and their associated probabilities can be combined and simplified to derive a model of inflation expectations that includes electoral expectations for both branches:

$$E[\pi] = \sum_{ij} p_{ij}\pi_{ij} = (\pi_D - \pi_R)(\alpha p_P + (1-\alpha)p_C) + \pi_R \tag{3}$$

This equation suggests that an increase in the probability that the Democrats win *either* branch of government will increase inflation expectations.

A THEORY OF POLICY RISK

Though rational partisan theory is persuasive in its focus on *electoral* uncertainty, it is silent on the issue of *policy* uncertainty. Alesina (1987) assumes future policies of election winners are fixed and known, but it is much more likely that there is some degree of uncertainty surrounding them. This uncertainty may result from not knowing exactly what economic policies a given party prefers and the inflation that would result if they were implemented. Although it may be easy to rank order the impact of left and right policies, it may be difficult to know if the victorious party will implement the moderate or extreme version of its proposals. Uncertainty may also arise because the effectiveness of a government in implementing policy varies, in part due to changing logistical competence and in part due to idiosyncrasies of the current institutional context (such as the personalities controlling legislative committees).

Policy uncertainty can have an effect on the real economy. A higher level of policy uncertainty increases the risk of holding assets with returns that depend on economic policies. For example, the decision to invest in a government bond is directly affected by the inflation rate since the real rate of return is equal to the nominal return minus the inflation rate. Any increase in the expected variance of inflation also increases the expected variance of the real return. This causes some investors to reallocate their money to other assets that have the same return but a lower level of total risk. As they do so, demand for the bond falls, as does its price. Thus, an increase in inflation risk increases interest rates, which can also have a negative impact on consumption, investment, and growth.

To derive an equation for inflation risk, we change rational partisan theory's assumption of known inflation outcomes for each party to random variables Π_D, Π_R with known means π_D, π_R, known variances σ_D, σ_R, and known covariance $c_{DR} = Cov(\Pi_D, \Pi_R)$. This assumption yields the same expected inflation rate as the model in which the inflation outcomes are known (equation 3), but it also yields variances implied by the equations in equation (2) for each of the four possible election outcomes:

$$\text{var}(\pi_{DD}) = \text{var}(\Pi_D) = \sigma_D$$
$$\text{var}(\pi_{DR}) = \text{var}\big(\alpha\Pi_D + (1-\alpha)\Pi_R\big) = \alpha^2\sigma_D + (1-\alpha)^2\sigma_R + 2\alpha(1-\alpha)c_{DR}$$
$$\text{var}(\pi_{RD}) = \text{var}\big(\alpha\Pi_R + (1-\alpha)\Pi_D\big) = \alpha^2\sigma_R + (1-\alpha)^2\sigma_D + 2\alpha(1-\alpha)c_{DR} \quad (4)$$
$$\text{var}(\pi_{RR}) = \text{var}(\Pi_R) = \sigma_R$$

These variances can be used to derive the variance of the inflation rate conditional on electoral probabilities (see Casela and Berger 2002: 167): $\text{var}(\pi \mid ij) = E[\text{var}(\pi \mid ij)] + \text{var}(E[\pi \mid ij])$. Each of the two terms in this equation has a substantive interpretation. The first term (expectation of the variances) can be thought of as *policy risk*. This is the inflation risk associated with each of the four electoral outcomes weighted by the probability each occurs:

$$
\begin{aligned}
\sigma_p = E[\text{var}(\pi \mid ij)] = \sum_{ij} p_{ij}\,\text{var}(\pi_{ij}) &= \alpha\big(\alpha(\sigma_D - \sigma_R) - 2(1-\alpha)(\sigma_R - c_{DR})\big)p_P \\
&+ (1-\alpha)\big((1-\alpha)(\sigma_D - \sigma_R) - 2\alpha(\sigma_R - c_{DR})\big)p_C \\
&+ 2\alpha(1-\alpha)\big((\sigma_D - \sigma_R) + 2(\sigma_R - c_{DR})\big)(p_P p_C + c_{PC})
\end{aligned}
\tag{5}
$$

Notice that policy risk is a function of partisanship, but the relationship is complicated. Increases or decreases in electoral probabilities can either increase or decrease the overall risk depending on how uncertain people are about the policies each party will implement.

The second term (variance of the expectations) can be thought of as *electoral risk*, σ_e:

$$
\begin{aligned}
\sigma_e = \text{var}(E[\pi \mid ij]) = \sum_{ij} p_{ij}(E[\pi_{ij}] - E[\pi])^2 \\
= \big(\alpha^2 p_P(1-p_P) + (1-\alpha)^2 p_C(1-p_C) + 2\alpha(1-\alpha)c_{PC}\big)(\pi_D - \pi_R)^2
\end{aligned}
\tag{6}
$$

Notice that electoral risk is increasing in the difference in the inflation rates expected under the Democrats and Republicans. Intuitively, as the difference in policy outcomes increases, so does the size of the change in expectations after the election results are known. Note also that electoral risk is increasing in the closeness of p_P and p_C to 0.5, reflecting the impact of electoral uncertainty. The contribution of each of these factors depends on α, the relative impact of the branches of government—if the president is more responsible for the inflation rate, then electoral uncertainty in the Congress does not have much of an effect on inflation risk, and vice versa.

DIVIDED GOVERNMENT

Several scholars have argued that divided governments react less quickly to economic shocks, which can increase levels of public debt and lead to higher real interest rates (Roubini and Sachs 1989a, 1989b; Grilli, Masciandaro, and Tabellini 1991; Alt and Lowry 1994). However, whereas divided governments may be less able to smooth *exogenous* economic shocks, they may also be less likely to create *endogenous* policy shocks because they are susceptible to gridlock. Responding to Mayhew (1991), a growing body of empirical work suggests that "important," "significant," "landmark," or "conflictual" legislation is less likely to pass under divided than unified government (Edwards, Barrett, and Peake 1997; Coleman 1999; Bowling and Ferguson 2001). The bureaucracy may also be affected—Epstein and O'Halloran (1996) find that under divided government agencies overseen by the executive, but constrained by the legislature, will not be able to make significant policy changes. Boix (1997) notes that divided governments tend to produce less policy change to the supply side of the economy, such as the level of public ownership of the business sector. These results also concord with the comparative politics literature on veto players, which suggests that the potential for policy change decreases as the number of groups with institutional veto power increases (Tsebelis 1995).

Analysis of the model presented here paints a more complicated picture. Whether or not divided government yields less policy risk than unified governments depends on both the risk associated with each party and the relative impact each branch of government has on policy. For example, suppose that *only* the presidency or *only* the Congress matters for policy. If so, then this substantially reduces the effect of divided and unified government. Expectations of policy risk will merely be a function of uncertainty and electoral expectations for a single branch of government. Suppose instead that both the presidency and Congress matter for policy, but the policies of one party are much more predictable than the other. Again, the effect of divided and unified government declines. Any increase in the probability that the unpredictable party wins either branch of government will increase risk, regardless of whether or not it also increases the probability of unified government. However, if (1) both branches matter and (2) there is similar uncertainty about both parties, then divided government forces the parties to negotiate and limits the range of policy changes that would be possible under unified government when one party has full control. Under these conditions divided government reduces policy risk by reducing the uncertainty associated with large policy changes.

INCUMBENCY

Incumbent governments reveal some information about both their policy preferences and their effectiveness because they implement policies in the period immediately prior to the election. Comparatively, challengers must be assessed using information from their prior turn in office, which could be several years ago. In the interim, the challenger's preferences may have changed, the competence of their new leadership may be harder to assess (cf., Rogoff and Sibert 1988; Rogoff 1990), and the interaction between branches of government may be harder to predict. Thus a challenger victory should be associated with more policy uncertainty. For simplicity, suppose that this effect applies equally across parties, so that when the incumbent party loses the presidency or the Congress, uncertainty increases by $\sigma_{ch,P}$ and $\sigma_{ch,C}$, respectively. This will not have any effect on electoral risk because it does not affect the mean inflation rate. However, it *will* affect policy risk because the variance is affected. Letting $p_{ch,P}, p_{ch,C}$ be the respective probabilities that the challenger party wins each branch, we can incorporate the effect of incumbency on the variance of inflation expectations. This has no impact on electoral risk, but it yields additional terms for policy risk:

$$E[\mathrm{var}(\pi \mid ij, p_{ch,P}, p_{ch,C})] = \sigma_p + p_{ch,P}\sigma_{ch,P} + p_{ch,C}\sigma_{ch,C} .$$

ELECTORAL MARGINS

So far we have only discussed the effect of winning an election on policies offered and implemented by competing parties. However, as we have argued throughout this book, the margin of victory may also be important, particularly for the presidency. A party that wins by a narrow margin of victory cannot afford to alienate its constituents at the very center of the political spectrum or else it may lose the next election. This reduces the credibility of the party's commitment to more extreme policy changes because any small sign of defection may force it to compromise with the opposition. A landslide victory gives a party more bargaining power because it can tolerate defections from the center without risking a loss of power. This intuition is confirmed both formally and empirically in Conley (2001) and in earlier chapters in this book.

To model the effect of shocks to the electoral margin on rational partisan theory, let the expected Democratic margin of victory be $\mu = (V_D - V_R)/(V_D + V_R)$ where V_D and V_R are the number of votes expected for the Democratic and Republican presidential candidates. Notice that μ is positive when the Democrat wins, negative when the Republican wins, and is proportional to the size of the victory. Suppose that parties offer economic policies during the campaign, but later shift them in response to the election outcome. Without loss of generality, assume that the size of this shift is proportional to the margin of victory μ and a random variable S denoting a shock with known mean s and known variance σ_s. The inflation expected under each electoral outcome conditional on this shock changes to $E[\pi_{ij}|S,\mu] = \pi_{ij} + s\mu$, which adds a term to the expression for expected inflation: $E[\pi|ij,S,\mu] = s\mu + \sum_{ij} p_{ij}\pi_{ij}$. The shock also changes the inflation risk associated with each electoral outcome: $\text{var}(\pi_{ij}|S,\mu) = \text{var}(\pi_{ij} + S\mu) = \text{var}(\pi_{ij}) + \sigma_S\mu^2$. This has no impact on electoral risk, but it does add a term to the overall expression for policy risk: $E[\text{var}(\pi|ij,S,\mu)] = \sigma_p + \sigma_S\mu^2$.

Notice that inflation expectations are increasing in the margin of Democratic victory, μ. More Democratic votes mean higher inflation. In contrast, policy risk is increasing in μ^2. This means that people expect more inflation risk when the margin of victory for *either* party increases because landslides yield bigger post-electoral shocks to policy. We thus expect larger margins of victory to be associated with higher nominal interest rates, *regardless of partisanship*.

EMPIRICAL IMPLICATIONS

The extended rational partisan theory implies that expectations of post-electoral inflation should increase with the probability of a Democratic victory in both branches of government and the expected vote share for the Democratic Party. The theory of policy risk implies that expectations of inflation risk should increase with the probability of unified government (under certain conditions), the probability a challenger party wins either branch of government, and the vote margin for the winning candidate. These implications can be tested by examining the impact of electoral expectations on nominal interest rates. Figure 8.1 summarizes the joint predictions of these theories. Expected nominal interest rates fall the most when an incumbent Republican wins reelection in a divided government by a narrow margin. Conversely, interest rates are expected to rise most when a Democratic challenger wins unified control of the government by a landslide. However, the crosscutting effects of partisanship and policy risk lead to ambiguous predictions in mixed cases, such as the reelection of an incumbent Democrat.

The finance literature (see Fischer 1975; Barro 1976; Benninga and Protopapadakis 1983; Cox, Ingersoll, and Ross 1985; Kandel, Ofer, and Sarig 1996) typically models nominal interest rates as a linear function of inflation expectations, inflation risk premia, and factors affecting the real interest rate. For factors affecting the real interest rate, we follow Plosser

Policy Risk

Partisan Orientation		High (Challengers, Landslide Elections, Unified Governments)	Low (Incumbents, Close Elections, Divided Governments)
	Left	Higher Nominal Interest Rates	Ambiguous
	Right	Ambiguous	Lower Nominal Interest Rates

FIGURE 8.1   Impact of partisan orientation and policy risk on expectations of nominal interest rates.

(1982, 1987), Baxter (1989), and Alesina, Roubini, and Cohen (1997), by assuming that the real interest rate is a linear function of the growth in the money supply ($M1$), growth in inflation (CPI), unemployment (UE), and industrial production (IP). Letting a constant K absorb the baseline inflation, inflation risk, and real interest rate yields the following full equation for estimation:

$$n = (\pi_D - \pi_R)(\alpha p_P + (1-\alpha)p_C) + \sigma_p + \sigma_e + \sigma_{ch,P} P_{ch,P} + \sigma_{ch,C} P_{ch,C}$$
$$+ s\mu + \sigma_s \mu^2 + \beta_{M1} M1 + \beta_{CPI} CPI + \beta_{UE} UE + \beta_{IP} IP + K + \varepsilon \tag{7}$$

To be clear, note that the main independent variables here are the observations of electoral probabilities (the p's) and vote share expectations (the μ's) implied by the IEM futures market. Parameter estimates in this specification provide explicit tests of separate parts of the rational partisan and policy-risk theories. If $\pi_D - \pi_R = 0$, then the rational partisan and electoral risk theories can be rejected because there is no expected difference in the inflation outcomes of the two parties. Notice, however, that this is a joint test of both hypotheses—if $\pi_D - \pi_R > 0$ then it is possible that only one of the two hypotheses is not rejected. If $\alpha = 1$ then the extended rational partisan theory can be rejected because the Congress is not expected to have an effect on policy. We can reject the policy-risk hypothesis only if $\alpha_p = 0$. Inspection of equation (5) shows that this is only true if *both* $\sigma_R - c_{DR} = 0$ and $\sigma_D - \sigma_R = 0$. The effect of incumbency on inflation risk can be rejected if $\sigma_{ch,P} = 0$ for the presidency and $\sigma_{ch,C} = 0$ for the Congress. Finally, the effect of the margin of victory on expected inflation can be rejected if $S < 0$ and its effect on inflation risk can be rejected if $\sigma_s < 0$.

FUTURES DATA

For the dependent variable, we need an appropriate measure for *post-electoral* nominal interest rates. Cohen (1993) solves this problem by combining spot prices for U.S. treasuries with some linear assumptions about the term structure to interpolate what forward interest rates will be when the victor takes office. Whereas this is a reasonable approximation of future interest rates, a simpler way to derive them is to use rates implied by treasury futures contracts.

A futures contract is a promise to buy or sell a specific asset on a given date (the settlement date) in the future at a price determined by the exchange (the settlement price). The price of these contracts includes consensus expectations of future prices and yields. Futures-based forecasts of nominal interest rates are typically more reliable than forecasts based on surveys or implicit forward rates (Hafer, Hein, and MacDonald 1992) and are used to predict important events such as changes in Federal Reserve policy (Krueger and Kuttner 1996). Therefore, we use futures contracts for treasuries that settle after each election to derive expectations for post-electoral nominal interest rates. In particular, we focus on 2-year and 5-year bonds because these are the closest in duration to the term length for the House and presidency.

MEASURING ELECTORAL PROBABILITIES

Turning to the independent variables, the literature has had difficulty assessing the impact of elections on financial markets because the only electoral probability that is known with certainty is the result itself: $p = 1$ for the winner and $p = 0$ for all others. Past studies have thus tended to focus on market changes *after* the election (see Niederhoffer 1971; Cutler, Poterba, and Summers 1989; Sheffrin 1989; Bachman 1992; Blomberg and Hess 1997; and Bernhard and Leblang 2002). However, if the market continuously updates its expectation of the electoral outcome *prior* to the election, it may help to explain why many of these studies do not observe large changes in interest rates on the day immediately following an election. For example, Clinton was the overwhelming favorite on the day prior to his election in 1996. It is thus reasonable to assume that most of whatever effect the market expected from a Clinton Presidency should already have been priced into the market *before* the election.

To improve on these approaches, we need a reliable method for measuring election probabilities before the election. Empirical models have typically been the most accurate predictors (Fair 1978, 1996; Rosenstone 1983; Erikson 1989; Campbell 1992; Gelman and King 1993; Erikson and Wlezian 1994; and Campbell and Garand 2000), but these models are usually based on long-term economic data from several months to a year before the election. Effects of the campaign or idiosyncratic qualities of the candidates are treated as error terms in these models, so the mean prediction does not tend to vary much on a day-to-day or even month-to-month basis. Other attempts have used preelectoral polling data to infer election probabilities. Chappell and Keech (1988), Suzuki (1992), Carlsen (1998), and Carlsen and Pedersen (1999) regress actual vote shares on presidential approval in the quarter before the election and use the coefficient and standard error to derive a probability that the incumbent will win more than 50% of the vote. Cohen (1993) goes a step further, using an option-pricing model to derive monthly implied election probabilities based on the current support level in polls and the volatility of past survey results. However, this model relies on specific parameterizations of the volatility and several restrictive assumptions about how new information is incorporated in each period.

ELECTORAL FUTURES MARKETS

We propose a simpler solution using election futures prices from IEM. IEM is a real futures exchange where traders buy and sell contracts based on the outcome of elections. For example, in 1996, IEM made available a Clinton winner-take-all (WTA) contract. On Election Day, a Clinton WTA contract is worth $1 if he wins and $0 if he loses. These contracts are traded and their prices fluctuate depending on consensus expectations of the probability that the candidate in question will win the election. WTA contracts are especially intuitive because their prices directly imply election probability.[1] That is, an individual who believes Clinton has a 65% chance of winning values the contract at $0.65. The market price thus implies the consensus expectation of the probability the candidate will win.

WTA contracts exist for major parties in the House and major candidates for the presidency. Daily closing prices on these contracts allow us to measure the probability of a Democratic victory for both institutions.

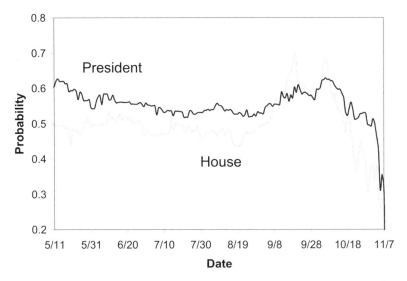

FIGURE 8.2   Probability that democrats would win U.S. elections in 2000. Probabilities derived from Iowa Electronic Market winner-take-all contracts for the 2000 U.S. presidential and House elections.

Figure 8.2 shows an example of these probabilities for U.S. presidential and House elections in 2000. In addition to WTA futures markets, IEM conducts markets in vote share (VS) for presidential elections. On settlement, these contracts pay a percentage of one dollar that is equal to the vote share received by the candidate in question. For example, a Democratic president vote share contract pays \$0.55 if the Democrats receive 55% of the vote. These contracts can be used to measure consensus expectations of the margin of victory. Chapter 8 Appendix describes how electoral probabilities and vote share expectations are derived from the IEM data and includes a number of technical details regarding the data.

WHY USE FUTURES DATA?

In spite of the creativity of poll-based measures of electoral probabilities, there are several reasons to use futures prices instead. IEM market prices are updated continuously and daily historical data is available. This dramatically increases the number of observations over the poll-based method and allows for more precise statistical inferences. Analytical comparisons of polls and election markets suggest that if market participants have access to polls, then the market price is always a better predictor (Kou and Sobel 2004). This is because the market price incorporates all information the poll could plus private information from experts and empirical political economy models.

One might object to using IEM data because the universe of participants in this market is limited and subject to partisan bias. For example, Forsythe et al. (1992) show that the individuals who participate in these markets are more likely to be white, higher income, conservative, and Republican. Forsythe, Rietz, and Ross (1999) also show that traders in these markets tend to invest in the candidate or party they support. However, a growing literature (Berg, Forsythe, and Rietz 1997; Berg et al. 2003; Berg, Nelson, and Rietz 2003; Forsythe et al. 1998; Forsythe, Rietz, and Ross 1999; Bohm and Sonnegaard 1999) demonstrates that there is *no partisan bias* in the market price and suggests that election futures markets are *more reliable than polls* for predicting election outcomes. For example, Berg et al. (2003) note that the election-eve IEM forecast has a lower mean prediction error than polls in 15 elections for which data on both exist (1.49% vs. 1.93%). Berg, Nelson, and Rietz (2003) also compare major poll predictions of U.S. presidential election outcomes to prices in the IEM vote share market. The IEM market prediction was closer to the election outcome 76% of the time ($n = 596$) and was not susceptible to predictable surges and declines (such as the postconvention surges for both parties observed in polling data). In sum, the literature on these markets suggests that IEM futures prices are the *best available data* for measuring preelectoral probabilities.

This presents a puzzling discrepancy—how can the market perform so well when its participants are biased? In spite of evidence that many traders invest in their favorites, Forsythe, Rietz, and Ross (1999) show that these individuals do not drive the market. Instead, the market price is strongly influenced by a group of "marginal traders" with no preference bias in their portfolios. Marginal traders invest twice as much as average traders, *make* prices rather than *taking* them, and are six times less likely to make a trading mistake. Forsythe, Rietz, and Ross (1999) show that this group acts to correct imbalances that may be related to preference-oriented investment and helps to explain why the market price across several elections does not show partisan bias.

ESTIMATION PROCEDURES

We use maximum likelihood to estimate the coefficients in equation (7). Daily financial time series are usually subject to a high degree of serial correlation, so we use an error correction model (see Beck 1992; Beck and Katz

1995; and King 1997). In this method, the change in the dependent variable is regressed on the change in all the independent variables and the lagged levels of the dependent and independent variables. Estimates are statistically valid as long as the coefficient on the lagged dependent-variable level is significantly different from zero. To check for remaining serial correlation, Beck and Katz (1995) suggest a Lagrange Multiplier Test in which the model residual is regressed on the lagged residual and the independent variables. If the coefficient on the lagged residual is not significantly different from zero, then serial correlation should no longer cause concern.

Daily financial time series are also subject to varying degrees of platykurtosis. That is, the probability of large shocks to nominal interest rates is larger than an assumption of normally distributed errors would imply. The statistics literature recommends correcting for these fatter tails in a variety of ways, but the most common for panel financial series is to assume a t-distribution of the error component of the model (see Adler, Feldman, and Taqqu 1998).

RESULTS

Maximum likelihood estimates are reported in Table 8.1 along with 95% confidence intervals derived from the profile likelihood. Lagrange Multiplier Tests for each of the specifications indicate that serial correlation in the errors is not significant. Estimates of the additional degrees of freedom parameter η (for the t-distribution) show that platykurtosis is indeed present. The five-year model yields coefficients closer to zero than the two-year model, suggesting that elections have a stronger impact on two-year rates. This is not surprising since a new set of elections that may yield policy changes occurs every two years. To discuss the substantive results, we use the model based on the two-year maturity to simulate first differences holding all variables constant at their means except the variables of interest (for a full description of this technique see King, Tomz, and Wittenberg 2000).

PARTISANSHIP

The first two rows of Figure 8.3 show how changing the probability of a Democratic president affects future two-year nominal interest rates. In the top row, we assume the Republicans have won the House, whereas in the next row, we assume the Democrats have won the House. The bottom two

TABLE 8.1 Impact of Electoral Outcomes on Interest Rates Implied by Futures Contracts

			Two-Year Maturity			Five-Year Maturity		
	Symbol		MLE	95% CI		MLE	95% CI	

Dependent Variable: Expected Post-Electoral Nominal Interest Rates

	Symbol		MLE	95% CI		MLE	95% CI	
Model coefficients								
Relative influence	α	Change	0.57	0.51	0.64	0.52	0.46	0.59
of presidency		Level	0.48	0.44	0.56	0.43	0.38	0.50
Partisan difference	$\pi_D - \pi_R$	Change	3.17	2.75	3.54	2.65	2.18	3.07
in inflation		Level	3.22	2.69	3.62	2.51	2.06	2.89
Partisan difference	$\sigma_D - \sigma_R$	Change	−1.21	−1.75	−0.56	−1.21	−1.68	−0.69
in inflation risk		Level	−2.12	−2.51	−1.60	−1.79	−2.12	−1.37
Republican inflation	$\sigma_R - c_{DR}$	Change	1.30	0.92	1.63	1.21	0.90	1.55
risk minus partisan		Level	1.50	1.18	1.80	1.29	0.99	1.60
covariance								
Effect of challenger	$\sigma_{ch,P}$	Change	0.08	−0.21	0.42	0.33	0.11	0.55
party in presidency		Level	−0.30	−0.49	0.12	−0.08	−0.22	0.04
Effect of challenger	$\sigma_{ch,H}$	Change	0.73	0.26	1.20	0.63	0.30	0.96
party in House		Level	−0.20	−0.65	0.30	−0.19	−0.51	0.15
Effect of electoral	s	Change	1.45	0.40	2.71	1.06	0.14	2.05
margin on inflation		Level	2.09	1.19	3.12	1.60	0.78	2.42
Effect of electoral	σ_S	Change	43.67	29.06	58.29	29.56	17.68	41.69
margin on inflation		Level	66.07	47.89	84.20	39.42	25.40	53.68
risk								
Economic controls	β_{M1}	Change	−0.03	−0.09	0.02	−0.02	−0.06	0.02
M1		Level	−0.02	−0.06	0.01	−0.02	−0.05	0.00
Inflation	β_{CPI}	Change	−0.06	−0.46	0.36	0.00	−0.29	0.33
		Level	0.07	−0.03	0.19	−0.01	−0.08	0.07
Unemployment	β_{UE}	Change	−0.34	−0.93	0.24	−0.14	−0.55	0.27
		Level	−0.14	−0.19	−0.10	−0.03	−0.06	0.00
Industrial production	β_{IP}	Change	−0.01	−0.12	0.10	0.00	−0.08	0.08
		Level	−0.04	−0.07	−0.01	−0.02	−0.05	0.00
Technical parameters		Change	−0.13	−0.17	−0.09	−0.08	−0.12	−0.05
Lagged dependent		Level	−0.34	−0.38	−0.29	−0.22	−0.27	−0.18
variable								
Constant			0.14	−0.38	0.67	−0.21	−0.61	0.14
σ_Y			0.25	0.23	0.26	0.18	0.17	0.20
η			6.43	4.69	9.69	3.62	2.80	4.90
Mean log likelihood			−296.17			−10.92		
Lagrange Multiplier Test (effect of ε_{t-1} on ε_t)			−0.04	−0.09	0.03	−0.03	−0.09	0.04

Note: Maximum likelihood estimates of coefficients in equation using an error correction model assuming t-distributed errors. Confidence intervals calculated from profile likelihood. CI—confidence interval; MLE—maximum likelihood estimation/estimate(s)

rows of Figure 8.3 show how changing the probability of a Democratic House affects interest rates. In the third row, we assume the Republicans have won the presidency, whereas in the bottom row, we assume the Democrats have won the presidency.

The first (left) column of Figure 8.3 shows the total effect of electoral probabilities on interest rates. Notice first that, regardless of the orientation of the other body, Democrats in both the House and presidency significantly increase nominal interest rates. For example, the upper left graph shows that increasing the probability of a Democratic president from 0 to 0.6 increases the two-year rate by 1.4%. However, the relationship is curvilinear—interest rates only rise about 0.7% when the probability changes from 0 to 1. Thus, it is important to analyze the different components of the model separately. Column 2 shows the partisan effect of electoral probabilities on expected inflation, $E[\pi]$, column 3 shows the partisan effect on electoral risk, σ_e, and the last (right) column shows the partisan effect on policy risk, σ_p.

As predicted by rational partisan theory, elections have a significant effect on inflation expectations. Inflation is expected to be 1.8% higher when Democrats control the presidency than when Republicans control it. This result is consistent with previous tests of rational partisan theory. In fact, Alesina, Roubini and Cohen (1997: 91) estimate that "after 1972, the difference in the steady state inflation rate between a Democratic and Republican regime is about 1.8% per year." Unlike past analyses, however, the extended model is the first to suggest that the party controlling Congress is also important. Inflation is expected to be 1.4% higher when Democrats control the House. This is close to the historical difference in inflation rates—from 1945 to 2004, inflation was 0.9% higher under the Democrats. The difference between the presidency and the House reflects the estimate of α, the parameter in the model that determines the relative influence of the presidency on inflation outcomes. This estimate suggests that the partisanship of the president accounts for about 60% of the policy impact on expected inflation, whereas the partisanship of the House accounts for only 40%.

The partisan difference in expected inflation outcomes also has an effect on electoral risk. Notice that the effect of electoral risk on the interest rate reaches a peak when there is a 50-50 chance that the Democrats will win either branch of government. Increasing the probability of a Democratic president from 0 to 0.5 increases the interest rate by 0.8%, whereas increasing it from 0 to 1 has no impact on the rate at all. A 50-50 probability in the

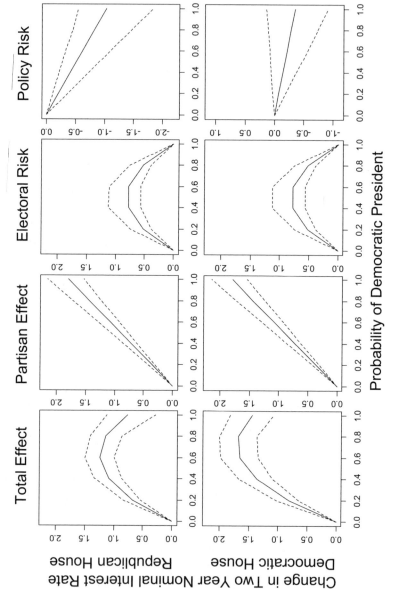

FIGURE 8.3   Effect of partisanship on two-year nominal interest rates.

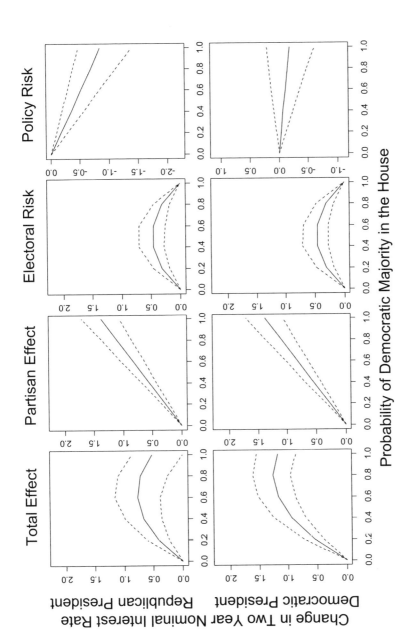

FIGURE 8.3 (continued)

House also increases the interest rate by about 0.5%, which suggests that electoral uncertainty in either branch of government has an effect. It is important to note that the effect of electoral risk is *nonpartisan*. Increasing the certainty of either a Republican or a Democratic victory lowers the interest rate because it reduces uncertainty about the identity of the party controlling policy, even if that party will ultimately choose policies that lead to higher inflation. Thus, previous work on the partisan effect on interest rates (e.g., Alesina, Roubini, and Cohen 1997) that did not include the effect of inflation risk may be missing an important control that could sharpen results.

DIVIDED GOVERNMENT

The policy-risk effect is more complicated than the partisan and electoral risk effects because it depends on the composition of both branches. When the *House* is under Republican control, increasing the probability of a Democratic president from 0 to 1 decreases policy risk by 1.0%. Conversely, when the *presidency* is under Republican control, increasing the probability of a Democratic House from 0 to 1 decreases policy risk by 0.9%. Thus, although Republicans are associated with lower absolute levels of inflation overall, *unified* Republican government is associated with *higher* inflation risk and nominal interest rates than either combination of divided government. In contrast, unified Democratic government seems to have no significant effect on nominal interest rates. This leaves open the possibility that the difference between unified Republican government and divided government is being driven instead by a perception that the Republican Party is associated with higher variance policy outcomes than the Democratic Party. That would explain the negative coefficient on the difference in the party variances ($\sigma_D - \sigma_R$) in Table 8.1 and would also be consistent with the recent finding that stock market volatility decreases as the probability of a Democratic president increases (Leblang and Mukherjee 2004). Thus, there is only partial support for the hypothesis that divided government decreases inflation risk.

INCUMBENCY

The model suggests that the probability that a *challenger* wins the presidency and House has a significant effect on the nominal interest rate. However, the effect of incumbency depends on the term of the interest rate. Increasing the probability that the challenger party wins the presidency from 0 to 1 has no significant effect on the two-year rate. In contrast, increasing the probability that the challenger party wins the House from 0 to 1 increases the two-year rate by 0.7%. These findings suggest that people have greater uncertainty about the policies that will result when there is turnover in the House than when there is turnover in the presidency. When we change the dependent variable to the five-year interest rate, the effect of incumbency gets stronger for the presidency and becomes significant at 0.3%, whereas the House effect declines to 0.6%. This may be due to the length of term for each office. House elections occur every two years, meaning that winners in the current election are expected to have a limited amount of time to affect policy. In contrast, presidential elections occur every four years, so the executive's effect on policy might be expected to last for a longer time. Overall, the model suggests that investors do expect to be compensated for the greater risk they bear when a new party takes office, *even if they expect that party to implement policies that will lead to lower inflation.*

PRESIDENTIAL MANDATE

The presidential margin of victory also has a significant impact on inflation expectations. Figure 8.4 shows how Democratic vote share affects nominal interest rates. In the left graph, notice that increasing the vote share for the Democrats from 40% to 60% increases the two-year interest rate by about 0.3%. However, the effect is curvilinear because it includes both the partisan effect on inflation and the policy effect on inflation risk. The center graph shows that the increase in Democratic support yields a linear increase in expected inflation. Investors apparently expect landslides to give each

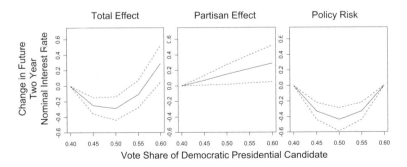

FIGURE 8.4   Effect of vote share on nominal interest rates.

party an opportunity to enact larger policy changes. This expectation also has a direct impact on inflation risk. The right graph shows that changing the election outcome from *either* 60–40 *or* 40–60 to 50–50 reduces the interest rate by about 0.4%. Thus, electoral margins appear to affect expectations of both inflation and policy risk. Just like the voters we surveyed in Chapter 6, participants in financial markets apparently expect both winning and losing parties to move with the mandate.

CONCLUSION

Rational partisan theory predicts that people expect the Left to enact policies that lead to higher inflation (and higher nominal interest rates) and they update their expectations prior to the election as electoral probabilities change. The empirical test presented here supports this prediction, showing that nominal interest rates rise when Democrats become more likely to win either branch of government. The theory of policy risk extends rational partisan theory and predicts that challenger parties and unified government will be associated with greater policy uncertainty, higher inflation risk, and thus, higher interest rates. Consistent with the policy-risk theory, the empirical model indicates that interest rates rise when the probability of incumbent victory falls. The model also suggests that an increase in the probability of divided government leads to lower interest rates, although support for this effect is limited by the possibility that the results are due to asymmetric risks associated with each party.

Both the rational partisan and policy-risk theories are utilized to demonstrate that presidential margins of victory have an effect on interest rate expectations. If people expect parties to adjust the policies they offer in response to the size of their victory (or loss) in the last election, then rational partisan theory implies that people should expect higher inflation as expected vote share for the Left increases. Similarly, the policy-risk theory suggests that people should expect greater policy uncertainty as the margin of victory for *either* party increases since a larger margin of victory may give the winning party more leeway to implement the more extreme version of its policies. The empirical model confirms both expectations and supports the main argument in this book that mandates have an important effect on the electoral system.

It is important not to draw too strong a conclusion from the evidence presented here since it is based on seven elections for a single country. However, the results are suggestive of new lines of research that could make contributions to several existing literatures. First, the policy-risk theory is an important complement to the rational partisan theory because it helps to make sharper predictions about interest rate expectations. For example, previous work that did not control for incumbency (e.g., Cohen 1993) may have underestimated the partisan effect since both Democratic Party incumbents and Republican Party challengers may have an ambiguous effect on nominal interest rates. Future tests of partisan theory should, therefore, control for incumbency, the institutional division of power, and margins of victory.

Second, evidence of partisan expectations may help to explain recent anomalies uncovered in the partisan business cycle literature. Clark and Hallerberg (2000) develop a formal model that incorporates capital mobility, exchange rate regimes, and central bank independence into rational partisan theory. In the U.S. case where capital is mobile, exchange rates are flexible, and the central bank is independent, their model predicts that the partisanship of government should have no effect on the money supply. They are surprised, however, when their empirical data show that even in these conditions, Leftist governments are associated with an expanded money supply. The empirical evidence presented here suggests a possible explanation. Suppose that, in reality, there is no difference in the economic outcomes associated with Left and Right control of the government. If people *expect* the Left to produce higher inflation, then the market might punish new Left governments with higher nominal interest rates that slow the economy, forcing the "independent" central bank to stimulate the economy at the beginning of their term as people believed they would. Similarly, the central bank may feel the need to tighten monetary policy in response to falling nominal interest rates associated with a Right-wing victory. Thus, *expectations* of partisan differences might be critically important for creating *real* partisan differences in the money supply. Future formal macroeconomic models should investigate whether such self-reinforcing equilibria exist.

Third, the policy-risk theory suggests the possibility of an *incumbent political business cycle*. If challenger governments cause higher interest rates until their preferred policies and competence become better known, then they might face a short-term reduction in growth and employment toward the beginning of their term in office. Alesina, Roubini, and Cohen (1997: 75–79) note that partisan effects on growth and employment appear to be strongest in the second year after a Challenger party takes control of the government. However, their data also supports the possibility of an incumbent cycle in the second year. From 1949–1994, incumbent Republican administrations experienced 1.68% more growth and 0.51% less unemployment than did new Republican administrations on average. Incumbent Democrat administrations experienced 2.61% more growth and 1.40% less unemployment than did new Democrat administrations. Thus, incumbent governments seem to be associated with better economic performance, and this may be due in part to lower policy-risk expectations. In future work, these arguments about the incumbent political cycle should be formalized and tested with the same analysis that has previously been applied to partisan and political business cycles.

Fourth, the policy-risk theory also suggests a reason for institutional balancing. There is a growing body of evidence for ticket-splitting as predicted by Alesina, Londregan, and Rosenthal (1993) and Alesina and Rosenthal (1995, 1996). For example, Scheve and Tomz (1999) show that the more surprised moderate voters are about the outcome of a presidential election, the lower the probability that they will support the president's party in the following midterm contest. These analyses are based on the assumption that extreme outcomes are moderated by the adjustment made by voters who want to bring policy back toward the center. The policy-risk theory suggests another reason for balancing. Voters may attempt to divide the government in order to reduce *policy risk* and the negative effects it might have on the economy. This incentive might be enough to convince less ideologically driven voters to switch to their less preferred alternative for one of the two branches of government.

Finally, we hope that this use of IEM electoral futures has shown how this unique data set might be used to study other questions related to electoral probabilities. We encourage scholars to use election futures to test relationships between electoral probabilities and macroeconomic outcomes, such as those related to electoral surprise (Chappell and Keech 1988; Roberts 1989; Alesina, Roubini, and Cohen 1997). Future work should also reverse the dependent and independent variables to see what effect the economy, campaigns, and other factors have on the probability of election. Election futures markets have been conducted for several non-U.S. elections, so there are many possibilities to use the data in both American and comparative contexts.

NINE

Conclusion

E lections determine not only *which* parties win but also *how* they win. In turn, how they win affects both current and future policies. Parties and candidates who barely win elections have much less leeway to enact their preferred policies than those who win big. Thus, *mandates matter*. In this book, we construct a theory of electoral mandates step-by-step and subject it to different assumptions and methodologies. Our theoretical models have testable empirical implications, several of which we have analyzed using field and experimental evidence. Our empirical analyses support our theoretical claims that electoral mandates play an important role in political competition and the policy-making process.

We use three models to develop our theoretical claims. First, we begin with a game theoretic model of repeated elections. Politicians in the model are assumed to be (a) policy-motivated, (b) uncertain about the exact location of the median voter, and (c) Bayesian learners, updating their beliefs about voters given evidence from past elections. In this model, we assume the voter distribution itself is exogenous. We find that the vote share is important for both the winning and losing parties. Depending on the margin of victory, parties change their platforms in the direction of the preferences of the winning party. The size of the change is primarily a function of vote share. The margin of victory is also important for voters. Extremists who align with the winning party clearly benefit from a large margin of victory, whereas moderates and extremists on the other side suffer from the policies adopted after the election.

In this model, we also show that other factors, in addition to the vote share, affect how mandates are declared. In particular, we find that electoral volatility, candidate confidence in prior beliefs about voters, and electoral polarization all have a dramatic effect on the nature of a mandate. For example, a more polarized electorate allows the winning party to choose a platform closer to its ideal point and also makes the losing party choose a more moderate platform.

To test the main prediction of our first model, we study the U.S. Senate to determine whether candidates move with the mandate. Do parties that win elections choose candidates who are more extreme, and do parties that lose elections choose candidates who are more moderate? How important is the margin of victory? We answer these questions by analyzing the relationship between Republican vote share in U.S. Senate elections and the ideology of candidates offered in the subsequent election. We observe that Republican victories in past elections lead to candidates who are more conservative in subsequent elections. Similarly, when Democrats win, both candidates in subsequent elections tend to be less conservative. Most importantly, the effect is proportional to the margin of victory.

In our second model, we relax the assumption of an exogenous voters' distribution. Here, we allow citizens in a social network to choose whether or not to vote, depending on local information available to them from their neighbors. In turn, policy-motivated parties use Bayesian learning to update their beliefs about the location of the median voter, receiving new evidence with each election. As a result, both parties and voters adapt to one another *dynamically* over a series of elections.

Endogenizing the uncertainty about the location of the median voter yields several interesting results, but it does not change the role that mandates play in voter-party interactions. Political candidates pay attention to electoral margins as they try to estimate the location of the median voter to remain competitive. As a result, proposed policies shift with changes in the positions of both the median voter and the median citizen. These results are consistent with our general theory of electoral mandates: using the margin of victory in the previous election, parties continuously try to adapt to the (endogenous) position of the median voter.

In our third model, we assume an exogenous reaction by parties to the previous election so that we can study how mandates affect the incentives facing citizens who are deciding whether or not to vote. This model suggests that voters may have a *signaling* motivation to vote if they believe that political candidates behave according to the theory of electoral mandates. Although a single vote may have no effect on the outcome, it will always have a small effect on the margin of victory, which, in turn, affects future policies offered by both parties. The signaling motivation may help to explain why some citizens turn out to vote despite the improbability of being pivotal. The model suggests that those individuals who have the highest levels of external efficacy, patience, and electoral pessimism are more likely to vote. All three of these implications are supported by an empirical analysis of National Elections Study data.

Another important implication of the third model is that moderates may switch their vote from their most preferred alternative if they think their preferred alternative is going to win big—this is because they do not want *future* policy to shift even farther from the center. Thus, we should find strategic voting among moderates in situations where they expect a large margin of victory for their preferred candidate (mandate balancing). To determine whether or not mandate balancing actually occurs, we use the Time-Sharing Experiments in the Social Sciences (TESS) internet instrument to learn what voters believe about mandates and party dynamics and see if this affects how they behave. We find that many voters do believe that politicians behave as the formal models suggest, with both parties moving in the direction of the winner and in proportion to the margin of victory. Our results also indicate that nonpartisan voters are more likely than partisans to switch their vote to the loser as the margin of victory increases.

The third model also suggests that electoral mandates magnify the effect that subjective time preferences have on the decision to vote. The costs of turnout are paid prior to and on the day of the election, whereas the policy benefits, if any, are not reaped until much later. People who care more about the future will have a greater incentive to vote because higher discount factors magnify the effect of the signaling motivation. A single vote has only a very small effect on shifts in post-electoral policies, but it will continue to affect policies in subsequent elections as well. Thus, individual discount factors may play an important role in voter turnout. Using a simple game from behavioral economics, we measure discount factors in the lab and find that they do help to predict which subjects vote.

Finally, we turn to a less obvious source of data to discover whether or not mandates matter. Rational partisan theory suggests that expectations about which party will win an upcoming election have an impact on inflation and interest rates. If mandates matter, then expectations about the vote share should also affect inflation and interest rates. We develop a formal extension to rational partisan theory that incorporates both the president and Congress and accounts for both inflation and inflation risk. This model suggests that increasing expected vote share for the Democrats should increase expectations of inflation. It also suggests that increasing the magnitude of the margin of victory for *either party* should increase inflation risk, since it will give them leeway to implement the more extreme version of their policies. We use data from Iowa Electronic Markets (IEM) to show that expectations of presidential mandates have these posited effects on interest rate expectations. Thus, market actors apparently think that mandates matter.

The total weight of the theoretical and empirical evidence points in one direction. Electoral mandates affect political behavior and expectations of political behavior in important ways. Politicians do move with the mandate, and voters and market actors both anticipate they will behave this way and adjust their own behavior accordingly. Thus, past elections shape both present policies and future electoral platforms. This is, perhaps, a very intuitive result—after all, even our subjects in the national survey that we conducted appear to believe that politicians respond to previous election results by shifting their policies in the direction of the winner and in proportion to the margin of victory. Nevertheless, scholars have not yet fully understood or widely accepted the role of electoral mandates in politics.

In addition to our substantive results, we develop new methods in this book that we hope will aid other scholars who are trying to model complex phenomena. Our underlying model is a dynamic variant of the Wittman equilibrium model with candidate preferences that are asymmetric around the expected location of the median voter. This model is not analytically tractable. We show how to proceed with analysis of such models and how to test hypotheses in a rigorous manner using numerical comparative statics. When we move to an even more complex model by endogenizing voter behavior, we show how an agent-based model (ABM) can be used to study the system. Like standard formal theory, the assumptions of an ABM have to be clearly stated in the language of mathematics, and the results can be replicated. Moreover, ABMs are powerful tools that can allow us to move beyond standard rational choice assumptions by including behavioral assumptions from other disciplines such as sociology, economics, psychology, and anthropology. However, we make a general plea to other scholars to use restraint. In electoral politics and other areas of study, a long formal theory literature already exists that should help to inform and constrain the choices of assumptions used in any ABM. We should take baby steps away from analytical models to make sure that we can connect our results to the established literature and that we can learn which of the added assumptions are actually generating the results.

This book also represents a plea for methodological pluralism. We use game-theoretic, agent-based, and decision-theoretic models to develop our theory. We then use data from the National Election Studies (NES), the laboratory, an internet-based national survey, and even market data to search for areas to test the implications of these models. We take the new emphasis in political science on Empirical Implications of Theoretical Models (EITM) seriously, and we hope that this book illustrates how purely political science phenomena can be tackled in a variety of creative ways.

Although we think the evidence presented makes a strong case for the importance of electoral mandates, we do not claim to have provided answers to all questions raised by these models and empirical results. There is a lot of room for improvement and future work is clearly needed. There are both general and specific concerns that we have about our work and ways to improve or build upon it.

Foremost, we believe that future work should include more analytical efforts to find closed-form alternatives to the results reported in this book. This is obviously not easy—otherwise, we would have already done that ourselves. Nevertheless, we believe that our theoretical hypotheses and empirical efforts to test them should prove to be helpful for formal theorists studying the problems of electoral competition. Our theoretical results can be seen as a basis for comparison, whereas our empirical results can be used to inform assumptions and test future models.

For example, future work should develop the formal aspects of dynamic responsiveness. Do both parties have to shift with a shock to the distribution of the location of the median voter? This question is, in fact, not trivial. If the losing party knows that the winning party is going to shift to its extreme, then it may simply stay put to increase its own probability of winning without sacrificing its own preferred policy. Similarly, if the winning party knows that the losing party is going to move to the center, then it may still have an incentive to keep its current policy in order not to compromise its electoral chances in the future. We do show in Chapters 2 and 4 that both parties shift in the direction of the winner's preference. However, this effort may not necessarily apply in contexts where divergence is caused by other factors like the threat of entry (Palfrey 1984; Greenberg and Shepsle 1987) or affected by other factors such as a valence advantage (e.g., Groseclose

2001). In general, the empirical results reported here should motivate formal theorists to extend their models to explore the relationship between updated beliefs implied by past vote shares and the positions parties choose to take.

Future work may also examine more specific questions. For example, in our general theory of electoral mandates, political parties observe past election results and then choose new candidates based on the information they provide about the location of the median voter. However, it is also possible that control of the process may be more dispersed—candidates themselves may exhibit self-selection by avoiding contests they think they will lose. If past election results indicate the median has shifted to the right, candidates in the left wing of the right party may be less likely to run because they believe they have a lower probability of winning their primary. Future work should focus on identifying whether party leaders or potential candidates are conscious of a relationship between past electoral margins and the ideology of future candidates.

The importance of electoral mandates might also be seen in other parts of political life not covered in this book. For example, future work should examine the effect of mandates on special-interest group behavior. Similar to voters, interest groups may be interested in promoting their preferred policy outcomes. Unlike voters, however, special interest groups can provide large political contributions to candidates and can mobilize substantial voting blocks in order to satisfy preferences of their members. If the margin of victory affects the ability to adopt certain policies, special-interest groups may have an interest in both the outcome of the election and the margin of victory for their favorite candidate. Although influence-peddling is illegal in a democracy, influencing policy through the creation/destruction of electoral mandates is not. Special-interest groups may be able to exert extra control over policy if they can affect the margin of victory and/or voter turnout.

Our theory of electoral mandates is primarily based upon a political system like the one we find in the United States, with two parties and a simple issue space. We believe, however, that our main theoretical claims may still be relevant in comparative perspective as well. Future work should examine whether electoral mandates matter in other political systems, including multiparty elections and proportional representation systems. A new theoretical model would examine whether the presence of multiple candidates affects the importance of vote share as well as the signaling motivation of voters. Moreover, although we focus on the importance of mandates in presidential and congressional elections in this book, we also believe that our theory is general enough to apply to local elections. Any officials or leaders chosen by an overwhelming majority of voters—whoever they are—should have greater authority to exercise power and implement preferred rules, and this should have a large effect on the behavior of their future opponents. Our argument may also be general enough to apply to other, nonpolitical, elections in such areas as business, sports, clubs, and small communities.

The various directions we might go all flow from a single idea at the core of this book: election results determine not only *who* gets into office, but *how* one gets into office. This idea may help us understand some of the most puzzling questions in political science such as voter turnout and platform divergence, but it also has broad applicability to the study of electoral competition and the theory of democracy. We show that elections play a much larger role in a society than the traditional instrumental role of determining a winner. In our analysis, it is the electoral mandate that is the driving force behind the expressive, or communicative, role of elections and a major link between voters and politicians.

APPENDIXES

APPENDIX: CHAPTER TWO

PROOF OF LEMMA 1

Note that under proximity voting, the vote share must equal the area under the voter distribution up to the halfway point between the two platforms in the previous election, given the implied location of the median voter, m, and electoral polarization, B:

$$s = \int_{-\infty}^{(x_L + x_R)/2} f(v \mid m, B) dv$$

If the voter distribution is normal then

$$s = \int_{-\infty}^{(x_L + x_R)/2} \frac{1}{\sqrt{2\pi B}} e^{-(v-m)^2/2B} dv.$$

As a result, the location of the median voter in the previous election, m, can be found if parties know the vote share, s, the platforms, x_L, x_R, and have beliefs about the degree of electoral polarization, B.

EQUILIBRIUM

We use a Nash equilibrium concept to analyze the behavior of policy-motivated parties. Using standard notation, we define equilibrium as a combination of candidates' platforms (y_L^*, y_R^*) such that $y_L^* = \max\arg U_L$ and $y_R^* = \max\arg U_R$:

$$\max_{y_L} EU_L = \pi(y_L, y_R^{\cdot})U_L(y_L) + (1 - \pi(y_L, y_R^{\cdot}))U_L(y_R^{\cdot})$$

$$\max_{y_R} EU_R = \pi(y_L^{\cdot}, y_R)U_R(y_L^{\cdot}) + (1 - \pi(y_L^{\cdot}, y_R))U_R(y_R), \tag{1}$$

where $\pi(y_L, y_R)$ is the probability that party L wins given the platforms y_L and y_R, $U_i(y_i) = -(y_W - p_i)^2$ is the utility of party $i = L, R$ if the party wins the election, $y_W = y_i$, and $U_i(y_{-i}) = -(y_W - p_i)^2$ is the utility of party $i = L, R$ if the party loses the election, $y_W = y_{-i}$.

The platform closest to the median voter's ideal point wins the election. Therefore, the probability that the Left wins the election is $\pi(y_L, y_R) = \Pr(M < (y_L - y_R)/2)$. Parties believe that the location of the median voter M is distributed according to which we assume to be normal.

In the first – or "previous" – election, the candidates' locations are the Wittman equilibrium platforms (x_L^*, x_R^*), and the probability that the Left wins the election is

$$\pi(x_L, x_R) = \int_{-\infty}^{(x_L + x_R)/2} \frac{1}{\sqrt{2\pi\beta}} e^{-(M-\mu)^2/2\beta^2} \, dM,$$

where μ is the prior belief about the location of the median voter and β is confidence in the prior belief. This gives us all the information we need to find the first order conditions for the utility equations in (1):

$$\frac{\partial EU_L}{\partial y_L} = \frac{e^{-(y_L + y_R - 2\mu)^2/8\beta}(y_R - y_L)(y_L + y_R - 2p_L)}{2\sqrt{2\pi\beta}}$$

$$+ 2(p_L - y_L)\left(\int_{-\infty}^{(y_L + y_R)/2} \frac{1}{\sqrt{2\pi\beta}} e^{-(M-\mu)^2/2\beta^2} \, dM \right)$$

$$\frac{\partial EU_R}{\partial y_R} = \frac{e^{-(y_L + y_R - 2\mu)^2/8\beta}(y_R - y_L)(y_L + y_R - 2p_R)}{2\sqrt{2\pi\beta}}$$

$$+ 2(p_R - y_R)\left(1 - \int_{-\infty}^{(y_L + y_R)/2} \frac{1}{\sqrt{2\pi\beta}} e^{-(M-\mu)^2/2\beta^2} \, dM \right)$$

For the current election, however, both μ and β need to be updated given the information that the previous election provided. As a result, the new expression for the probability of victory by the Left becomes:

$$\pi\left(y_L, y_R\right) = \int_{-\infty}^{(y_L + y_R)/2} \frac{1}{\sqrt{2\pi\beta'}} e^{-(M-\mu')^2/2\beta'^2} dM,$$

where μ' and β' are the product of Bayesian inference as defined previously. The first order conditions for the current election will be identical to those for the previous election except we use the posterior mean and variance instead of the prior.

R CODE TO FIND EQUILIBRIUM

```
## FOC for party 0
deu0 <- function(x0,x1,p0,p1,mu,bt)
(exp(-((x0+x1-2*mu)^2)/(8*bt))*(x1-x0)*(x0+x1-2*p0))/(2*sqrt(2*bt*pi))+
2*(p0-x0)*pnorm((x0+x1)/2, mean=mu, sd=bt^(1/2))

## FOC for party 1
deu1 <- function(x0,x1,p0,p1,mu,bt)
(exp(-((x0+x1-2*mu)^2)/(8*bt))*(x1-x0)*(x0+x1-2*p1))/(2*sqrt(2*bt*pi))+
2*(p1-x1)*(1-pnorm((x0+x1)/2, mean=mu, sd=bt^(1/2)))

## find Wittman equilibrium policies, utilities
fweq <- function(p0,p1,mu,bt,b,B,s) {

        ## previous election:
        ## optimize by minimizing loss function
        ## (start near median voter)
        eq<-optim(c(mu,mu+.01),function(x)
            abs(deu0(x[1],x[2],p0,p1,mu,bt)) +
            abs(deu1(x[1],x[2],p0,p1,mu,bt)) +
            if(x[1]<p1||x[2]>p0) .01 else 0)
        xs<-eq$par

        ## infer median voter from vote share
        m <- qnorm(1-s,mean=(sum(xs))/2,sd=sqrt(B))

        ## Bayesian update mean and variance
        mup<-(bt*m+b*mu)/(bt+b); btp<-bt*b/(bt+b)

        ## current election:
        ## optimize by minimizing loss function
        ## (start at median voter)
```

```
        peq<-optim(c(mup,mup+.01),function(x)
          abs(deu0(x[1],x[2],p0,p1,mup,btp)) +
          abs(deu1(x[1],x[2],p0,p1,mup,btp)) +
          if(x[1]<p1llx[2]>p0) .01 else 0)
        ## return vector of eq platforms
        print(peq$par)
}
## example: preferences at -1,1, median voter at 0,
## electoral variance, conf. in prior, voter distribution = 1,1,1
## vote share for left = 0.5
fweq(p0=-1,p1=1,mu=0,bt=1,b=1,B=1,s=0.5)
```

APPENDIX: CHAPTER FOUR

CODE FOR "DYNAMIC PARTIES AND SOCIAL TURNOUT" MODEL

```
DPAST<-function(n=32,p=c(-1,1),cost=0.1,vMem=0.0,prefCor=0.0,
partiesFixed=FALSE,turnoutFixed=FALSE,B=1,nPeriods=100,nSims=1,
graphs=FALSE,fileName=NULL) {

## key parameters
## n<-32 ## length, width of grid
## p<-c(-1,1) ## party preferences
## cost<-0.1 ## cost of turnout
## vMem<-0.0 ## voter memory weights past vs. present observations
## prefCor<-0.75 ## degree of correlation of voter preferences
## partiesFixed=FALSE ## choose whether or not to fix parties
## turnoutFixed=FALSE ## choose whether or not to fix turnout
## B<-1 ## voter polarization (var of voter distribution)
## nPeriods<-100 ## number of periods
## nSims<-1 ## number of repetitions of simulation

for (sims in 1:nSims) {

## initialize time series and other variables
N<-n^2 ## number of voters
x<-array(0,dim=c(nPeriods,2)) ## platforms
## prior mean, variance, turnout, vote share, median voter
mu<-bt<-turnout<-s<-mv<-rep(0,nPeriods)

## initialize count arrays
nt<-npt<-npa<-array(0,dim=c(n,n))

## set initial turnout unless fixed
iTurnout<-0.5 ## initial turnout
if (turnoutFixed) iTurnout=1.0

## set initial party platforms
x[1,]<-p

## initialize voter preferences as combination of sorted and
## unsorted preferences depending on preference correlation
sorted<-rbinom(N,1,prefCor)
pref<-array(sorted*sort(rnorm(N,0,sqrt(B)))+
        (1-sorted)*rnorm(N,0,sqrt(B)),dim=c(n,n))

## FOCs for left and right party
deuL <- function(x,pL,mu,bt) -(exp(-((sum(x)-2*mu)^2)/(8*bt))*
    (x[1]-x[2])*(-2*pL+sum(x)))/(2*sqrt(2*bt*pi))+
    2*(pL-x[1])*pnorm(mean(x), mean=mu, sd=bt^(1/2))
```

```
deuR <- function(x,pR,mu,bt) -(exp(-((sum(x)-2*mu)^2)/(8*bt))*
  (x[1]-x[2])*(-2*pR+sum(x)))/(2*sqrt(2*bt*pi))+
  2*(pR-x[2])*(1-pnorm(mean(x), mean=mu, sd=bt^(1/2)))

## function for collecting neighborhood stats
neighbors<- function(mat) {
mat<-rbind(rep(0,(n+2)),cbind(rep(0,n),mat,rep(0,n)),rep(0,(n+2)))
mat[1:n,1:n]+mat[1:n,2:(n+1)]+mat[1:n,3:(n+2)]+
  mat[2:(n+1),1:n]+mat[2:(n+1),2:(n+1)]+mat[2:(n+1),3:(n+2)]+
  mat[3:(n+2),1:n]+mat[3:(n+2),2:(n+1)]+mat[3:(n+2),3:(n+2)]
}

## index array of number of neighbors in each neighborhood
nn<-neighbors(array(1,dim=c(n,n)))

##INITIAL ELECTION

## initialize turnout actions
action<-array(rbinom(N,1,iTurnout)==1,dim=c(n,n))

## voters choose parties (flip coin if equidistant)
choice<- (-(x[1,2]-pref)^2 > -(x[1,1]-pref)^2) +
         (-(x[1,2]-pref)^2 == -(x[1,1]-pref)^2)*rbinom(N,1,0.5)

## determine turnout, vote share, winner (flip coin if tie)
turnout[1]<-mean(action)
if (turnout[1]>0) {
  s[1]<-mean(action*choice)/turnout[1]
} else {
  s[1]<-0.5 ## ignorance result when no one votes
}
s[1]<-max(min(s[1],(N-1)/N),1/N) ## restrict s[t] to avoid inf in m

winner<-(s[1]>0.5)+(s[1]==0.5)*rbinom(1,1,0.5)

## voter payoffs
payoff<- -(x[1,winner+1]-pref)^2-action*cost

## ELECTION CYCLE
for (t in 2:nPeriods) {

## PARTIES

if (partiesFixed) {
x[t,]<-x[t-1,]
} else {
  ## infer median voter from previous vote share and platforms
  m <- qnorm(s[t-1],mean(x[t-1,]),sqrt(B))
```

```
## Bayesian update beliefs
mu[t]<-((t-2)*mu[t-1]+m)/(t-1) ## mean
bt[t]<-((t-2)*bt[t-1]+(m-mu[t-1])^2)/(t-1) ## variance

## optimize by minimizing loss function
peq<-optim(c(mu[t],mu[t]+.01),function(z)
  abs(deuL(z,p[1],mu[t],max(bt[t],.000001))) +
  abs(deuR(z,p[2],mu[t],max(bt[t],.000001))) +
  if(z[1]<p[1]||z[2]>p[2]) .01 else 0)

  ## set eq platforms
  x[t,]<-peq$par
}


## VOTERS

if (!turnoutFixed) {

  ## count number of voters in each neighborhood
  nt<-vMem*nt+(1-vMem)*neighbors(action)

  ## sum payoffs of voters and abstainers in each neighborhood
  npt<-vMem*npt+(1-vMem)*neighbors(payoff*action)
  npa<-vMem*npa+(1-vMem)*neighbors(payoff*(1-action))

  ## turn out if ave payoff of voting neighbors is higher than
  ## ave payoff of abstaining neighbors
  action<-((npt/nt)>(npa/(nn-nt)))
  action<-action&(nt>0) ## turn out only if someone else turns out
  action<-action|(nn-nt==0) ## turn out if no one else abstains
}

## voters choose parties (flip coin if equidistant)
choice<- (-(x[t,2]-pref)^2 > -(x[t,1]-pref)^2) +
         (-(x[t,2]-pref)^2 == -(x[t,1]-pref)^2)*rbinom(N,1,0.5)

## determine percent turnout, vote share, winner (flip coin if tie)
turnout[t]<-mean(action)
if (turnout[t]>0) {
  s[t]<-mean(action*choice)/turnout[t]
} else {
  s[t]<--0.5 ## ignorance result when no one votes
}
s[t]<-max(min(s[t],(N-1)/N),1/N) ## restrict s[t] to avoid inf in m
winner<-(s[t]>0.5)+(s[t]==0.5)*rbinom(1,1,0.5)

  ## median voter
  mv[t]<-median(pref[which(action)])
```

```
## voter payoffs
payoff<- -(x[t,winner+1]-pref)^2-action*cost
}



## median preference
medPref<-median(pref)

if (graphs) {
  par(mfrow=c(2,3)) ## clear graphs
  plot(x[,1],
type="1",ylim=c(min(c(x[2:nPeriods,],mv)),max(c(x[2:nPeriods,],mv))))
  lines(x[,2], type="1", lty=2)
  plot(mv,
type="1",ylim=c(min(c(x[2:nPeriods,],mv)),max(c(x[2:nPeriods,],mv))))
  lines(rep(median(pref),nPeriods), type="1", lty=2)
  plot(mu,
type="1",ylim=c(min(c(x[2:nPeriods,],mv)),max(c(x[2:nPeriods,],mv))))
  plot(turnout, type="1")
  plot(s, type="1")
  lines(rep(0.5,nPeriods), type="1", lty=2)
  plot(bt, type="1")
}

## turnout correlation
turnoutCor<-cor(c(action[2:n,2:n],action[2:n,1:n],action[2:n,1:(n-1)],
  action[1:n,2:n]),c(action[1:(n-1),1:(n-1)],action[1:(n-1),1:n],
  action[1:(n-1),2:n],action[1:n,1:(n-1)]))

## preference correlation
prefCorr<-cor(c(pref[2:n,2:n],pref[2:n,1:n],pref[2:n,1:n-1],pref[1:n,2:n]),
  c(pref[1:(n-1),1:(n-1)],pref[1:(n-1),1:n],pref[1:(n-1),2:n],
  pref[1:n,1:(n-1)]))

## interior exterior turnout
intTurnout<-mean(action[2:(n-1),2:(n-1)])
extTurnout<-mean(c(action[1,],action[,1],action[n,],action[,n]))

## write data if file name provided
if (!is.null(fileName))
write.table(t(c(n,p,cost,vMem,prefCorr,partiesFixed,

turnoutFixed,B,nPeriods,turnoutCor,prefCor,intTurnout,extTurnout,medPref,
  x,turnout,s,mv,mu,bt)),file=fileName,append=TRUE,row.names=FALSE,
col.names=FALSE)

} ## end sim
} ## end function
```

APPENDIX: CHAPTER FIVE

MODEL AND PROOF OF PROPOSITIONS

In the model, each "citizen" i has an ideal point in one-dimensional issue space $Q_i \in \Re^1$ and faces a decision problem to maximize subjective expected utility. The decision problem takes place in the context of infinitely repeated elections starting with the current election at time $t = 0$. In every election, two parties (J and $\sim J$) compete with each party proposing a platform $F \in \Re^1$. Each citizen has three choices: vote for the closest ("favorite" or "preferred") party (J), vote for the party furthest away ($\sim J$), or abstain. Citizen i's single period utility from voting is $U_i^V = -|F - Q_i| - c$, where $c > 0$ is the cost of voting in the current election, and F is platform of the winning party. Correspondingly, the single period utility from abstention is the same except that a citizen does not incur the cost $U_i^A = -|F - Q_i|$. For simplicity, we assume that a voter believes his or her vote will not change the outcome of the current election (the probability of being pivotal is $P = 0$). Nor does the voter get extra benefits from voting related to a normative obligation to vote ($D = 0$).

The total number of "voters" is the sum of votes for each party $N = V_J - V_{\sim J}$, which is different from the total number of "citizens" if there is at least one abstention. Candidate J wins elections by simple majority rule and the margin of victory for candidate J is

$$\mu = \frac{V_J - V_{\sim J}}{N}. \tag{2}$$

Notice that if party J loses the election, μ is negative: in this case, the "margin of victory" is, in fact, a margin of a loss. We assume that voters believe that parties use the margin of victory from the previous election to adjust the platform they offer in the next election. Specifically, voters think parties act in accordance with an exogenously given response function

$$F_{t+1} = F_t + \mu E, \tag{3}$$

where F_{t+1} is a new platform, F_t is the previous platform, μ is the past margin of victory, and E is an "efficacy" parameter denoting how much the voter thinks parties pay attention to citizen preferences. Furthermore, the sign of E indicates the voter's belief about the preferred direction of movement for party J ($E \geq 0$ if J is the right party and $E \leq 0$ if J is the left party). This means that μE is positive for both parties when the right wins (they both move right) and negative when the left wins (they both move left).

Let $p = V_J/N$ be the citizen's expectation of the proportion of votes his or her favorite party will receive in the current election. Note that this can also be thought of as the probability that any other given voter will vote for candidate J. One vote for party J has the following effect on the margin of victory:

$$\Delta\mu = \mu^{V(J)} - \mu^A = \frac{V_J - V_{\sim J} + 1}{N+1} - \frac{V_J - V_{\sim J}}{N} = \frac{2V_{\sim J}}{N(N+1)} = \frac{2(1-p)}{N+1} \quad (4)$$

By the same logic, one vote for party $\sim J$ has the exact opposite effect on the margin of victory, changing it by:

$$\mu^{V(\sim J)} - \mu^A = \frac{V_J - V_{\sim J} - 1}{N+1} - \frac{V_J - V_{\sim J}}{N} = \frac{-2V_{\sim J}}{N(N+1)} = -\Delta\mu. \quad (5)$$

A citizen's decision to vote thus has a direct effect on the platforms both parties offer in the next election. A vote for party J changes both party platforms by

$$\left[F_t + (\mu + \Delta\mu)E \right] - \left[F_t + \mu E \right] = \Delta\mu E. \quad (6)$$

Moreover, this change in the party platform persists into the future since it becomes the new basis for future platforms. For example, the effect of a vote today on the platform 2 elections from now is the same:

$$\begin{aligned}
F_{t+2}^{A,t} &= F_{t+1} + \mu_{t+1}E = F_t + \mu_t E + \mu_{t+1}E \\
F_{t+2}^{V(J),t} &= F_{t+1} + \mu_{t+1}E = F_t + (\mu_t + \Delta\mu)E + \mu_{t+1}E \\
F_{t+2}^{V(J),t} - F_{t+2}^{A,t} &= \Delta\mu E
\end{aligned} \quad (7)$$

Given a subjective rate of time preference (discount factor $0 < \delta < 1$), a citizen who abstains expects utility

$$U_i^A = \sum_{t=1}^{\infty} \delta^t \left(-q \, | \, F_t^J + \mu_t E - Q_i \, | -(1-q) \, | \, F_t^{\sim J} + \mu_t E - Q_i \, | \right), \quad (8)$$

where q is the subjective probability that party J wins future elections ($t > 0$). A citizen who abstains does not change the margin of victory so he or she has no effect on the new platforms of either candidate. If the citizen votes for the preferred candidate J, his or her utility is:

$$U_i^{V(J)} = \sum_{t=1}^{\infty} \delta^t \left(-q \,|\, F_t^J + (\mu_t + \Delta\mu)E - Q_i \,| - (1-q) \,|\, F_t^{\sim J} + (\mu_t + \Delta\mu)E - Q_i \,| \right).$$

(9)

If he or she votes for the least-preferred candidate J, that utility is:

$$U_i^{V(\sim J)} = \sum_{t=1}^{\infty} \delta^t \left(-q \,|\, F_t^J + (\mu_t - \Delta\mu)E - Q_i \,| - (1-q) \,|\, F_t^{\sim J} + (\mu_t - \Delta\mu)E - Q_i \,| \right).$$

(10)

To determine the utility from voting, we divide citizens into four types. Each citizen prefers either the left or right candidate and is either an "extremist" (with preferences to the left or right of both parties) or a "moderate" (with preferences between both parties). First, we consider an extremist who prefers the right party, $F^{\sim J} < F^J < Q_i$. The utility gain from voting for one's preferred party is:

$$U_i^{V(J)} - U_i^A$$

$$= \sum_{t=1}^{\infty} \delta^t (q((F_t^J + (\mu + \Delta\mu)E - Q_i) - c) + (1-q)((F_t^{\sim J} + (\mu + \Delta\mu)E - Q_i) - c))$$

$$- \sum_{t=1}^{\infty} \delta^t (q(F_t^J + \mu E - Q_i) + (1-q)(F_t^{\sim J} + \mu E - Q_i)) = \frac{\delta}{1-\delta} \Delta\mu E - c.$$

(11)

The case for a left extremist $(Q_i < F^J < F^{\sim J})$ yields a similar result:

$$U_i^{V(J)} - U_i^A$$

$$= \sum_{t=1}^{\infty} \delta^t (q(-F_t^J - (\mu + \Delta\mu)E + Q_i - c) + (1-q)(-F_t^{\sim J} - (\mu + \Delta\mu)E + Q_i - c))$$

$$- \sum_{t=1}^{\infty} \delta^t (q(-F_t^J - \mu E + Q_i) + (1-q)(-F_t^{\sim J} - \mu E + Q_i)) = -\frac{\delta}{1-\delta} \Delta\mu E - c.$$

(12)

Since $E \leq 0$ for left extremists and all other variables in the first term are non-negative, the signaling motivation to vote for all extremists is:

$$\frac{\delta}{1-\delta} \Delta\mu |E| \geq 0 \tag{13}$$

If extremists vote for their less preferred party ($\sim J$), the sign on $\Delta\mu$ simply changes and yields nonpositive utility:

$$-\frac{\delta}{1-\delta} \Delta\mu |E| \leq 0 \tag{14}$$

Thus, if no other incentives exist, extremists will choose to vote for their preferred candidate when $(\delta/(1-\delta))\Delta\mu |E| > c$. Otherwise, they will abstain.

Moderates have different incentives. Consider the case of a right moderate ($F^{\sim J} < Q_i < F^J$). The utility of voting for one's preferred candidate is:

$$U_i^{V(J)} - U_i^A$$

$$= \sum_{t=1}^{\infty} \delta^t (q(-F_t^J - (\mu+\Delta\mu)E + Q_i - c) + (1-q)(F_t^{\sim J} + (\mu+\Delta\mu)E - Q_i - c))$$

$$- \sum_{t=1}^{\infty} \delta^t (q(-F_t^J - \mu E + Q_i) + (1-q)(F_t^{\sim J} + \mu E - Q_i))$$

$$= \frac{\delta}{1-\delta} \Delta\mu(1-2q)E - c. \tag{15}$$

For left moderates ($F^J < Q_i < F^{\sim J}$), the result is similar:

$$U_i^{V(J)} - U_i^A$$

$$= \sum_{t=1}^{\infty} \delta^t (q(F_t^J + (\mu-\Delta\mu)E - Q_i - c) + (1-q)(-F_t^{\sim J} - (\mu-\Delta\mu)E + Q_i - c))$$

$$- \sum_{t=1}^{\infty} \delta^t (q(F_t^J + \mu E - Q_i) + (1-q)(-F_t^{\sim J} - \mu E + Q_i))$$

$$= -\frac{\delta}{1-\delta} \Delta\mu(1-2q)E - c. \tag{16}$$

Since $E \leq 0$ for left moderates and all other variables in the first term are nonnegative, the signaling motivation for all moderates is:

$$\frac{\delta}{1-\delta}\Delta\mu\,|\,E\,|\,(1-2q) \geq 0 \tag{17}$$

If a moderate votes for his or her less preferred party ($\sim J$), the sign on $\Delta\mu$ changes and so does the signaling motivation utility:

$$\frac{\delta}{1-\delta}\Delta\mu\,|\,E\,|\,(2q-1) \geq 0. \tag{18}$$

Recall that q is the citizen's belief about the probability that party J will win future elections. When $q < 0.5$, the utility for voting for party J is positive and the utility for voting for party $\sim J$ is negative. The reverse is true when $q > 0.5$. Thus, moderates only get positive utility from voting for the party they think is more likely to lose future elections, and they do so only when $(\delta/(1-\delta))\Delta\mu|E|\,|1-2q| > c$. Otherwise, they abstain.

We include one last technical proposition about citizen types. When parties shift their platforms, this causes some citizens with ideal points very close to the platform to change from being a moderate to an extremist or vice versa as we have defined them. The following proposition shows that it is the type in the election at time $t + 1$ that determines a citizen's strategy.

PROPOSITION 3: *The citizen's strategy in period t is contingent upon his or her type in period t + 1.*

A right extremist believes that he or she will become a moderate if the winning candidate's new platform will be to the right from the voter's ideal point. This happens when

$$F_t^J + (\mu_t \pm \Delta\mu)E - Q_i < 0. \tag{19}$$

If this inequality holds, we change the signs of the variables inside the absolute values in equation (11). This changes equation (11) to equation (15), which corresponds to the case of a right moderate. A right moderate believes that he or she will become an extremist if the winning candidate's new platform will be to the left from the voter's ideal point. This happens when

$$F_t^J + (\mu_t \pm \Delta\mu)E - Q_i > 0. \tag{20}$$

If this inequality holds, we change signs of the variables inside the absolute values in formula (15). This changes formula (15) to formula (11), which corresponds to the case of a right extremt.

The same logic applies for left extremists and moderates.

DATA USED IN THE STATISTICAL MODELS PRESENTED IN
TABLE A-5.1

TABLE A-5.1   Turnout Models for the National Election Studies, 1976–1988

Variable	Pooled Model Using Multiple Imputation		Model for 1976 Using Listwise Deletion	
Pivotal motivation				
Candidate differential (B)	0.21*	(0.08)	0.29	(0.19)
Closeness of election (P)	0.01	(0.04)	0.15	(0.13)
Signaling motivation				
External efficacy (E)	0.33*	(0.07)	0.32*	(0.14)
Discount factor (δ)	0.20*	(0.07)	0.24*	(0.12)
Probability favorite party wins (p)	−0.18*	(0.07)	−0.49*	(0.24)
Duty motivation				
Civic duty (D)	0.20*	(0.04)	0.20*	(0.09)
Socioeconomic variables				
Education	0.05*	(0.01)	0.06*	(0.02)
Income	0.02	(0.01)	0.03	(0.06)
Employed	0.06	(0.04)	0.13	(0.10)
Home ownership	0.36*	(0.04)	0.58*	(0.10)
Age	0.03*	(0.01)	0.05*	(0.02)
Age-squared/1,000	−0.20*	(0.06)	−0.04*	(0.02)
Marital status (married)	0.15*	(0.05)	0.19	(0.10)
Gender (female)	0.02	(0.04)	0.05	(0.10)
Race (black)	−0.15*	(0.05)	−0.11	(0.15)
South	−0.31*	(0.04)	−0.39*	(0.09)
Institutional affiliation				
Church attendance	0.50*	(0.05)	0.67*	(0.13)
Nonpolitical organization	0.13*	(0.04)	0.16	(0.10)
Psychological variables				
Political interest	0.48*	(0.05)	0.15	(0.14)
Political information	0.33*	(0.06)	0.31*	(0.12)
Internal efficacy	0.01	(0.05)	0.04	(0.11)
Strength of party ID	0.36*	(0.06)	0.38*	(0.16)
Intercept	−2.70*	(0.17)	−3.41*	(0.48)
Pseudo R^2	0.20		0.23	
N	8,158		1,040	

Note: Coefficient estimates are from a probit model of *validated* turnout with heteroskedastic-consistent errors. Missing data are imputed using Expectation Maximization algorithm (King et al. 2001).

*$p < .05$. **$p < .01$. Standard errors are in parenthesis.

For variables with an asterisk, we follow the coding procedure in Timpone (1998). Numbers in parentheses indicate the NES variables in order by year, 1976 first, 1980 second, 1984 third, and 1988 last. *Candidate differential** (B) is the absolute value of the difference in evaluations of the candidates on the 100-point thermometer scale (3,298, 3,299; 154, 155; 290, 293; 154, 155). *Closeness of election* (P) is coded 1 = the presidential race will be close, 0 = one candidate will win by quite a bit (3,027; 55; 77; 99). For *external efficacy* (E), we follow Craig, Niemi and Silver (1990) and Niemi, Craig, and Mattei (1991) by creating an index that averages responses from four questions: "People like me don't have any say about what the government does" (3,815; 1,030; 312; 937), "I don't think public officials care much what people like me think" (3,818; 1,033; 313; 938), "How much do you feel that having elections makes the government pay attention to what the people think?" (3,743; 890; 309; 959), and "Over the years, how much attention do you feel the government pays to what the people think when it decides what to do?" (3,741; 888; 310; 960). The first two questions are coded 0 = agree, 0.5 neither, and 1 = disagree in 1976–1984. For 1988, they are 0 = agree strongly, 0.25 = agree somewhat, 0.5 = neither, 0.75 = disagree somewhat, and 1 = disagree strongly. The third and fourth questions are coded 1 = a good deal, 0.5 = some, and 0 = not much. Coding for the *discount factor* (δ) (3,736; 3,737 in 1976 only) and the *probability favorite party wins* (p) (3,026, 3,027, 3,044, 3,045; 54; 55; 137; 76; 77; 425; 98; 99; 763) are described in the text. *Civic duty* (D) is coded 1 = yes and 0 = no for "If a person doesn't care how an election comes out he shouldn't vote in it" (3,350; 145; 311; 936).

*Education** is the number of years completed (3,384; 429; 431; 419). *Income** is family income in constant 1976 dollars, using the Bureau of Labor Statistics measure of the Consumer Price Index to transform income in later years (686; 725; 680; 520). *Employed* is coded 1 = employed and 0 otherwise (3,409; 515; 457; 429). *Home Ownership** is coded 1 for homeowners, 0 for others (3,509; 719; 706; 552). *Age** is in number of years and *age-squared** is mean-centered to reduce collinearity (3,369; 408; 429; 417). *Marital status** is 1 for married and 0 for all others (3,370; 409; 430; 418). *Gender** is 1 for female, 0 for male (3,512; 720; 707; 413). *Race** is 1 for black, 0 for others (3,513; 721; 708; 534). *South** is 1 for people from southern states, 0 for others.

*Church attendance** is an index of religious attendance, 0 = never/no religious preference, 0.25 = a few times a year, 0.5 = once or twice a month, 0.75 = almost every week, and 1 = every week. Group membership* is coded 1 if people belong to any organizations representing the group they feel closest to and 0 otherwise (3,868; 1,169; 1,103; 1,114). *Political interest* in the campaign is coded 1 = very much interested, 0.5 = somewhat interested, 0 = not much interested (3,031; 53; 75; 97). Following Verba, Schlozman, and Brady (1995), *political information* is based on answers to factual questions: "Do you happen to know which party elected the most members to the House of representatives in the elections this/last month?" (3,683; 1,028; 1,006; 878) and "Do you happen to know which party had the most members in the House of Representatives in Washington before the elections?" (3,684; 1,029; 1,007). The second question was not asked in 1988 so we substitute and "Do you happen to know which party had the most members in the Senate before the elections?" (879 in 1988 only). We code the variable 1 = correct answer to both questions, 0.5 = correct answer to one question, 0 = no correct answers. *Internal efficacy** is a binary response (0 = true, 1 = false) to the question "Sometimes politics and government seem so complicated that a person like me can't really understand what's going on." (3,817; 1,032; 314; 939) *Strength of party identification** is coded 0 = independents and apoliticals, 1/3 = independents leaning towards a party, 2/3 = weak partisans, and 1 = strong partisans (3,174; 266; 318; 274).

Spatial positioning for variables in the vote choice model are determined by self-placement and placement of the major party candidates on the liberal-conservative scale (3,286; 3,287; 3,288; 267; 268; 269; 369; 371; 372; 228; 231; 232). *Strategic voting* is coded 0 if respondents vote for the candidate they place closest to their own position. Otherwise, it is coded a 1 (3,044, 3,045; 137; 425; 397). *Moderates* are coded 1 if they place themselves between the two candidates and 0 otherwise. *Directional voting* is coded 1 for those who intend to vote for a candidate on the same side of (and including) the "cutpoint" of 4 on the 7-point liberal-conservative scale. *Institutional balancing* is coded 1 for those who vote for a different party for President than they do for the House or Senate, and 0 for straight-ticket voters (3,044; 3,045; 3,670; 3,673; 137; 998; 1,002; 425; 792; 798; 397; 768; 773).

For multiple imputation, we use a procedure called *Amelia* developed by Honaker et al. (2000). King et al. (2001) show that multiple imputation is more efficient and no more biased than listwise deletion, *regardless of the nature of the variables being imputed*. It is a misconception to assume that "objective" variables can be imputed, whereas "subjective" variables like attitudinal responses cannot. If attitudinal variables correlate with other observed variables, then the Expectation Maximization algorithm can impute them like any other variable. Gelman, King, and Liu (1999) also note that multiple imputation has the further benefit of permitting us to use data that was observed in only one year by estimating how respondents might have answered a question had it been asked in other years. This depends on the assumption that the same types of respondents (as reflected by their answers to other questions in the imputation model) would respond similarly to a question when it was not observed as when it was observed. This assumption may seem restrictive, but we note that it is also made implicitly for all pooled models (e.g., Timpone 1998), regardless of whether or not they use multiple imputation. We also note that multiple imputation estimates not only point values but the uncertainty of those imputations. Estimates are thus conservative in the sense that they are based on uncertainty from both the imputation and analysis models.

We include all variables from the turnout model in the imputation model for turnout and all variables from the vote choice model in the imputation model for vote choice. In both cases, we impute five datasets and use the analysis model to generate five sets of coefficients and standard errors. The final coefficients are simply the mean of the coefficients generated. Final standard errors must include uncertainty about the imputation, so they are the mean of the standard errors generated plus their variance across the datasets. For additional details, please refer to King et al. (2001).

APPENDIX: CHAPTER SIX

TIME-SHARING EXPERIMENTS IN THE SOCIAL SCIENCES (TESS) SURVEY INSTRUMENT

Imagine it is the year 2016. Suppose a U.S. presidential election is about to be held in which the two main candidates are a liberal Democrat and a conservative Republican. Given what you know about the election from media reports, poll results, and personal conversations, suppose that you expect . . .

[Draw a random integer v uniformly distributed from 35 to 65. If $v < 50$, give stimulus A. If $v > 50$, give stimulus B. If $v = 50$, give stimulus C.]

> STIMULUS A: *The Democrat to receive* [v] *percent of the vote and the Republican to receive only* [$1 - v$] *percent of the vote in the upcoming election.*

> STIMULUS B: *The Republican to receive* [$1 - v$] *percent of the vote and the Democrat to receive only* [v] *percent of the vote in the upcoming election.*

> STIMULUS C: *The Democrat and Republican each to receive 50 percent of the vote in the upcoming election.*

1) *Suppose you decide to vote. Would you choose the Democrat or the Republican? (I definitely would choose the Democrat./I probably would choose the Democrat./I probably would choose the Republican./I definitely would choose the Republican.)*

[Randomly choose question 2a or 2b. Randomly choose question 3a or 3b. Then randomize the order of these two randomly chosen questions]

Suppose the election occurs just as you expected. The Democrat receives [v] *percent of the vote and the Republican receives* [$1 - v$] *percent of the vote. How do you think the election results will affect policies supported by Republicans?*

2a) Republican politicians will try to enact laws that are (much more liberal, somewhat more liberal, about the same, somewhat more conservative, much more conservative).

Suppose the election occurs just as you expected. The Democrat receives [v] *percent of the vote and the Republican receives* [$1 - v$] *percent of the vote. How do you think the election results will affect policies supported by Democrats?*

2b) Democratic politicians will try to enact laws that are (much more liberal, somewhat more liberal, about the same, somewhat more conservative, much more conservative).

Suppose the election occurs just as you expected. The Democrat receives [v] percent of the vote and the Republican receives [1 − v] percent of the vote. How do you think the election results will affect future Republican candidates?

3a) In future elections, Republican candidates will be (much more liberal, somewhat more liberal, about the same, somewhat more conservative, much more conservative).

Suppose the election occurs just as you expected. The Democrat receives [v] percent of the vote and the Republican receives [1 − v] percent of the vote. How do you think the election results will affect future Democratic candidates?

3b) In future elections, Democratic candidates will be (much more liberal, somewhat more liberal, about the same, somewhat more conservative, much more conservative).

Imagine it is the year 2024. Suppose a different U.S. presidential election is about to be held in which the two main candidates are a Democrat and a Republican. Given what you know about the election from media reports, poll results, and personal conversations, suppose that in this new election you expect . . .

[Repeat experiment a second time with new randomly drawn stimulus. Repeat quions 1–3 (keep the same randomly drawn questions in 2 and 3 and number them 4–6.]

7) Generally speaking, do you usually think of yourself as a Republican, a Democrat, or an independent?

APPENDIX: CHAPTER SEVEN

VARIABLE DESCRIPTION AND QUESTION WORDING

The discount factor is based on behavior in the choice game. The game was described to subjects as follows: "A prize will be awarded in class at the conclusion of this study. If you are chosen to receive the prize, your answers to the following series of questions will determine the amount of the award and the date of payment. You will be asked to choose the payment option that you would prefer in each of 20 different payoff alternatives. Note that each of the 20 payoff alternatives will pay $100 in 30 days (option A) or $100 + $x in 60 days (option B), where x differs under each payoff alternative. For each payoff alternative, you will select the payment option (A or B) that you would prefer if you are chosen to receive the prize. When the study is completed, a random drawing will be held in class to choose which one of the 20 payoff alternatives will determine the prize and another random drawing will be held to determine the one person who will receive the second prize. When and how much the winner will be paid will be based on the payment option he or she chooses under the payoff alternative selected.

"In the table of alternatives there is a column labeled "Annual Interest Rate." This is the interest rate required on the initial balance of $100 (option A) that would yield the amount in option B, after accounting for the fact that interest is compounded daily on the initial balance. For comparison, most banks are currently paying 1% to 2% interest on savings accounts or certificates of deposits. Most credit card companies are charging college students 12% to 16% interest to borrow money. Thus, you have an opportunity to earn money at much higher rates of interest in this study. Below is the table of the payment options for the 20 different alternatives. For payoff alternative 1, would you prefer option A ($100 in 30 days) or option B ($100.17 in 60 days)?" Subjects were asked to make choices over twenty sets of alternatives. Table A-7.1 shows each set of alternatives as they were displayed to the subjects.

Political information is the number of correct answers to the following eight multiple choice and open-answer questions. "Which party currently has the most members in the House of Representatives in Washington?" (Republican/Democrat) "Which party currently has the most members in the Senate in Washington?" (Republican/Democrat) "Who has the final responsibility to decide if a law is constitutional or not?" (President/Congress/Supreme Court) "Whose responsibility is it to nominate judges to the Federal Courts?" (President/Congress/Supreme Court) "What is the job held

TABLE A-7.1   Choices Available to Participants in the Experiment

Payoff Alternative	Payment Option A (pays amount below in 30 days)	Payment Option B (pays amount below in 60 days)	Annual Interest Rate	Payment Option Preferred (choose A or B)
1	$100.00	$100.17	2.0%	A B
2	$100.00	$100.25	3.0%	A B
3	$100.00	$100.33	4.0%	A B
4	$100.00	$100.42	5.0%	A B
5	$100.00	$100.63	7.5%	A B
6	$100.00	$100.84	10.0%	A B
7	$100.00	$101.05	12.5%	A B
8	$100.00	$101.26	15.0%	A B
9	$100.00	$101.47	17.5%	A B
10	$100.00	$101.68	20.0%	A B
11	$100.00	$102.10	25.0%	A B
12	$100.00	$102.96	35.0%	A B
13	$100.00	$104.25	50.0%	A B
14	$100.00	$106.44	75.0%	A B
15	$100.00	$108.68	100.0%	A B
16	$100.00	$110.96	125.0%	A B
17	$100.00	$113.29	150.0%	A B
18	$100.00	$115.66	175.0%	A B
19	$100.00	$118.08	200.0%	A B
20	$100.00	$123.07	250.0%	A B

by William Rehnquist?" "What is the job held by Tony Blair?" "What is the job held by John Ashcroft?" "What is the job held by Bill Frist?"

Reads the News and Watches the News were based on answers to these two questions: "During the past week, about how many days did you read a daily newspaper (other than the CALIFORNIA AGGIE) or consult an online news source?" and "During the past week, about how many days did you watch a national network news program on television?"

Parents' Income is the answer to: "Please choose the category that describes the total amount of INCOME earned in 2003 by your PARENTS or GUARDIANS. Consider all forms of income, including salaries, tips, interest and dividend payments, scholarship support, student loans, parental support, social security, alimony, and child support, and others." (1=$15,000 or under, 2= $15,001−$25,000, 3=$25,001−$35,000, 4=$35,001−$50,000, 5=$50,001 − $65,000,   6=$65,001−$80,000,   7=$80,001−$100,000, 8=over $100,000). Parents' Education is the average for both parents on "What was the highest level of education that your father [mother] (or male [female] guardian) completed?" 1=Less than high school, 2=High school diploma, 3=Vocational school, 4=Attended college, 5=Bachelor's, 6=Graduate school.

For external efficacy, we follow Craig, Niemi and Silver (1990) and Niemi, Craig, and Mattei (1991) by creating an index that sums responses from four questions: "People like me don't have any say about what the government does," "I don't think public officials care much what people like me think," "How much do you feel that having elections makes the government pay attention to what the people think?", and "Over the years, how much attention do you feel the government pays to what the people think when it decides what to do?" The first two questions are coded 0=agree, 0.5=neither, and 1=disagree in 1976–1984. For 1988, they are 0=agree strongly, 0.25=agree somewhat, 0.5=neither, 0.75=disagree somewhat, and 1=disagree strongly. The third and fourth questions are coded 1=a good deal, 0.5=some, and 0=not much.

For the remaining variables, we follow the coding procedure in Timpone (1998) and the question wording used in the *National Election Studies*. Age is in number of years. Married is 1 for married and 0 for all others. Church attendance is an index of religious attendance, 1=never/no religious preference, 2=a few times a year, 3=once or twice a month, 4=almost every week, and 5=every week. Internal efficacy is a binary response (0=true, 1=false) to the question "Sometimes politics and government seem so complicated that a person like me can't really understand what's going on." Strength of party identification is coded 1=independents and apoliticals, 2=independents leaning towards a party, 3=weak partisans, and 4=strong partisans. Civic duty is coded 1=agree strongly, 2=agree somewhat, 3=neither, 4=disagree somewhat, and 5=disagree strongly for "If a person doesn't care how an election comes out he shouldn't vote in it." Female is 1 for female, 0 for male. Race is 1 for black, 0 for others. Interest in Politics is the answer to the question "Some people don't pay much attention to political campaigns. How interested are you in the 2004 presidential election campaign?" (1=not much interested, 2=somewhat interested, 3=very much interested).

APPENDIX: CHAPTER EIGHT

Tables A-8.1 and A-8.2 explain how data used in the statistical models are derived from futures prices. Panels are based on the following periods: 6/10/88–11/9/88, 1/22/92–11/4/92, 6/21/94–11/9/94, 1/2/96–11/6/96, 2/3/98–11/4/98, 1/3/00–11/10/00, 7/20/02–11/6/02. These periods start on the first day in which at least one bond futures price and one election futures contract price are observed within the year of the election and they end the day the election outcome is known. Iowa Electronic Markets (IEM) records daily historical data prices at midnight after the market has absorbed all the prime-time news. This contrasts with financial markets that close in the afternoon before critical campaign information is released. Therefore, electoral probabilities are lagged by one day relative to interest rates to make sure that today's financial markets know about yesterday evening's political news. This should also address concerns about possible endogeneity.

A major difficulty with approaches based on monthly data (such as Cohen 1993) is that they assume a one-month lag in economic variables because the market gets data for the prior month. However, based on release dates published in the Bureau of Labor Statistics, CPI data has been released as late as eight weeks after-the-fact. Therefore, these models probably give the market more prescience than it actually has. To solve this problem, unrevised control data are matched with release dates to specify precisely when the market receives the information. This is especially important since the tests here are based on daily data.

Incumbent probabilities are not observed but they can be derived given partisan probabilities and information about the incumbent parties. Let I_P, $I_C \in \{0,1\}$ denote the current party in the presidency and the Congress (0 for Republicans and 1 for Democrats). The probability of the challenger party winning the presidency is $p_{ch,P} = ((1-I_P)p_P + I_P(1-p_P))$ and the probability of the challenger party winning the Congress is $p_{ch,C} = ((1-I_C)p_C + I_C(1-p_C))$.

The number of observations for each panel varies depending on trading volume, contract availability, and rules regarding the first date a contract may be traded. As a result, if we use listwise deletion for the analysis, missingness in the data forces us to eliminate most of the observations in the data set. One possible solution is to eliminate some of the independent variables from consideration. However, missingness in the dependent variable is correlated with several of the independent variables, suggesting that listwise deletion may cause omitted variable bias. Thus, we follow the advice of King et al. (2001) who recommend multiple imputation as a

TABLE A-8.1   Economic and Futures Market

| | Observations | | | | | | | |
Variable	1988	1992	1994	1996	1998	2000	2002	Description
3-month maturity	107	201	100	204	163	60	53	Change in future 3-month Treasury bill yield in percent. Calculated as (100 – futures price).
2-year maturity	—	102	81	93	89	69	66	Change in future 2-year Treasury note yield in percent. Calculated as the effective yield at the current futures price of a 2-year bond with a biennial coupon of 8 percent.
5-year maturity	107	170	100	159	142	97	78	Change in 5-year Treasury note future yield in percent. Calculated as the effective yield at the current futures price of a 5-year bond with a biennial coupon of 8 percent for 1988–1998 and 6 percent for 2000.
10-year maturity	107	200	100	216	191	114	78	Change in 10-year Treasury note future yield in percent. Calculated as the effective yield at the current futures price of a 10-year bond with a biennial coupon of 8 percent for 1988–1998 and 6 percent for 2000.
30-year maturity	107	200	100	216	191	216	78	Change in 30-year Treasury note future yield in percent. Calculated as the effective yield at the current futures price of a 30-year bond with a biennial coupon of 8 percent for 1988–1998 and 6 percent for 2000.
M1	153	288	142	310	275	311	112	Most recent one week rate of growth in the M1 money supply as reported by the Federal Reserve Board.
Inflation	153	288	142	310	275	311	112	Most recent one month rate of growth in the consumer price index as reported by the Bureau of Labor Statistics.
Unemployment	153	288	142	310	275	311	112	Most recent unemployment rate as reported by the Bureau of Labor Statistics.
Industrial production	153	288	142	310	275	311	112	Most recent one month rate of growth in the industrial production index as reported by the Federal Reserve Board.

TABLE A-8.2   Election Futures Variables

Variables	Panels	Observations	Description
Probability	1994	142	[HM.DEM+(1 − HM.REP)]/2
Left wins	1996	93	[RH.lose +(1 − (RH.hold+RH.gain)) +
House (p_C)	1998	274	(NhNs +NhRs)+(1 − (RhRs +RhNs)]/4
	2000	309	"
	2002	112	"
			"
Probability	1992	117	[P.CL + (1 − (P.BU + P.PE)]/2
Left wins	1994	142	1
presidency	1996	310	[(CLIN + OTDEM) + (1 − (REP + ROF96)]/2
(p_P)	1998	275	1
	2000	189	[Dem + (1 − (Rep + Reform)]/2
	2002	112	0
Democratic	1988	153	[(Dukakis + Jackson)/(Dukakis + Jackson + Bush)]
presidential	1992	288	[(D.BR + D.CL + D.HA + D.KE + D.RF + D.TS) +
Vote			(1 − R.BU)]/2
Share (μ)	1996	276	[V.CLIN + (1 − V.DOLE)]/2
	2000	305	[DemVS/(DemVS + RepVS)]

Note: Negative implied values and implied values greater than one are set to zero and one, respectively. Abbreviations in calculations for probabilities and vote shares based on election futures contracts are taken directly from Iowa Electronic Markets (http://www.biz.uiowa.edu/iem/archive/historicaldata.html).

superior alternative to listwise deletion. The imputation model is based on the Expectations Maximization algorithm with importance sampling and includes all of the variables used in the analysis model. Specifically, this means we include variables for the yields implied by two- and five-year treasury futures, variables related to electoral probabilities and vote share $(p_P, p_C, p_P p_C, p_P (1-p_P), p_C(1-p_C), cov(p_P, p_C), ((1-I_P)p_P + I_P(1-p_P)), ((1-I_C)p_C + I_C(1-p_C)), I_P, I_C, \mu, \mu^2$ and economic controls $(M1, CPI, UE, IP)$. To improve estimation, the imputation model also includes variables for yields implied by 3-month, 10-year, and 30-year treasury futures.

To deal with serial correlation, the imputation model assumes an ADL(1,1) structure to the data. Lagrange Multiplier Tests in the unimputed data suggest that one lag of each of the variables is sufficient to reduce serial correlation to insignificance. Note that there is only one observation (the election outcome) for p_C in 1988 and 1992 so all these data are imputed. However, Table A-8.3 shows that model results are not substantively different when these two elections are excluded. Election Day changes in electoral probabilities are much larger than typical changes prior to Election Day, but

TABLE A-8.3   Impact of Electoral Outcomes on Interest Rates 1994–2002

		Two-Year Maturity			Five-Year Maturity		
		MLE	95% CI		MLE	95% CI	
Model coefficients							
α	Change	0.74	0.63	0.87	0.72	0.14	0.88
	Lagged level	0.55	0.00	0.77	0.50	0.44	0.60
$\pi_D - \pi_R$	Change	2.09	1.24	2.71	1.76	0.94	2.51
	Lagged level	2.93	1.74	3.52	2.71	2.02	3.17
S	Change	1.19	−0.14	2.61	1.03	0.04	2.17
	Lagged level	2.32	1.06	3.54	1.46	0.45	2.48
$\sigma_D - \sigma_R$	Change	¬0.31	−1.27	0.77	−0.47	−1.37	0.83
	Lagged level	−1.31	−1.89	−0.24	−1.58	−2.01	−0.92
σ_R	Change	0.74	0.10	1.90	0.81	−0.03	2.20
	Lagged level	0.95	0.56	1.36	1.07	0.78	1.42
σ_S	Change	20.99	6.38	35.81	14.33	2.15	26.85
	Lagged level	34.18	15.01	53.31	21.94	7.07	36.87
$\sigma_{ch,p}$	Change	0.49	−0.07	1.13	0.51	0.02	0.93
	Lagged level	−0.04	−0.41	0.46	−0.13	−0.41	0.16
$\sigma_{ch,H}$	Change	0.56	0.11	0.95	0.57	0.26	0.89
	Lagged level	−0.25	−0.82	0.61	−0.46	−0.83	0.02
Economic controls							
M1	Change	−0.03	−0.09	0.02	−0.01	−0.05	0.03
	Lagged level	−0.03	−0.06	0.01	−0.02	−0.05	0.00
Inflation	Change	0.05	−0.34	0.48	0.06	−0.23	0.38
	Lagged level	0.18	0.06	0.30	0.03	−0.05	0.13
Unemployment	Change	−0.41	−1.06	0.16	−0.19	−0.66	0.26
	Lagged level	−0.06	−0.12	0.01	0.01	−0.02	0.05
Industrial	Change	0.00	−0.12	0.11	−0.01	−0.09	0.08
production	Lagged level	−0.06	−0.10	−0.03	−0.04	−0.07	−0.01
Technical parameters							
Lagged dependent	Change	−0.14	−0.19	−0.09	−0.11	−0.16	−0.06
Variable	Level	−0.38	−0.43	−0.32	−0.27	−0.33	−0.22
Constant		−0.29	−0.95	0.38	−0.23	−0.76	0.30
σ_Y		0.23	0.21	0.25	0.17	0.15	0.19
η		6.88	4.56	13.07	4.11	2.98	6.18
Mean log likelihood		−113.78			94.46		
LaGrange Multiplier Test (effect of ε_{t-1} on ε_t)		−0.02	−0.08	0.04	−0.02	−0.08	0.04

Note: Maximum likelihood estimates of coefficients in equation (7) using an error correction model and restricting attention to the 1994–2002 elections. Confidence intervals calculated from profile likelihood.

TABLE A-8.4 Impact of Electoral Outcomes on Market Prices Interest Rates (without Outliers)

Dependent Variable: Expected Post-Electoral Nominal Interest Rates

	Symbol		Two-Year Maturity			Five-Year Maturity		
			MLE	95% CI		MLE	95% CI	
Model coefficients								
Relative influence of Presidency	α	Change	0.53	0.47	0.60	0.47	0.53	0.39
		Level	0.53	0.47	0.74	0.43	0.51	0.37
Partisan difference in inflation	$\pi_D - \pi_R$	Change	3.40	2.87	3.85	2.43	1.88	2.89
		Level	3.23	2.49	3.73	2.51	2.03	2.90
Partisan difference in inflation risk	$\sigma_D - \sigma_R$	Change	-2.04	-2.60	-1.39	-1.40	-1.87	-0.93
		Level	-2.10	-2.59	-1.39	-1.78	-2.11	-1.34
Republican inflation risk minus partisan covariance	$\sigma_R - c_{DR}$	Change	1.80	1.44	2.21	1.14	0.79	1.53
		Level	1.66	1.29	2.05	1.27	0.99	1.60
Effect of challenger party in Presidency	$\sigma_{ch,P}$	Change	-0.18	-0.59	0.14	0.26	0.03	0.55
		Level	-0.51	-0.75	0.30	-0.12	-0.27	0.01
Effect of challenger party in House	$\sigma_{ch,H}$	Change	0.52	0.24	0.82	0.40	0.07	0.80
		Level	-0.16	-0.71	0.48	-0.36	-0.71	0.10
Effect of mandate on inflation	s	Change	1.16	0.11	2.60	1.03	0.28	2.08
		Level	2.00	1.04	3.18	1.46	0.59	2.35
Effect of mandate on inflation risk	σ_S	Change	41.12	24.77	57.65	23.45	11.21	35.89
		Level	52.88	32.75	73.41	29.48	14.57	44.27
Economic controls								
M1	β_{M1}	Change	0.00	-0.07	0.06	0.00	-0.04	0.04
		Level	-0.02	-0.06	0.01	-0.01	-0.04	0.01
Inflation	B_{CPI}	Change	0.25	-0.20	0.72	0.05	-0.26	0.37
		Level	-0.06	-0.17	0.08	0.00	-0.08	0.10
Unemployment	B_{UE}	Change	-0.17	-0.83	0.41	-0.20	-0.63	0.13
		Level	-0.15	-0.20	-0.10	-0.04	-0.07	-0.01

TABLE A-8.4 (Cont.)

Dependent Variable: Expected Post-Electoral Nominal Interest Rates

	Symbol		Two-Year Maturity		Five-Year Maturity	
			MLE	95% CI	MLE	95% CI
Industrial production	B_{IP}	Change	0.01	-0.11 0.13	0.00	-0.08 0.08
		Level	-0.02	-0.05 0.01	-0.02	-0.05 0.00
Technical parameters						
Lagged dependent variable		Change	-0.23	-0.27 -0.19	-0.14	-0.19 -0.09
		Level	-0.34	-0.39 -0.29	-0.19	-0.24 -0.15
Constant			0.37	-0.23 0.96	-0.20	-0.62 0.21
σ_Y			0.28	0.26 0.30	0.18	0.16 0.20
η			5.80	4.32 8.34	2.39	1.94 3.01
Mean log likelihood			-493.96		-248.64	
Lagrange multiplier test (effect of ε_{t-1} on ε_t)			0.34	-0.05 0.72	0.31	-0.10 0.69

Table A-8.4 shows that when these outliers are excluded the substantive results remain the same.

To estimate the covariance $\text{cov}(p_P, p_C)$ in the model, we use the product moment of the two probability estimates at each time point during the election period measured under the assumption that it remains fixed for each election. Although we can estimate the difference in inflation risk for the two parties $\sigma_D - \sigma_R$, neither the absolute level of inflation risk σ_R nor the covariance in inflation risk between the two parties c_{DR} can be estimated separately. These two parameters always appear together as the term $\sigma_R - c_{DR}$ in equation (5), which causes the model to become unidentified if we estimate them separately. The same technical difficulty also prevents us from estimating separate variances for each party by chamber.

Whereas, it is possible for serial correlation to affect the estimates, analysis of the cross-correlations at several lags suggests that it does not—they do not differ significantly from the zero-lag estimates. Robust covariance estimation with nearest neighbor variance (Wang and Raferty 2002) also yields similar results. Under all of these procedures, the range of the covariances across all elections is very close to zero $[-0.02, 0.01]$ and does not change significantly for different subsets of each election time series (e.g., the last 20 days before the election). This evidence suggests that covariance should not have much impact on the estimation since there is no evidence that it changes significantly over time. In other words, fixed covariance appears to be a reasonable assumption. The bottom line here is that the substantive findings would probably not change even if we knew the time-varying covariance with certainty.

Finally, it is important to note that one might have an ecological inference problem if we did not assume that the covariance remains fixed for a given election. However, if we do assume it is fixed, then we can use all of the individual daily observations of the electoral probabilities to estimate the covariance for the two series. If we did not impose this constraint, then there would be no way to go from the marginal probabilities p_P and p_C to the joint probability p_{DD}. By assuming the covariance is fixed, we essentially lock in the relationship between the marginal probabilities and the joint probabilities. In a more perfect world, we would observe the joint probabilities directly, but given that the estimated covariance does not appear to change much over time, it is doubtful that such observations would significantly change the results.

NOTES

CHAPTER ONE: INTRODUCTION

1. Although in an n-dimensional issue space, the behavior of policy-motivated candidates is better behaved with parties converging to a "minmax set," which either coincides with the Pareto optimal set or lies within its interior (Kramer 1977).

CHAPTER TWO: MOVING WITH THE MANDATE: POLICY-MOTIVATED PARTIES IN DYNAMIC POLITICAL COMPETITION

1. For notable exceptions, see Groseclose (2001) and Adams and Merrill (2003) who study the valence advantage in the context of Wittman equilibrium.

2. This choice of utility function is a standard approach for modeling policy-motivated candidates (cf., Wittman 1983; Calvert 1985; Duggan and Fey 2000).

3. A variety of mechanisms have been advanced to explain learning behavior. Although these vary in the degree of efficiency, many of them converge to Bayesian updating in the limit (Fudenberg and Levine 1997).

4. Notice also that the posterior variance β' is always less than the prior variance β since $\beta' = b\beta/(b+\beta)$ and $b/(b+\beta) < 1$. One implication of the result is that if preferences in the electorate are permanently fixed, then in the limit the posterior variance will approach zero and, therefore, the parties will know the location of the median voter with certainty, which would lead to platform convergence (cf., Duggan and Fey 2000). Letting the true location of the median voter be uncertain would prevent convergence, but we do not model this because it would require a fourth probability distribution and further unnecessary complexity without affecting the results.

5. Technically, the term "polarization" may be more appropriate for a bimodal distribution of voters. We use the term to describe the variance of a normal distribution due to its intuitive simplicity as opposed to such terms as the "spread" or "variance" of the electorate.

6. The set of parameters used in all the figures is $p_L = -1, p_R = 1, \mu = 0, s = 0.5, \beta = 0.25, b = 0.25$, and $B = 0.5$. The examples assume that prior platforms x_L, x_R are in equilibrium.

7. By "close enough" we mean that the result always holds for some set of perceived locations of the median voter near the midpoint between the preferences of the two parties. When the perceived median is not near the midpoint it means that one of the parties has preferences that are located much closer to the center of the voter distribution. Under these circumstances close elections may yield smaller divergence.

CHAPTER THREE: DYNAMIC RESPONSIVENESS IN THE U.S. SENATE

1. This dynamic has also been suggested in the literature on presidential mandates (see Stigler 1972; Kramer 1977; Stone 1980; Conley 2001).

2. Another implicit assumption is that parties tend to have polarized preferences. A wide variety of measures of ideology tend to corroborate this assumption—party leaders and candidates have preferences that are more extreme than rank-and-file party members (Iversen 1994; Hetherington 2001; Layman and Carsey 2002) who are in turn more extreme than the median voter (DiMaggio, Evans, and Bryson 1996; Abramowitz and Saunders 1998).

3. Poole notes that the first dimension explains 85% of the variation in roll-call votes, so restricting analysis to a single dimension may not be completely unrealistic.

4. Another difficulty with using House data is the decennial redistricting that takes place. Shifting district boundaries would weaken the relationship between the median voter implied by the previous election and the location of the median voter in the newly formed district.

5. Only elections in which both a Democrat and a Republican run are used (i.e., election results when one candidate runs election unopposed are excluded).

6. Because of overlap in the six-year terms, these cases can be divided into three groups. In 424 cases, the previous election occurred two years ago, in 384 cases, the previous election occurred four years ago, and in the remaining cases, there was an irregular time interval due to a special election in the current or the former period.

7. For example, the retrospective voting literature shows that economic performance—and not ideology—determines the fate of many incumbents (Fiorina 1978; Atkeson, Rae, and Partin 1995).

8. Mean Senate ideology is based on Common Space scores. Public policy mood data is available at James Stimson's website: http://www.unc.edu/~jstimson/.

9. Models with either state dummies alone or year dummies alone yield substantively identical results.

CHAPTER FOUR: DYNAMIC PARTIES AND SOCIAL TURNOUT: AN AGENT-BASED MODEL

1. $u_i = -(x_W - p_i)^2 - c$, where u_i is the utility of voter i, x_W is the platform of the winning party, p_i is the preference of voter i, and $c > 0$ is the cost of voting. If a citizen abstains, $c = 0$.

2. The location of the median voter m is the solution to the equation

$$s = \int_{-\infty}^{(x_L + x_R)/2} f(v \mid m)dv$$

where s is the vote share for the left party, x_L and x_R are the party platforms, and $f(v)$ is the voter distribution (which we assume to be normal with variance 1).

3. Unlike the model in Chapter 2, the model here is not based on the assumptions that politicians know the variance of the voter distribution. Instead, we assume that parties model the location of the median voter as though it were drawn from a normal distribution with unknown mean and variance. It is well known that under these conditions the expected median voter is the sample mean of all previous observations of the location of the median voter, and the variance in the expected median voter will be the sample variance.

4. As in Chapter 2 we assume that the expected payoff of each party is the probability of winning times the winning payoff plus the probability of losing times the losing payoff. Parties choose a set of equilibrium policies in which neither party can achieve a higher expected payoff by changing its platform. For a detailed description of the dynamic model of policy-motivated candidates under uncertainty and Wittman political equilibrium see the appendix for Chapter 2.

5. We assume voter preferences are independent and drawn from a standard normal distribution. Later in the chapter we will relax the independence assumption by assuming preferences are correlated between neighbors.

6. We assume a Moore neighborhood structure, which means individuals typically have 8 neighbors (top, bottom, left, right, top left, top right, bottom left, and bottom right). We also assume the grid is bounded, so individuals on the edges have fewer neighbors (e.g., an individual on the left edge has five neighbors—top, bottom, bottom right, top right, and bottom right).

7. There are several learning algorithms that we could choose to model this behavior, so we have deliberately chosen a simple one. Citizens have discussions with each of their neighbors and learn how satisfied they were (i.e., their utility) with the results of the previous election. Each citizen then estimates the average satisfaction with voting S^{vote} by summing the satisfaction of all voters in the neighborhood (including themselves, if applicable) and dividing by the number of voters. Similarly, they find the average satisfaction with abstaining $S^{abstain}$ by summing the satisfaction of all abstainers in the neighborhood (including themselves, if applicable) and dividing by the number of abstainers. If the number of voters or abstainers in the neighborhood is zero, then the individual repeats his or her action from the previous election.

8. It is important to emphasize here that while citizen decisions are deterministic in our model, the distribution of preferences is stochastic. Thus, utility itself is a random variable: a citizen in an n person neighborhood with v voters will vote in the next election with probability

$$\Pr\left(\frac{1}{v}\sum_{i=1}^{v} u^i > \frac{1}{n-v}\sum_{j=v+1}^{n-v} u^j \right).$$

9. The negative feedback mechanism not only leads to turnout when it is costly but also to abstention when it is not costly – in fact, even if we make the cost of voting negative (pay people to vote) – turnout will still be significantly less than 100% for this reason.

10. This may seem like a trivially small cost of voting, but consider the fact that the mean distance between the left and right party platforms in our sample is about 0.2. If voters must bear a cost of 0.1 in order to vote, they are paying one half of the total benefit they would receive if they could choose the election winner. For most of the formal models cited above, the highest cost-benefit ratios that would yield positive turnout are typically several orders of magnitude smaller than this.

11. Let M be a memory parameter. As above, citizens find the average satisfaction level of voting and abstaining for the current election, but they now weight the new information with previous estimates of the average satisfaction levels for voting and abstaining:

$$ s_{t+1}^{vote} = (1-M)\frac{1}{v}\sum_{i=1}^{v} u_t^i + Ms_t^i, \ s_{t+1}^{abstain} = (1-M)\frac{1}{a}\sum_{i=1}^{a} u_t^i + Ms_t^i $$

CHAPTER FIVE: A DYNAMIC CALCULUS OF VOTING

1. See also Lohmann 1993, Piketty 2000, Razin 2003, and Shotts 2000 for game-theoretic signaling models of participation.

2. Note that the literature on "protest voting" suggests that some citizens vote for a party other than their first choice in order to send a signal to one or both parties (e.g., Niemi, Whitten, and Franklin 1992; Heath and Evans 1994). In contrast, our model suggests that this signaling motivation exists for *all* citizens.

3. See Chapter 5 Appendix (equation 9) or Hamilton (1994: 443) for a more detailed explanation of persistence of innovations in unit root processes.

4. To be sure our reasoning applies to all citizens including those who may be moderates at time t and extremists at time $t + 1$ (or vice versa) we show that a citizen's type is technically determined in the election at time $t + 1$. See Proposition 3 in Chapter 5 Appendix.

5. One might argue that the discount factor could also be important for the pivotal motivation since benefits gained from a vote today may not accrue until well into the winner's term in office. However, the benefits from being pivotal will be less sensitive to the discount factor than the benefits related to the signaling motivation. Small changes in the discount factor may change the pivotal motivation directly through δ, but they will affect the signaling motivation through $\delta/(1-\delta)$. For example, a 1% change in δ from 0.9 to 0.91 changes the pivotal motivation by 1% but changes the signaling motivation by 12%.

6. This is similar to the measure of electoral expectations used in Scheve and Tomz (1999).

7. Including each of these categories as a dummy variable does not change the results.

8. Specifically, the NES is significantly ($p < .01$) more likely to try to validate respondents' votes if they are white, rich, well-educated, or own their homes. The NES is also less likely ($p < .01$) to validate votes in the south.

9. The models differ only in their uncertainty of the estimate. The model using listwise deletion suggests a 95% confidence interval of ± 5% whereas the model using multiple imputation suggests an interval of ± 3%.

CHAPTER SIX: PARTY RESPONSIVENESS AND MANDATE BALANCING

1. We do not have information about candidate or self-placement on the liberal conservative scale in the TESS data, but we do have data from the National Election Studies (NES). The NES cumulative file shows that nonpartisans are significantly more likely than partisans to self-identify as "moderate, middle of the road" (20.1% vs. 14.2%).

CHAPTER SEVEN: PATIENCE AND TURNOUT

1. The expressive benefits of voting and benefits related to fulfilling a social obligation may also play a role in the turnout decision, but controlling for these factors does not eliminate the influence of benefits related to the election outcome (Blais, Young, and Lapp 2000).

2. Although these experimental discount factors may be high relative to those implied by annual market rates of interest, they fall within the wide range of discount factors estimated by other scholars in the literature (see Frederick, Loewenstein, and O'Donoghue 2002 for a comprehensive review) and should still be useful for resolving whether or not people who prefer the earlier prize behave differently than people who prefer the later prize.

CHAPTER EIGHT: MARKETS AND MANDATES: HOW ELECTORAL MARGINS AFFECT THE ECONOMY

1. This may seem unreasonably simplistic to readers familiar with optimal pricing models. For example, Malinvaud (1974) provides a general equilibrium proof that the futures market price should be a function of consensus forecasts, the risk-free interest rate, and the risk premium associated with the aggregate risk factor of the futures position. However, Berg et al. (2003) and Berg, Nelson, and Rietz (2003) use Capital Asset Pricing Models to show that no risk adjustment is required for the IEM futures market because the risk-free rate in the market is zero and neither an aggregate risk factor nor a premium for one can exist.

REFERENCES

Abramowitz, Alan I., and Kyle L. Saunders. 1998. "Ideological Realignment in the US Electorate." *Journal of Politics* 60 (3): 634–652.

Abramson, Paul R. 1983. *Political Attributes in America: Formation and Change.* San Francisco: W. H. Freeman.

Adams, James, and Samuel Merrill, III. 2003. "Policy-seeking Motivations When One Platform Has a Valence Advantage: Strategic Implications and Empirical Applications to Presidential Elections." Manuscript. Santa Barbara: University of California.

Adams, James, Michael Clark, Lawrence Ezrow, and Garrett Glasgow. 2003. "Understanding Change and Stability in Party Ideologies: Do Parties Respond to Public Opinion or to Past Election results?" Manuscript. Santa Barbara: University of California.

Adler, Robert, Raisa Feldman, and Murad S. Taqqu, eds. 1998. *A Practical Guide to Heavy Tails: Statistical Techniques and Applications.* Boston: Birkhauser.

Aldrich, John H. 1993. "Rational Choice and Turnout." *American Journal of Political Science* 37 (1): 246–278.

Alesina, Alberto. 1987. "Macroeconomic Policy in a Two-Party System as a Repeated Game." *Quarterly Journal of Economics* 102: 651–678.

Alesina, Alberto, and Howard Rosenthal. 1995. *Partisan Politics, Divided Government, and the Economy.* New York: Cambridge University Press.

Alesina, Alberto, and Howard Rosenthal. 1996. "A Theory of Divided Government." *Econometrica* 64 (November): 1311–1341.

Alesina, Alberto, John Londregan, and Howard Rosenthal. 1993. "A Model of the Political Economy of the United States." *American Political Science Review* 87 (March): 12–33.

Alesina, Alberto, Nouriel Roubini, and Gerald D. Cohen. 1997. *Political Cycles and the Macroeconomy.* Cambridge: MIT Press.

Alt, James E., and Robert C. Lowry. 1994. "Divided Government, Fiscal Institutions, and Budget Deficits—Evidence from the States." *American Political Science Review* 88 (4): 811–828.

Alvarez, R. Michael. 1997. *Information and Elections.* Ann Arbor: University of Michigan Press.

Alvarez, R. Michael, and Jonathan Nagler. 2000. "A New Approach for Modeling Strategic Voting in Multiparty Elections." *British Journal of Political Science* 30: s57–75.

Ansolabehere, Stephen, James M. Snyder, and C. Stewart. 2001a. "Candidate Positioning in U.S. House Elections." *American Journal of Political Science* 45 (1): 136–159.

Ansolabehere, Stephen, James M. Snyder, and C. Stewart. 2001b. "The Effects of Party and Preferences on Congressional Roll-Call Voting." *Legislative Studies Quarterly* 26 (4): 533–572.

Arnold, R. Douglas. 1990. *The Logic of Congressional Action.* New Haven: Yale University Press.

Atkeson, Lonna Rae, and Randall W. Partin. 1995. "Economic and Referendum Voting— A Comparison of Gubernatorial and Senatorial Elections." *American Political Science Review* 89 (1): 99–107.

Axelrod, Robert. 1997. *The Complexity of Cooperation: Agent-Based Models of Competition and Collaboration.* Princeton: Princeton University Press.

Bachman, Daniel. 1992. "The Effect of Political Risk on the Forward Exchange Rate Bias: The Case of Elections." *Journal of International Money and Finance* 11: 208–219.

Barro, Robert J. 1976. "Rational Expectations and the Role of Monetary Policy." *Journal of Monetary Economics* 2:1–32.

Bartels, Larry M. 1991. "Constituency Opinion and Congressional Policy Making—The Reagan Defense Buildup." *American Political Science Review* 85 (2): 456–474.

Bartels, Larry M., and John Zaller. 2001. "Al Gore and George Bush's Not-So-Excellent Adventure—Presidential Vote Models: A Recount." *PS: Political Science & Politics* 34 (1): 8–20.

Baxter, Marianne. 1989. "The Neoclassical Approach to Unprecedented Policies: The 1979 Change in Federal Reserve Operating Procedures." *Carnegie-Rochester Conference Series on Public Policy* 31: 247–296.

Beck, Nathaniel. 1992. "Comparing Dynamic Specifications: The Case of Presidential Approval." *Political Analysis* 3: 51–87.

Beck, Nathaniel, and Jonathan Katz. 1995. "What To Do (and Not to Do) with Time-Series-Cross-Section Data in Comparative Politics." *American Political Science Review* 89 (3): 634–647.

Beck, Paul Allen, Russell J. Dalton, Steven Greene, and Robert Huckfeldt. 2002. "The Social Calculus of Voting: Interpersonal, Media, and Organizational Influences on Presidential Choices." *American Political Science Review* 96: 57–74.

Becker, G. S., and C. B. Mulligan. 1997. "The Endogenous Determination of Time Preference." *Quarterly Journal of Economics* 112 (3): 729–758.

Bendor, Jonathan, Daniel Diermeier, and Michael Ting. 2003. "A Behavioral Model of Turnout." *American Political Science Review* 97 (2): 261–280.

Benninga, Simon, and Aris Protopapadakis. 1983. "Real and Nominal Interest Rates Under Uncertainty: The Fisher Theorem and the Term Structure." *Journal of Political Economy* 91: 856–867.

Berch, Neil. 1993. "Another Look at Closeness and Turnout—The Case of the 1979 and 1980 Canadian National Elections." *Political Research Quarterly* 46: 421–432.

Berelson, Bernard, Paul F. Lazarsfeld, and William N. McPhee. 1954. *Voting.* Chicago: University of Chicago Press.

Berg, Joyce, Robert Forsythe, and Thomas A. Rietz. 1997. "What Makes Markets Predict Well? Evidence from the Iowa Electronic Markets." In *Understanding Strategic*

Interaction: Essays in Honor of Reinhard Selten, W. Guth, ed., 444–463. West Berlin: Springer-Verlag.

Berg, Joyce, Forrest Nelson, and Thomas A. Rietz. 2003. "Accuracy and Forecast Standard Error of Prediction Markets." Working paper (July).

Berg, Joyce, Forrest Nelson, Robert Forsythe, and Thomas A. Rietz. "Results from a Decade of Election Futures Markets Research." In *Handbook of Experimental Economic Results*, Charles A. Plott and Vernon Smith, eds New York: Elsevier, forthcoming.

Berger, Bennett M. 1960. *Working-Class Suburb: A Study of Auto Workers in Suburbia.* Berkeley: University of California Press.

Bernhard, William and David Leblang. 2002. "Democratic Processes, Political Risk, and Foreign Exchange Markets." *American Journal of Political Science* 46 (2): 316–333.

Bernhard, W. T., B. Sala, and T. Nokken. 2002. "Strategic Senators and House Elections." Mimeo, University of Illinois at Urbana-Champaign.

Blais, A., R. Young, and M. Lapp. 2000. "The Calculus of Voting: An Empirical Test." *European Journal of Political Research* 37 (2): 181–201.

Blomberg, S. Brock, and Gregory Hess. 1997. "Politics and Exchange Rate Forecasts." *Journal of International Economics* 43 (1/2): 189–205.

Bohm, Peter, and Joakim Sonnegaard. 1999. "Political Stock Markets and Unreliable Polls." *Scandinavian Journal of Economics* 101: 205–222.

Boix, Charles. 1997. "Privatizing the Public Business Sector in the Eighties: Economic Performance, Partisan Responses and Divided Governments." *British Journal of Political Science* 27 (October): 473–496.

Bowling, Cynthia J., and Margaret R. Ferguson. 2001. "Divided Government, Interest Representation, and Policy Differences: Competing Explanations of Gridlock in the Fifty States." *Journal of Politics* 63 (February): 182–206.

Box, George E. P., and George C. Tiao. 1973. *Bayesian Inference in Statistical Analysis.* Reading, MA: Addison-Wesley Publishing Company.

Boyd, Richard W. 1989. "The Effects of Primaries and Statewide Races on Voter Turnout." *Journal of Politics* 51 (3): 730–739.

Boyd, Robert, and Peter J. Richerson. 1985. *Culture and the Evolutionary Process.* Chicago: University of Chicago Press.

Brody, Richard A., and Benjamin I. Page. 1973. "Indifference, Alienation and Rational Decisions: The Effects of Candidate Evaluations on Turnout and the Vote." *Public Choice* 15: 1–18.

Calvert, Randall L. 1985. "Robustness of the Multidimensional Voting Model: Platform Motivations, Uncertainty, and Convergence." *American Journal of Political Science* 29 (1): 69–95.

Camerer, C. F., and R. M. Hogarth. 1999. "The Effects of Financial Incentives in Experiments: A Review and Capital-Labor-Production Framework." *Journal of Risk and Uncertainty* 19 (1–3): 7–42.

Campbell, A. 1960. "Surge and Decline: A Study of Electoral Change." *Public Opinion Quarterly* 24: 379–418.

Campbell, Angus, Philip E. Converse, Warren E. Miller, and Donald E. Stokes. 1960. *The American Voter.* New York: Wiley.

Campbell, Angus, Gerald Gurin, and Warren E. Miller. 1954. *The Voter Decides.* Evanston: Row, Peterson and Company.

Campbell, James E. 1992. "Forecasting the Presidential Vote in the States," *American Journal of Political Science* 36: 386–407.

Campbell, James E., and Garand, James C., eds. 2000. *Before the Vote: Forecasting American National Elections.* Thousand Oaks, CA: Sage.

Carlsen, Fredrik. 1998. "Rational Partisan Theory: Empirical Evidence for the United States." *Southern Economic Journal* 65 (July): 64–82.

Carlsen, Fredrik, and Elin F. Pedersen. 1999. "Rational Partisan Theory: Evidence from Seven OECD Economies." *Economics and Politics* 11 (1): 13–32.

Casela, George, and Roger L. Berger. 2002. *Statistical Inference.* Pacific Grove, CA: Duxbury.

Cassel, C., and Luskin, R. 1988. "Simple Explanations of Turnout Decline." *American Political Science Review* 82:1321–1330.

Cave, Damien. 2004. *Flip-Flopper.* New York Times, December 26, 2004, 5.

Chappell, Henry W., Jr., and William R. Keech. 1988. "The Unemployment Consequences of Partisan Monetary Policy." *Southern Economic Journal* 55: 107–122.

Chappell, Henry W., Jr., and William R. Keech. 1986. "Policy Motivation and Party Differences in a Dynamic Spatial Model of Party Competition." *American Political Science Review* 80: 881–899

Clark, William R., and Mark Hallerberg. 2000. "Mobile Capital, Domestic Institutions, and Electorally Induced Monetary and Fiscal Policy." *American Political Science Review* 94 (June): 323–346.

Cohen, Gerald D. 1993. "Pre- and Post-Electoral Macroeconomic Fluctuations." PhD diss., Harvard Univ.

Coleman, John J. 1999. "Unified Government, Divided Government, and Party Responsiveness." *American Political Science Review* 93 (December): 821–835.

Coller, Maribeth, and Melonie B. Williams. 1999. "Eliciting Individual Discount Rates." *Experimental Economics* 2: 107–127.

Conley, Patricia. 2001. *Presidential Mandates: How Elections Shape the National Agenda.* Chicago: University of Chicago Press.

Cosmides, Leda, and John Tooby. 1996. "Are Humans Good Intuitive Statisticians After All? Rethinking Some Conclusions from the Literature on Judgment under Uncertainty." *Cognition* 58: 1–73.

Cox, Gary. 1984. "An Expected Utility Model of Electoral Competition." *Quality and Quantity* 18: 337–349.

Cox, Gary W., and Munger Michael C. 1989. "Closeness, Expenditures, and Turnout in the 1982 United-States House Elections." *American Political Science Review* 83 (1): 217–231.

Cox, John C., Jonathan E. Ingersoll, and Stephen A. Ross. 1985. "A Theory of the Term Structure of Interest Rates." *Econometrica* 53: 385–408.

Craig, S. C., and M. A. Maggiotto. 1982. "Measuring Political Efficacy." *Political Methodology* 8: 85–110.

Craig, Stephen C., Richard G. Niemi, and Glenn E. Silver. 1990. "Political Efficacy and Trust: A Report on the NES Pilot Study Items." *Political Behavior* 12: 289–314.

Cutler, David M., James M. Poterba, and Lawrence H. Summers. 1989. "What Moves Stock Prices?" *The Journal of Portfolio Management* 15: 4–12.

Dahl, Robert A. 1990. "Myth of the Presidential Mandate." *Political Science Quarterly* 105 (3): 355–372.

Davis, Otto, M. J. Hinich, and P. C. Ordeshook, 1970. "An Expository Development of a Mathematical Model of the Electoral Process." *American Political Science Review* 64: 426–448.

De Marchi, Scott. 2005. *Computational and Mathematical Modeling in the Social Sciences.* New York: Cambridge University Press.

Dew-Becker, Ian. 2006. "Kalman Learning and Downsian Competition: How Do Politicians Learn about Voters' Preferences?" Working paper, Northwestern University.

DiMaggio, Paul, John Evans, and Bethany Bryson. 1996. "Have Americans' Social Attitudes Become More Polarized?" *American Journal of Sociology* 102 (3): 690–755.

Downs, Anthony. 1957. *An Economic Theory of Democracy.* New York: Harper Collins.

Duggan, John, and Mark Fey. 2005. "Electoral Competition with Policy-Motivated Candidates." *Games and Economic Behavior* 51: 490–522.

Durlauf, Steven N. 2001. "A Framework for the Study of Individual Behavior and Social Interactions," *Sociological Methodology* 31: 47–87.

Edwards, George C., Andrew Barrett, and Jeffrey S. Peake. 1997. "The Legislative Impact of Divided Government." *American Journal of Political Science* 41 (April): 545–563.

Epstein, David, and Sharyn O'Halloran. 1996. "Divided Government and the Design of Administrative Procedures: A Formal Model and Empirical Test." *Journal of Politics* 58 (May): 373–397.

Erikson, Robert S. 1989. "Economic Conditions and the Presidential Vote." *American Political Science Review* 83: 567–573.

Erikson, Robert S., and Christopher Wlezian. 1994. "Forecasting the Presidential Vote, 1992." *Political Methodologist* 5: 10–11.

Estrella, Arturo, and Gikas A. Hardouvelis. 1991. "The Term Structure as a Predictor of Real Economic Activity." *Journal of Finance* 46 (2): 555–576.

Estrella, Arturo, and Frederic S. Mishkin. 1998. "Predicting US Recessions: Financial Variables as Leading Indicators." *Review of Economics and Statistics* 80 (1): 45–61.

Fair, Ray C. 1978. "The Effect of Economic Events on Votes for President." *Review of Economics and Statistics* 60: 59–172.

Fair, Ray C. 1996. "Econometrics and Presidential Elections." *Journal of Economic Perspectives* 10: 89–102.

Feddersen, Timothy J., and Wolfgang Pesendorfer. 1996. "The Swing Voter's Curse." *American Economic Review* 86: 408–424.

Fenno, Richard F., Jr. 1978. *Home Style: House Members in Their Districts.* Boston: Little, Brown.

Fenno, Richard F., Jr. 1986. "Observation, Context, and Sequence in the Study of Politics." *American Political Science Review* 80 (1): 3–15.

Fenster, Mark J. 1994. "The Impact of Allowing Day of Registration Voting on Turnout in United-States Elections from 1960 to 1992—A Research Note." *American Politics Quarterly* 22 (1): 74–87.

Ferejohn, John, and Morris Fiorina. 1974. "The Paradox of Not Voting: A Decision Theoretic Analysis." *American Political Science Review* 68: 525–536.

Finkel, Steven E. 1987. "The Effects of Participation on Political Efficacy and Political Support: Evidence from a West German Panel." *Journal of Politics* 49: 441–464.

Fiorina, Morris P. 1977. "*Congress, Keystone of the Washington Establishment.*" New Haven: Yale University Press.

Fiorina, Morris P. 1978. "Economic Retrospective Voting in American National Elections—Microanalysis." *American Journal of Political Science* 22 (2): 426–443.

Fiorina, Morris P. 1988. "The Reagan Years: Turning to toward the Right or Groping toward the Middle? In *The Resurgence of Conservatism in Anglo-American Democracies*, A. Kornberg and W. Mishler, eds. Durham, NC: Duke University, 430–460.

Fischer, Stanley. 1975. "The Demand for Index Bonds." *Journal of Political Economy* 83: 503–534.

Forgette, Richard and Brian R. Sala. 1999. "Conditional Party Government and Member Turnout on Senate Recorded Votes, 1873–1935." *Journal of Politics* 61 (2): 467–484.

Forsythe, Robert, Murray Frank, Vasu Krishnamurthy, and Thomas W. Ross. 1998. "Markets as Predictors of Election Outcomes: Campaign Events and Judgement Bias in the 1993 UBC Election Stock Market." *Canadian Public Policy* 24: 329–351.

Forsythe, Robert, Forrest Nelson, Neumann, George R., and Jack Wright. 1992. "Anatomy of an Experimental Political Stock Market." *American Economic Review* 82: 1142–1161.

Forsythe, Robert, Thomas A. Rietz, and Thomas W. Ross. 1999. "Wishes, Expectations and Actions: A Survey on Price Formation in Election Stock Markets." *Journal of Economic Behavior and Organization* 39:83–110.

Fotos, Michael A., and Mark N. Franklin. 2002. "Naïve Political Science and the Paradox of Voting." Paper prepared for the *Midwest Political Science Meeting*, Chicago, IL.

Fowler, James H. 2005. "Turnout in a Small World." In *Social Logic of Politics*, Alan Zuckerman, ed., 269–287. Philadelphia: Temple University Press.

Fowler, James H. 2006. "Habitual Voting and Behavioral Turnout," *Journal of Politics.* 68 (2): 335–344.

Franklin, Daniel P., and Eric E. Grier. 1997. "Effects of Motor Voter Legislation—Voter Turnout, Registration, and Partisan Advantage in the 1992 Presidential Election." *American Politics Quarterly* 25 (1): 104–117.

Frederick, S., G. Loewenstein, and T. O'Donoghue. 2002. "Time Discounting and Time Preference: A Critical Review." *Journal of Economic Literature* 40 (2): 351–401.

Fudenberg, Drew, and David K. Levine. 1997. *Theory of Learning in Games*. Cambridge, MA: MIT Press.

Gans, Herbert J. 1967. "Levittown and America." In *The City Reader*, Richard T. LeGates and Frederic Stout, ed., 63–69. London and New York: Routledge.

Gelman, Andrew, and Gary King. 1990. "Estimating Incumbency Advantage without Bias." *American Journal of Political Science* 34 (4): 1142–1164.

Gelman, Andrew, and Gary King. 1993. "Why Are American Presidential Election Campaign Polls So Variable When Votes Are So Predictable?" *British Journal of Political Science* 23: 409–451.

Gelman, Andrew, Gary King, and Chuanhai Liu. 1999. "Not Asked and Not Answered: Multiple Imputation for Multiple Surveys." *Journal of the American Statistical Association* 93: 846–857.

Gigerenzer, Gerd, et al. 1999. *Simple Heuristics that Make Us Smart*. New York, NY: Oxford University Press.

Gilbert, Nigel, and Klaus Troitzsch. 1999. *Simulation for the Social Scientist*. Philadelphia: Open University Press.

Glaser, William A. 1959. "The Family and Voting Turnout." *Public Opinion Quarterly* 23 (4): 563–570.

Granberg D., and Holmberg S. 1991. "Self-Reported Turnout and Voter Validation." *American Journal of Political Science* 35: 448–459.

Greenberg, Joseph, and Kenneth Shepsle. 1987. "The Effect of Electoral Rewards in Multiparty Competition with Entry." *American Political Science Review* 81 (2): 525–538.

Grilli, Vittorio, Donato Masciandaro, and Guido Tabellini. 1991. "Political and Monetary Institutions and Public Finance Policies in the Industrial Democracies." *Economic Policy* 13: 342–392.

Grofman, Bernard, Christian Collet, and Robert Griffin. 1998. "Analyzing the Turnout-Competition Link with Aggregate Cross-Sectional Data." *Public Choice* 95 (3–4): 233–246.

Grofman, Bernard, Robert Griffin, and Amihai Glazer. 1990. "Identical Geography, Different Party: A Natural Experiment on the Magnitude of Party Differences in the U.S. Senate, 1960–84." In *Developments in electoral geography*, R. J. Johnston, F. M. Shelley, and P. J. Taylor. ed., 207–217. London: Routledge.

Groseclose, Timothy. 2001. "A Model of Platform Location when One Platform Has a Valence Advantage." *American Journal of Political Science* 45:862–886.

Groseclose, Timothy, Steve D. Levitt, and James M. Snyder. 1999. "Comparing Interest Group Scores across Time and Chambers: Adjusted Ada Scores for the US Congress." *American Political Science Review* 93 (1): 33–50.

Hafer, R. W., Scott E. Hein, and S. Scott MacDonald. 1992. "Market and Survey Forecasts of the Three-Month Treasury-Bill Rate." *Journal of Business* 65 (1): 123–138.

Hamilton, James D. 1994. *Time Series Analysis*. Princeton, NJ: Princeton University.

Hanks, Christopher, and Bernard Grofman. 1998. "Turnout in Gubernatorial and Senatorial Primary and General Elections in the South, 1922–90: A Rational Choice Model of the Effects of Short-Run and Long-Run Electoral Competition on Relative Turnout." *Public Choice* 94 (3–4): 407–421.

Hanley, J. A., and A. Lippmanhand. 1983. "If Nothing Goes Wrong, Is Everything All Right— Interpreting Zero Numerators." *Journal of the American Medical Association* 249 (13): 1743–1745.

Hansen, S., T. R. Palfrey, and H. Rosenthal. 1987. "The Downsian Model of Electoral-Participation—Formal Theory and Empirical-Analysis of the Constituency Size Effect." *Public Choice* 52 (1): 15–33.

Hansen, Steven, Thomas R. Palfrey, and Howard Rosenthal. 1987. "The Relationship between Constituency Size and Turnout: Using Game Theory to Estimate the Cost of Voting." *Public Choice* 52: 15–33.

Hansson, Ingemar, and Charles Stuart. 1984. "Voting Competitions with Interested Politicians: Platforms Do Not Converge to the Preferences of the Median Voter." *Public Choice* 44: 431–441.

Harrison, G. W., M. I. Lau, and M. B. Williams. 2002. "Estimating Individual Discount Rates in Denmark: A Field Experiment." *American Economic Review* 92 (5): 1606–1617.

Harrison, Glenn W., Morten Igel Lau, E. Elisabet Rutström, and Melonie B. Sullivan. 2004. "Eliciting Risk and Time Preferences Using Field Experiments: Some Methodological Issues." In *Field Experiments in Economics*, J. Carpenter, G. W. Harrison, and J. A. List, eds., Greenwich, CT: JAI Press, 125–218.

Harvey, Campbell, R. 1988. "The Real Term Structure and Consumption Growth." *Journal of Financial Economics* 22 (2): 305–333.

Heath, Anthony, and Geoffrey Evans. 1994. "Tactical Voting: Concepts, Measurement and Findings." *British Journal of Political Science* 24: 557–561.

Herron, Michael C., James Lavin, Donald Cram, and Jay Silver. 1999. "Measurement of Political Effects in the United States Economy: A Study of the 1992 Presidential Election." *Economics and Politics* 11 (1): 51–81.

Hetherington, Marc J. 2001. "Resurgent Mass Partisanship: The Role of Elite Polarization." *American Political Science Review* 95 (3): 619–631.

Hibbs, Douglas A. 1987. *The American Political Economy*. Cambridge, MA: Harvard University Press.

Hibbs, Douglas A. 1977. "Political Parties and Macroeconomic Policy." *American Political Science Review* 71 (4): 1467–1487.

Highton, Benjamin. 1997. "Easy Registration and Voter Turnout." *Journal of Politics* 59 (2): 565–575.

Highton, Benjamin. 2000. "Residential Mobility, Community Mobility, and Electoral Participation." *Political Behavior* 22 (2): 109–120.

Highton, Benjamin, and Raymond E. Wolfinger. 2001. "The First Seven Years of the Political Life Cycle." *American Journal of Political Science* 45 (1): 202–209.

Honaker, James, Anne Joseph, Gary King, and Kenneth Scheve. 2000. *Amelia: A Program for Missing Data (Gauss Version).* Cambridge, MA: Harvard University. Also available online at http://gking.harvard.edu.

Hotelling, Harold. 1929. "Stability in Competition." *The Economic Journal* 39: 41–57.

Huang, Chi, and Todd G. Shields. 2000. "Interpretation of Interaction Effects in Logit and Probit Analyses—Reconsidering the Relationship between Registration Laws, Education, and Voter Turnout." *American Politics Quarterly* 28 (1): 80–95.

Huckfeldt, Robert, and John Sprague. 1995. *Citizens, Parties, and Social Communication.* New York: Cambridge University Press.

Huckfeldt, Robert, and John Sprague. 1992. "Political Parties and Electoral Mobilization: Political Structure, Social Structure and the Party Canvass." *American Political Science Review* 86: 70–86.

Huggins, V., and Eyerman, J. 2001. "Probability Based Internet Surveys: A Synopsis of Early Methods and Survey Research Results." *Federal Committee of Statistical Methods Conference* 2001.

Huckfeldt, R. Robert and John Sprague. 1987. "Networks in Context: The Social Flow of Political Information." *American Political Science Review* 81 (Dec.): 1197–1216.

Iannaccone, L. R. 1998. "Introduction to the Economics of Religion." *Journal of Economic Literature* 36 (3): 1465–1495.

Iversen, Torben. 1994. "The Logics of Electoral-Politics—Spatial, Directional, and Mobilizational Effects." *Comparative Political Studies* 27 (2): 155–189.

Iyengar, Shanto. 1980. "Subjective Political Efficacy as a Measure of Diffuse Support." *Public Opinion Quarterly* 44: 249–256.

Jackson, John E. 1983. "Election Night Reporting and Voter Turnout." *American Journal of Political Science* 27 (4): 615–635.

Jackson, John E., and David C. King. 1989. "Public-Goods, Private Interests, and Representation." *American Political Science Review* 83 (4): 1143–1164.

Jackson, Robert A. 2000. "Differential Influences on Participation in Midterm Versus Presidential Elections." *Social Science Journal* 37 (3): 385–402.

Jacobson, Gary C. 1990. "Does the Economy Matter in Midterm Elections?" *American Journal of Political Science* 34: 400–404.

Jacobson, Gary C. 1991. "The Persistence of Democratic House Majorities." In *The Politics of Divided Government*, G. W. Cox and S. Kernell, eds., 57–84. Boulder, Colorado: Westview Press.

Jacobson, Gary C., and Samuel Kernell. 1981. *Strategy and Choice in Congressional Elections.* New Haven: Yale University Press.

Johnson, Paul. 1998. "Rational Actors Versus Adaptive Agents: Social Science Implications." Mimeo. Lawrence, KS: University of Kansas.

Kaempfer, William H., and Anton D. Lowenberg. 1993. "A Threshold-Model of Electoral Policy and Voter Turnout." *Rationality and Society* 5 (1): 107–126.

Kamara, Avraham. 1997. "The Relation between Default-Free Interest Rates and Expected Economic Growth Is Stronger Than You Think." *Journal of Finance* 52 (4): 1681–1694.

Kandel, Shmuel, Aharon R. Ofer, and Oded Sarig. 1996. "Real Interest Rates and Inflation: An Ex-Ante Empirical Analysis." *Journal of Finance* 51 (1): 205–225.

Karp, Jeffrey A., and Susan A. Banducci. 2000. "Going Postal: How All-Mail Elections Influence Turnout." *Political Behavior* 22 (3): 223–239.

Kedar, Orit. 2005. "When Moderate Voters Prefer Extreme Parties: Policy Balancing in Parliamentary Elections." *American Political Science Review* 99 (2): 185–199.

Keith, Bruce E., David B. Magleby, Candice J. Nelson, Elizabeth Orr, Mark C. Westlye, and Raymond Wolfinger. 1992. *The Myth of the Independent Voter*. Berkeley: University of California.

Kelly, Stanley. 1983. *Interpreting Elections*. Princeton, NJ: Princeton University Press.

Kenny, Christopher B. 1992. "Political Participation and Effects from the Social Environment." *American Journal of Political Science* 36: 259–267.

Key, V. O. 1949. *Southern Politics in State and Nation*. New York: Knopf.

King, Anthony Stephen. 1997. *Running Scared: Why America's Politicians Campaign Too Much and Govern Too Little*. New York: Martin Kessler Books.

King, Gary. 1997. *Unifying Political Methodology*. Ann Arbor: University of Michigan Press.

King, Gary, James Honaker, Anne Joseph, and Kenneth Scheve. 2001. "Analyzing Incomplete Political Science Data: An Alternative Algorithm for Multiple Imputation." *American Political Science Review* 95:49–69.

King, Gary, James Honaker, Anne Joseph, and Kenneth Scheve. 2001. "Analyzing Incomplete Political Science Data: An Alternative Algorithm for Multiple Imputation." *American Political Science Review* 95 (March): 49–69.

King, Gary, Robert O. Keohane and Sidney Verba. 1994. *Designing Social Inquiry: Scientific Inference in Qualitative Research*. Princeton: Princeton University Press.

King, Gary, Michael Tomz, and Jason Wittenberg. 2000. "Making the Most of Statistical Analyses: Improving Interpretation and Presentation." *American Journal of Political Science* 44 (March): 341–355.

Kingdon, J. 1966. *Candidates for Office: Beliefs and Strategies*. New York: Random House.

Kirchgassner, Gebhard, and Anne Meyer zu Himmern. 1997. "Expected Closeness and Turnout: An Empirical Analysis for the German General Elections, 1983–1994." *Public Choice* 91 (1): 3–25.

Knack, Stephen. 1992. "Civic Norms, Social Sanctions, and Voter Turnout." *Rationality and Society* 4:133–156.

Knack, Stephen. 1994. "Does Rain Help the Republicans—Theory and Evidence on Turnout and the Vote." *Public Choice* 79 (1–2): 187–209.

Knack, Stephen. 2001. "Election-Day Registration—The Second Wave." *American Politics Research* 29 (1): 65–78.

Knack, Stephen. 1997. "The Reappearing American Voter: Why Did Turnout Rise in '92?" *Electoral Studies* 16 (1): 17–32.

Knack, Stephen, and White James. 2000. "Election-Day Registration and Turnout Inequality." *Political Behavior* 22 (1): 29–44.

Kollman, Kenneth, John H. Miller, and Scott E. Page. 1992. "Adaptive Parties in Spatial Elections." *American Political Science Review* 86: 929–937.

Kollman, Kenneth, John H. Miller, and Scott E. Page, eds. 2003. *Computational Models in Political Economy*. Cambridge, MA: MIT Press.

Kou, Steven G., and Michael E. Sobel. 2004. "Forecasting the Vote: An Analytical Comparison of Election Markets and Public Opinion Polls." *Political Analysis* 12: 277–295.

Kramer, Gerald. 1977. "A Dynamical Model of Political Equilibrium." *Journal of Economic Theory* 16 (2): 310–334.

Krueger, J. T., and K. N. Kuttner. 1996. "The Fed Funds Futures Rate as a Predictor of Federal Reserve Policy." *Journal of Futures Markets* 16 (Dec): 865–879.

Kunce, Mitch. 2001. "Pre-Election Polling and the Rational Voter: Evidence from State Panel Data (1986–1998)." *Public Choice* 107 (1–2): 21–34.

Laibson, David. 1997. "Golden Eggs and Hyperbolic Discounting." *Quarterly Journal of Economics* 112 (2): 443–477.

Lane, Robert E. 1959. *Political Life: Why People Get Involved in Politics*. Glencoe, IL: The Free Press.

Layman, Geoffry C., and Tom M. Carsey. 2002. "Party Polarization and "Conflict Extension" in the American Electorate." *American Journal of Political Science* 46 (4): 786–802.

Lazarsfeld, Paul F., Bernard Berelson, and Hazel Gaudet. 1948. *The People's Choice*. New York: Columbia University.

Leblang, David, and Bumba Mukherjee. 2004. "Presidential Elections and the Stock Market: Comparing Markov-Switching and Fractionally Integrated GARCH Models of Volatility." *Political Analysis* 12 (3): 296–322.

Ledyard, John D. 1984. "The Pure Theory of Large Two Party Elections." *Public Choice* 44: 7–41.

Lindbeck, Assar, and Jorgen W. Weibull. 1993. "A Model of Political Equilibrium in a Representative Democracy," *Journal of Public Economics* 51: 195–209.

Loader, C. 1999. *Local Regression and Likelihood*. Springer-Verlag: New York.

Lohmann, Susanne. 1993. "A Signaling Model of Informative and Manipulative Political Action." *American Political Science Review* 88: 319–333.

Londregan, John, and Thomas Romer. 1993. "Polarization, Incumbency, and the Personal Vote." In *Political Economy: Institutions, Competition, and Representation,* William A. Barnett, Melvin Hinich, and Norman Schofield, eds., 355–377. New York: Cambridge University Press.

Lucas, Robert E. 1977. "Understanding Business Cycles." In *Stabilization of the Domestic and International Economy,* K. Brunner and A. Meltzer, eds., Carnegie-Rochester Conference Series on Public Policy 5: 7–29.

Lupia, Arthur, and Mathew D. McCubbins. 1998. *The Democratic Dilemma: Can Citizens Learn What They Need to Know?* New York: Cambridge University Press.

Mackie, Tom, and Richard Rose. 1997. *A Decade of Elections Results: Updating the International Almanac.* Centre for the Study of Public Policy. Glasgow: University of Strathclyde.

Macy, Michael W. 1995. "Pavlov and the Evolution of Cooperation: An Experimental Test." *Social Psychological Quarterly* 58: 74–87.

Malinvaud, E. 1974, "The Allocation of Individual Risks in Large Markets." In *Allocation under Uncertainty: Equilibrium and Optimality,* J. H. Dréze, ed., 110–125. London, England: MacMillan Press.

Mason, Ronald M. 1982. *Participatory and Workplace Democracy*. Carbondale: University of Southern Illinois.

Matsusaka, John G. 1993. "Election Closeness and Voter Turnout—Evidence from California Ballot Propositions." *Public Choice* 76 (4): 313–334.

Mayhew, David R. 1974. *Congress: The Electoral Connection.* Yale Studies in Political Science 26. New Haven: Yale University Press.

Mayhew, David R. 1991. *Divided We Govern: Party Control, Lawmaking, and Investigations, 1946–1990.* New Haven: Yale University.

McKelvey, Richard. 1976. "Intransitivities in Multidimensional Voting Models and Some Implications for Agenda Control." *Journal of Economic Theory* 12: 472–482.

Mebane, Walter R. 2000. "Coordination, Moderation, and Institutional Balancing in American Presidential and House Elections." *American Political Science Review* 94 (March): 37–57.

Mebane, Walter R., and Jasjeet Sekhon. 2002. "Coordination and Policy Moderation at Midterm." *American Political Science Review* 96 (March): 141–157.

Meirowitz, Adam. 2004. "Polling Games and Information Revelation in the Downsian Framework." Princeton, NJ: Princeton University.

Meirowitz, Adam, and Joshua Tucker. 2003. "Voting and Information Transition in Sequential Elections: Run Boris Run." Princeton, NJ: Princeton University.

Miller, Warren E., and Donald E. Stokes. 1963. "Constituency Influence in Congress." *American Political Science Review* 57: 45–56.

Morton, Rebecca B. 1993. "Incomplete Information and Ideological Explanations of Platform Divergence." *American Political Science Review* 87 (2): 382–392.

Myerson, Roger. 1998. "Population Uncertainty and Poisson Games." *International Journal of Game Theory* 27:375–392.

Nagler, Jonathan. 1991. "The Effect of Registration Laws and Education on United-States Voter Turnout." *American Political Science Review* 85 (4): 1393–1405.

Nelson, Richard R., and Sidney G. Winter. 2002. "Evolutionary Theorizing in Economics." *Journal of Economic Perspectives* 16:23–46.

Niederhofer, Victor. 1971. "The Analysis of World Events and Stock Prices." *Journal of Business* 44: 193–219.

Niemi, Richard G., Stephen C. Craig, and Franco Mattei. 1991. "Measuring Internal Political Efficacy in the 1988 National Election Study." *American Political Science Review* 85: 1407–1413.

Niemi, Richard G., Guy Whitten, and Mark N. Franklin. 1992. "Constituency Characteristics, Individual Characteristics and Tactical Voting in the 1987 British General Election." *British Journal of Political Science* 22: 229–254.

Noelle-Neumann, Elisabeth. 1984. *The Spiral of Silence: Public Opinion—Our Social Skin.* Chicago: University of Chicago Press.

Oliver, J. Eric. 1996. "The Effects of Eligibility Restrictions and Party Activity on Absentee Voting and Overall Turnout." *American Journal of Political Science* 40 (2): 498–513.

Olsen, Marvin E. 1972. "Social Participation and Voting Turnout: A Multivariate Analysis." *American Sociological Review* 37 (June): 317–333.

Osborne, Martin J. 1995. "Spatial Models of Political Competition under Plurality Rule— A Survey of Some Explanations of the Number of Candidates and the Positions They Take." *Canadian Journal of Economics* 28 (2): 261–301.

Page, Benjamin I., and Robert Y. Shapiro. 1992. *The Rational Public: Fifty Years of Trends in Americans' Policy Preferences.* Chicago: University of Chicago Press.

Palfrey, Thomas R. 1984. "Spatial Equilibrium with Entry." *Review of Economic Studies* 51 (1): 139–156.

Palfrey, Thomas R., and Howard Rosenthal. 1983. "A Strategic Calculus of Voting." *Public Choice* 41: 7–53.

Palfrey, Thomas R., and Howard Rosenthal. 1985. "Voter Participation and Strategic Uncertainty." *American Political Science Review* 79: 62–78.

Pateman, Carole. 1970. *Participation and Democratic Theory.* New York: Cambridge University.

Peltzman, Samuel. 1984. "Constituent Interest and Congressional Voting." *Journal of Law and Economics* 27: 181–210.

Peterson, David A. M., Lawrence J. Grossback, James A. Stimson, and Amy Gangl. 2003. "Congressional Response to Mandate Elections." *American Journal of Political Science* 47: 411–426.

Piketty, Thomas. 2000. "Voting as Communicating." *Review of Economic Studies* 67: 169–191.

Plosser, Charles I. 1987. "Fiscal Policy and the Term Structure." *Journal of Monetary Economics* 20: 343–367.

Plosser, Charles I. 1982. "Government Financing Decisions and Asset Prices." *Journal of Monetary Economics* 9: 325–352.

Plott, Charles. 1967. "A Notion of Equilibrium Under Majority Rule," *American Economic Review* 57: 787–806.

Plutzer, Eric. 2002. "Becoming a Habitual Voter: Inertia, Resources, and Growth in Young Adulthood." *American Political Science Review* 96 (1): 41–56.

Poole, Keith T. 2003. "Changing Minds? Not in Congress!" Houston, Texas: University of Houston.

Poole, Keith T. 1998. "Recovering a Basic Space from a Set of Issue Scales." *American Journal of Political Science* 42 (3): 954–993.

Poole, Keith T., and Howard Rosenthal. 1997. *Congress: A Political-Economic History of Roll Call Voting.* New York: Oxford University Press.

Poole, Keith T., and Howard Rosenthal 1984. "The Polarization of American Politics." *Journal of Politics* 46 (4): 1061–1079.

Quattrone, George A., and Amos Tversky. 1988. "Contrasting Rational and Psychological Analysis of Political Choice." *American Political Science Review* 82: 719–736.

Rabinowitz, George, and Stuart Elaine MacDonald. 1989. "A Directional Theory of Issue Voting." *American Political Science Review* 83: 93–121.

Razin, Ronny. 2003. "Signaling and Electing Motivations in a Voting Model with Common Values and Responsive Candidates." *Econometrica* 71: 1083–1120.

Reif, K., and H. Schmitt. 1980. "Nine Second-order National Elections: A Conceptual Framework for the Analysis of European Election Results." *European Journal of Political Research* 8: 3–44.

Rhine, Staci L. 1995. "Registration Reform and Turnout Change in the American States." *American Politics Quarterly* 23 (4): 409–426.

Riker, William H., and Peter C. Ordeshook. 1968. "A Theory of the Calculus of Voting." *American Political Science Review* 62: 25–42.

Roberts, Brian E. 1989. "Voters, Investors, and the Consumption of Political Information." In *Models of Strategic Choice in Politics,* Peter C. Ordeshook, ed., 31–47. Ann Arbor, MI: University of Michigan Press.

Robertson, David. 1976. *A Theory of Party Competition.* London: J. Wiley.

Roemer, John E. 2001. *Political Competition: Theory and Applications.* Cambridge: Harvard University Press.

Roemer, John E. 1997. "Political-Economic Equilibrium When Parties Represent Constituents: The Unidimensional Case." *Social Choice and Welfare* 14: 479–502.

Rogoff, Kenneth. 1990. "Equilibrium Political Budget Cycles." *American Economic Review* 80 (1): 21–36.

Rogoff, Kenneth, and Anne Sibert. 1988. "Elections and Macroeconomic Policy Cycles." *Review of Economic Studies* 55 (1): 1–16.

Rosenstone, Steven J. 1983. *Forecasting Presidential Elections.* New Haven, CT: Yale University Press.

Rosenstone, Steven J., and John Mark Hansen. 1993. *Mobilization, Participation, and Democracy in America.* New York: Macmillan.

Rosenstone, Steven J., and Raymond E. Wolfinger. 1978. "The Effect of Registration Laws on Voter Turnout." *American Political Science Review* 72 (March): 22–45.

Roubini, Nouriel, and Jeffry Sachs. 1989a. "Government Spending and Budget Deficits in the Industrialized Countries." *Economic Policy* 8: 99–132.

Roubini, Nouriel, and Jeffry Sachs. 1989b. "Political and Economic Determinants of Budget Deficits in the Industrial Democracies." *European Economic Review* 33: 903–933.

Scheve, Kenneth, and Michael Tomz. 1999. "Electoral Surprise and the Midterm Loss in US Congressional Elections." *British Journal of Political Science* 29 (July): 507–521.

Shachar, Ron, and Barry Nalebuff. 1999. "Follow the Leader: Theory and Evidence on Political Participation." *American Economic Review* 89: 525–547.

Sheffrin, Steven M. 1989. "Evaluating Rational Partisan Business Cycle Theory." *Economics and Politics* 1 (3): 239–259.

Shotts, Kenneth. 2000. *A Signaling Model of Repeated Elections.* Chicago, IL: Northwestern University.

Simon, Herbert. 1982. *Models of Bounded Rationality.* Cambridge: MIT Press.

Skvoretz, John. 2002. "Complexity Theory and Models for Social Networks." *Complexity* 8 (1): 47–55.

Smirnov, Oleg, and James Fowler. 2007. "Moving with the Mandate: Policy-motivated Parties in Dynamic Political Competition." Forthcoming in the *Journal of Theoretical Politics* 19(1): 9–31.

Southwell, Priscilla L., and Justin Burchett. 2000b. "The Effect of All-Mail Elections on Voter Turnout." *American Politics Quarterly* 28 (1): 72–79.

Squire, Peverill, Raymond E. Wolfinger, and David P. Glass. 1987. "Residential Mobility and Voter Turnout (in Articles)." *American Political Science Review* 81 (March): 45–66.

Stigler, George. 1972. "Economic Competition and Political Competition." *Public Choice* 13: 91–106.

Stimson, James A., Michael B. Mackuen, and Robert S. Erikson. 1995. "Dynamic Representation." *American Political Science Review* 89 (3): 543–565.

Stokes, Susan C. 1999. "Political Parties and Democracy." *Annual Review of Political Science* 2: 243–267.

Stone, Walter J. 1980. "The Dynamics of Constituency: Electoral Control in the House." *American Politics Quarterly* 8: 399–424.

Straits, Bruce C. 1990. "The Social-Context of Voter Turnout." *Public Opinion Quarterly* 54 (1): 64–73.

Suzuki, Motoshi. 1992. "Political Business Cycles in the Public Mind." *American Political Science Review* 86: 989–996.

Taber, Charles S., and Richard J. Timpone. 1996. *Computational Modeling.* Sage University Paper Series on Quantitative Applications in the Social Sciences, 07–113. Newbury Park, CA: Sage.

Tesfatsion, Leigh. 1980. "A Conditional Expected Utility Model for Myopic Decision Makers." *Theory and Decision* 12: 185–206.

Tesfatsion, Leigh. 1984. "Games, Goals, and Bounded Rationality." *Theory and Decision* 17: 149–175.

Tesfatsion, Leigh, and Kenneth L. Judd, eds. 2006. *Handbook of Computational Economics, Vol. 2: Agent-Based Computational Economics.* Amsterdam: North-Holland.

Thompson, Dennis F. 1970. *The Democratic Citizen: Social Service and Democratic Theory.* Cambridge: Cambridge University.

Timpone, Richard J. 1998. "Structure, Behavior, and Voter Turnout in the United States." *American Political Science Review* 92 (1): 145–158.

Tsebelis, George. 1995. "Decision-Making in Political-Systems—Veto Players in Presidentialism, Parliamentarism, Multicameralism and Multipartyism." *British Journal of Political Science* 25: 289–325.

Verba, Sidney, and Norman H. Nie. 1972. *Participation in America: Political Democracy and Social Equality.* New York: Harper & Row.

Verba, Sidney, Kay Lehman Schlozman, and Henry E. Brady. 1995. *Voice and Equality: Civic Voluntarism in American Politics.* Cambridge, Mass.: Harvard University Press.

Wang, Naisyin, and Adrian E. Raferty, 2002. "Nearest Neighbor Variance Estimation (NNVE): Robust Covariance Estimation Via Nearest Neighbor Cleaning." *Journal of the American Statistical Association* 97: 994–1019.

Wittman, Donald. 1983. "Platform Motivation: A Synthesis of Alternative Theories." *American Political Science Review* 77: 142–157.

Wittman, Donald. 1977. "Platforms with Policy Preferences: A Dynamic Model." *Journal of Economic Theory* 14 (1): 180–189.

Wittman, Donald. 1973. "Parties as Utility Maximizers." *American Political Science Review* 67: 490–498.

Wolfinger, Raymond E., and Steven J. Rosenstone. 1980. *Who Votes?* New Haven: Yale University Press.

INDEX

adaptive rationality, 61, 64
agent-based modeling, 54–55: simulation code, 148–151

balancing. *See under* mandate balancing
bounded rationality, 14, 57–64

citizen's utility, 56. *See also* Euclidian utility function
closeness of election, 26, 53, 63, 84: and pivotal motivation, 72, 83–86; and signaling motivation, 73
common space scores. *See under* ideology scores
computational results: agent-based, 58–59; numerical simulation, 16, 24–25. *See also* agent-based modeling
Conley, P., 2
constituent interests, 36–37

democratic government, 36
directional voting, 74, 83, 86
discount factor, 80, 84, 105–106
divergence, 26, 37, 51, 66–67: and preference correlation among voters, 68–69
divided government, 118–119, 122, 132
Downsian model, 75. *See also* electoral competition: office-motivated parties

dynamic elections. *See under* Wittman equilibrium: dynamic model
dynamic responsiveness, 36–38: and change in candidate ideology, 41–42, 47–49; and incumbency, 44; and institutions, 46–47; and partisanship, 45–46; and voter beliefs, 91–99

economy and elections, 113, 120–121
economic shocks, 119
efficacy, 108–110: external, 11, 73–75; formulas 76–80; internal, 81, 86, 109, 111, 159, 165; political, 75
electoral competition: divergence of platforms. *See under* divergence; office-motivated parties, 3; policy-motivated parties. *See under* Whittman equilibrium; probability of winning, 19; uncertainty about outcome, 4. *See also* margin of victory
electoral pessimism, 73, 77
electoral polarization, 22, 32–33
electoral risk, 118
electoral variance. *See under* electoral volatility
electoral volatility, 20–22, 29
endogenous interaction of voters and politicians, 10, 55, 66–69, 138. *See also* interdependence of voters and politicians

James H. Fowler is Associate Professor of Political Science at University of California, San Diego.

Oleg Smirnov is Assistant Professor of Political Science at University of Miami.